Pete Oxford is an award-winning conservation photographer specialising in conservation issues, wildlife and indigenous cultures around the world. With his wife, Reneé, they also organise bespoke travel, for small groups, to some of the world's top wildlife and cultural destinations. They have worked many times on every continent. This book is a collection of short stories from their exhaustive travels, some with clients and some alone. At times, you will laugh out loud at the hilarity of the tales, then be blind-sided by a short, thought-provoking sentence. Pete reveals his most embarrassing moments, his fears, his triumphs, his insights and his uninhibited passion for the wild. He is a very knowledgeable naturalist and has spent his life in the company of wildlife. He is often asked, what does it take to be an international photographer capturing unique images of endangered wildlife. This book has many of the answers, however, it is not in the least a 'how to' book but rather the adventures that life has taken him on whilst in pursuit of experiencing the breadth of this vulnerable planet, since before he even used a camera.

*Pete telling panda jokes*

To Reneé, my wife, who, over nearly three decades, has made these tales all the more rewarding by sharing most of them with me. And Yvonne.

Pete Oxford

## Trampled by Tapir and Other Tales from a Globe-Trotting Naturalist

AUSTIN MACAULEY PUBLISHERS™
LONDON * CAMBRIDGE * NEW YORK * SHARJAH

Copyright © Pete Oxford 2022

The right of Pete Oxford to be identified as author of this work has been asserted by the author in accordance with section 77 and 78 of the Copyright, Designs and Patents Act 1988.

All rights reserved. No part of this publication may be reproduced, stored in a retrieval system or transmitted in any form or by any means, electronic, mechanical, photocopying, recording or otherwise, without the prior permission of the publishers.

Any person who commits any unauthorised act in relation to this publication may be liable to criminal prosecution and civil claims for damages.

The story, experiences, and words are the author's alone.

A CIP catalogue record for this title is available from the British Library.

ISBN 9781398428683 (Paperback)
ISBN 9781398428690 (ePub e-book)

www.austinmacauley.com

First Published 2022
Austin Macauley Publishers Ltd®
1 Canada Square
Canary Wharf
London
E14 5AA

Each encounter with a fellow human, or animal, however brief, is absorbed into my being. No matter if infinitesimal, somehow it causes change, like a 'butterfly effect', to make me who I am. Yet it is hard, even for me, to know who that is, as, by consequence, I am forever changing. I thank all creatures who have helped guide me on this journey thus far.

There are, of course, too many to name in person. Those who have been most constant in nudging my direction have been my parents Meg and John Oxford, sisters, Sue Cunningham and Cath Moore and Reneé, my wife, who has not so much nudged but given a big push where necessary. I am thankful to all and can only hope that I have spawned a reciprocal difference. Lastly, to all those of you who made it into the pages of this book. I thank you for our shared adventures.

# Table of Content

| | |
|---|---|
| Introduction | 11 |
| The Coast Ecuador | 14 |
| Galapagos Ecuador | 18 |
| Sparkling Spirit Pacific Ocean | 27 |
| Catching Crocodiles Australia | 31 |
| Jigging for Squid Falkland Islands | 39 |
| Jungle Days Ecuador | 45 |
| Two Weddings Ecuador | 49 |
| Beny and Sacha Ecuador | 53 |
| The Crush Madagascar | 59 |
| Drips and Diapers India | 64 |
| Muslim Uprising Assam, India | 67 |
| The Scalping India | 74 |
| At Night with the Holy Grail Brazil | 78 |
| The Machine Peru | 81 |
| Huaorani, Missionaries and Self-Determination Amazon Rainforest | 83 |
| The Brute Peru | 95 |
| Wild Dogs, Lions and Valium Botswana | 99 |
| Kidnapped Russia | 106 |
| Siberian Surprise Russia | 112 |
| A Maggot in My Head Amazon Rainforest, Ecuador | 118 |
| Ice Is Nice Antarctica | 121 |
| Guyana's Rupununi Guyana | 133 |
| Anaconda, Giant Otters and Animal Planet Guyana | 138 |

| | |
|---|---|
| They Wiped Me Down with a Fish Brazil | 148 |
| A Pig Valve for a BFF Delhi, India | 152 |
| Living Bridges Meghalaya | 156 |
| The Last of the Head-Hunters Nagaland, India | 160 |
| Pig-Nosed Women Arunachal Pradesh, India | 164 |
| Horse's Sweat, Hairy Pasta and a Bottle of Wine Mongolia | 169 |
| Camel Blood Wine China | 183 |
| Fossa, a Frenchman and Farting Frogs Madagascar | 192 |
| Ocean's Ambassadors Mexico | 199 |
| Himba – The Ochre People Namibia | 204 |
| Stolen Binoculars and a Black Panther Amazon, Ecuador | 213 |
| Sharks and Dragons Indonesia | 223 |
| Afterword South Africa | 234 |

# Introduction

I decided not to start at the beginning, as the first half of my life was unextraordinary and can be summed up in the following 500 words.

A few things stand out, but not many. We had a good family. My mother, Meg, and father, John, loved my two sisters and I very much and only ever wanted the best for any of us. My father was in the British Army. Every two years or so, we moved. Friends were transient and nowhere, really, was home. A sense of self-reliance developed from an early age and although kicking and screaming at the thought of returning to my military boarding school in Dover, the actual journey was cherished. At 11 years old, I was driven to the coach station, close to the military barracks, waved goodbye and left alone, but defiant, as I crossed Germany, Belgium and a corner of France to catch the Channel ferry, then a train, to arrive at my 'prison'. I have had wanderlust ever since.

The greatest gift my father gave me was that he taught me how to watch animals and how to be patient. At a very young age, we would sit together, motionless, on the bank of an English brook, for hours on end, to wait for water voles to appear. He loved nature and, because of him, so do I.

University was everything I wanted it to be. I started at Birmingham studying dentistry! Peer pressure got me there but I hated the concept. The highlight, strangely, was being the volunteer to cut the head in half, of a man that had very considerately donated his deceased body as a resource for the furtherment of medical training. My tool was a woodworking tenon saw and it was imperative that I cut through the head in an exact sagittal section, as we were later to share a half head each per three dental students, once I had removed it from the body. A year was too much for me and I quit, took a year out working on Berlin building sites and picking grapes in France then pursued what I always wanted to do and attended Bangor University to study marine zoology. Degree-related job recruitment rates were appalling in the field. I was lucky to be one of the few and designed, built and ran a lobster hatchery in Menai Bridge, on Anglesey.

Later being granted a patent for co-designing a novel lobster release technique. At this point, I became desperate to leave the UK. I had to get out into the wider world. I was driven by an overwhelming curiosity of natural history and wanted to experience the Attenborough and Cousteau documentaries first-hand rather than through a glass screen in my living room. The tropics beckoned and I wrote to Indonesia, Nigeria, Singapore, the Philippines and Ecuador looking for work – anywhere I could think of that was big in aquaculture. Long story short, I got a letter from friends in Ecuador. Ten days later, I was there, leaving behind a newly purchased house and temporarily, a first wife.

I was already 26 years old and embarrassed for having forsaken my dream for so long. Finally, enthralled by my new chapter, life became extraordinary.

*Pete with Huaorani women in the Ecuadorian Amazon rainforest*

*Pete as part of a white rhino capture team in South Africa*

# The Coast
# Ecuador

After arriving to South America, I spent a short spell in Guayaquil, at that time a rough, dirty, dangerous and oppressively hot port town, known as the 'Pearl of the Pacific' I moved out to the coast and felt like a king. It was 1985 and the 100 km road heading west from Guayaquil was still dirt, bridging two entirely different worlds. On the one hand, a bustling city with fancy, air-conditioned malls and the other a string of shanty fishing villages where black vultures gathered at your feet for scraps from the *al-fresco* tables set in the sand – heaven! My first home was perched on a low cliff above the Pacific Ocean, where humpback whales passed by in season. It was a six-bedroom house, complete with a delightful caretaker family headed by Pedro and Maria. I built a shrimp hatchery (king prawns) with a friend in the arid dirt below the house which was where I worked. The deal was that the house was mine except for holiday times when the owner, with his important friends would descend on the property and luxuriate in the hedonic lifestyle. Still not much more than a puppy in my new surroundings, it was the week before Easter (Holy Week) and I was invited out to enjoy the traditional Ecuadorian soup known as *Fanesca*. It was heavy and rich, full of a multitude of grains, beans, gourds and salt cod (*bacalao*). I lapped it up and got as far as my third bowl before I was satiated. Being Easter the house was full. The next morning, not feeling quite right, I was down in my lab at work. At the same instant that I felt an incredible urge to shit, down came the whole household of fancy friends to meet me in person. They called my name in greeting. I froze in fear, exerting as much sphincter control as was humanly possible. They approached, hands outstretched, it was all too much and while standing there face-to-face an explosive brown torrent gushed out of my shorts and down the back of both legs. Not the impression I had hoped to give but the lead woman was gracious enough to simply say, "Oh! You seem to have a problem." They turned and left, I headed straight into the ocean. The laxative effects of *Fanesca* are well known enough that cartoons appeared in the local newspaper drawing humour from similar 'accidents'. Never again!

It was very much the Wild West on the coast in those days, lawless and exciting. Roads were crazy and full of hazards, especially at night, donkeys were the worst but cows were bad too. One night, squashed in the front seat of a small fiberglass truck with a crazy Frenchman at the wheel and another friend between us tension was high as Hervé refused to heed my warning of livestock on the road. "If zer iz one zing I will do, it is get you home alive," he said and there was a dramatic thud, as we scooped up a whole cow broadside. At 120 km per hour, the momentum was enough to roll it up the bonnet, smash the windshield, for an instant replacing it with cowhide then thud, thud, thud as it rolled right over the car landing on four broken legs. It was still alive but we couldn't kill it and stood there, transfixed, grieving, as Hervé searched for his broken antenna in the darkness. Most likely, it was killed and butchered by somebody less squeamish in a later car.

If a bridge is down a car tyre is painted white and left on the road as a signal. One friend, missing the fallen tyre, careered over the end and rolled down a ditch where he spent two days before he was found. Another, an ex-pat, killed a girl that ran out in front of his car. He was nearly lynched by the community but the police saved him. He went to jail and was there for a month before the closest relatives of the child, from another town, were tracked down to negotiate. He was only released after agreeing a price for the body. $5000, an inflated 'gringo' price, was enough. It took a while to understand the Ecuadorian ways.

At work one day, I heard an explosion next door. Pedro and I ran over and found a local worker with his arm almost completely blown off. He had tried to open up a sealed 45-gallon fuel drum with a circular saw. The gas fumes ignited with the sparks and *Boom*! I got my truck and laid him in the back with his colleagues to help. Our nearest 'best' clinic was in a little fishing village called Anconcito. We took him there to hand him over with little hope of a satisfactory outcome. The disappointing thing was that his 'friends' in the back with him robbed him on the way. It was the same hospital that I later took Pedro. Never one to complain, he came to me one day with a sharp abdominal pain. Fearing appendicitis, we drove to Anconcito. After I signed fiscal responsibility for Pedro, the doctor accepted his new inpatient. It was late and I drove home. The following day, I received a call to return. Pedro's appendix had been on the point of rupture and was removed in the night. I went to see him. He was lying on a hospital cot on a plastic sheet caked in dried blood. "Pedro," I said, "that is a lot of blood to lose over an appendectomy!"

Forever cheerful. "No, no, no," he said, "that's not my blood." And I took him home to Maria.

Eventually, it was considered appropriate that Jane, my first wife, should join me. It was idyllic yet rustic and we moved into a new house a little down the coast, also on the same low cliff. Andy and Clarice, our best friends, were neighbours and we lived in each other's houses sharing chores like cooking with a Hāngi oven on the beach, preheating the rocks and preparing the suckling pig with copious amounts of beer enjoyed in the long wait. I found this new lifestyle was immensely satisfying and easy to handle, it was different and exciting to me. The grocery shopping was perhaps the biggest culture shock for Jane. The market in La Libertad was semi-open with narrow passageways between vendors. Produce was good and tastier than I was used to but not (thankfully) hermetically sealed and perfect like the supermarkets of Wales. I would leave Jane to navigate the muddy substrate, pushing to one side the free-range cows stealing from the stalls and haggle, as best she could, with the wily vendors. I meanwhile would go to the fish section where live green turtles, sometimes having been dropped down to the ground from the top of a bus, were flapping, hopelessly, upside down on the floor. I checked them for cracks in the shell and particularly that their eyes were still in good condition. If sound I bought them, $5.00 a pop, loaded them into my truck and released them far away from the fisherman. Creating a demand in the market, you say. Well, I never took them without a passionate lecture, a plea really, to leave them alone. I just couldn't stand it. Moving to our new home, we were closer to Bobbie, a Texan biologist who had the 'A' frame house a few kilometres north on the beach. I paid him a visit late one evening and he was visibly upset. He had been robbed. It turned out that this was the third time in as many weeks. There was nothing left to rob he stated woefully. Bobbie's Spanish was effluent at best, so I took it upon myself to visit the guard of the house next door. He *must* know *something* I reasoned. A crowd developed around me as I ranted theatrically. I overheard newcomers being brought up to speed with what was going on. The list of items stolen was longer than I had told them – they knew something! I confirmed the missing items with Bobbie. The following day, in La Libertad I sought the services of a cop. In his spare time, off duty, he could be hired as a torturer and enforcer. We discussed the problem, I paid upfront on Bobbie's behalf and out we all trucked, three armed henchmen in tow back to the guard. Under the threat of a severe beating, electrocution and thumbscrews (all within budget) he sang like a canary. The whole scenario was revealed where a gang known as *Los Lobos* (The Wolves) would sit halfway up the hill behind the house, wait for a gap, rob and then load the 'hot' loot straight on to a boat which gapped it for Guayaquil's black market. We had them busted.

Meanwhile, I had earned a certain notoriety locally for being the crazy 'gringo' that rescues animals. I had an eclectic collection and once the popular Vistazo magazine published a full-blown story, it only got worse as more injured waifs were brought for care. My menagerie included a burrowing owl, a boa constrictor that survived a stoning, three juvenile pelicans with broken wings, two blue-footed boobies, a wayward Humboldt penguin, a swallow-tailed gull, two spectacled caimen and several green iguanas. Sweetpea, one of my pelicans, was a particular favourite of everyone. I would carry the three juveniles all down to the beach under my arms and swim with them for a while every day. The fishermen got to know them well and for Sweetpea, especially, would save their gash fish for her to eat. Her wing had a compound fracture at the elbow, a common cause of death in juvenile pelicans learning their complicated dive technique. I decided to operate. The vet gave me drugs that he claimed were enough to knock out a horse. Administered gradually until they were all gone, they had no effect on a pelican. Discouraged, I waited three days before trying again. On a sterilised table, with sterile medical tools and three scrubbed up friends for helpers, I decided to knock her out with vodka. She was very quick to get drunk and before long was in a complete state of abandon. I cut into her wing, cut the bone, meshed it together, swabbed out the wound repeatedly and sewed her back up applying a stiff splint. She would never fly but it healed beautifully and she was obviously more comfortable as a result.

Always just over the horizon, 1000 km due west of where we were, the Galapagos Islands loomed tantalisingly closer than I had ever thought possible, Jane and I went for a visit. I fell in love with the place and she, in no uncertain terms, made it clear that the idea of ever living there was untenable. Months later, she was gone, disappearing out of my life with a painful note hastily scribbled in pencil and left on the table. I quit my job and Andy's brother, Graham and I persuaded a tour boat company that they should sponsor us both as Galapagos National Park naturalist guides – which they did.

# Galapagos
# Ecuador

Graham and I graduated as naturalist guides in the Galapagos in 1987. We were first and second in the course with 97.25% and 97% respectively. He always was smarter than me. Hungry for knowledge we soaked up everything that there was to know about the archipelago – the good and the bad. Galapagos to me was the stuff of legends, a playground for heroes like Darwin and Attenborough. Yet, here I was – me! These remote, highly volcanic islands lie 1000 km off the west coast of Ecuador and straddle the equator. They were never attached to the mainland. Everything that lives there today, plant or animal had to arrive and then establish. The wide saltwater barrier between the islands and Ecuador's mainland proved too much of an obstacle to many groups that are common on the mainland. There are no native amphibians for example, nor woodpeckers or native larger mammals. We call it a disharmonic community with regard to the nearest faunal and floral source of colonisation. Humans have indeed only had a recent history themselves. Year 1807 saw the first permanent inhabitant, an Irishman called Patrick Watkins, who was deliberately marooned on Floreana Island due to his unsavoury character. A significant influx of colonisers arrived pre-WWII as Europeans looked for a utopia to escape Nazism. Three brothers from a German family – the Angermeyers settled in Puerto Ayora, on Santa Cruz Island, now the most populous town. Their progeny, true *Galapagueños,* born in the islands, included Fiddi who shone above the rest. Today the population of Galapagos has soared to approximately 30,000 people, spread over the five inhabited islands. It is shocking to most visitors, many of whom do not even realise there are *any* inhabitants.

Having moved to the islands and living in town, soon after arriving, I met up with Fiddi's ex-wife, Judy. She was surprised to learn that I had no idea that Jane was now with Fiddi and lauding it up as Queen of Galapagos. It was a shock to my system. Today the population is mixed. There are of course the passionate conservationists but on the other side of the coin there is an abundance of highly fecund, poorly educated fishermen types imported from the mainland. They were encouraged to colonise by a politician who wanted to increase his voter base. They now have a powerful lobby. For example when fishing quotas were reduced by the park, on a scientific basis to protect the resource, the fishermen rose to arms, burnt park buildings, kidnapped officials, killed wild tortoises and even threatened to kill the iconic Lonesome George. They were rewarded for their violence and quotas were restored. The precedent is set and the more you act aggressively in Galapagos, the more you get. The politician had an issue with foreign guides and me in particular. While most guides left the islands, I stayed and stood up to him. I repeatedly got death threats, was hounded by him with the police in tow and could never sleep in the same place on two consecutive nights. The British Embassy issued me two passports in case I needed an escape option quickly. When he yelled at me in Spanish from the seat of his empire on the downtown boulevard, "Get out of the islands you son-of-a-bitch," I would politely reply, "Hi Brother," implying we had the same dubious mother. When our craziest President allegedly stole $300,000,000 in cash from the country's coffers and fled to Panama, the politician went with him. I heard that he was jailed for child prostitution. Having completed seven years in exile however crimes are exonerated in Ecuador, so, guess what, he came back to run again for office. Galapagos – it's a hell of a place!

Despite the downside, my two and a half years living and guiding in the islands passed dreamily and, to this day, I still go every year to lead trips on a boat that Reneé and I charter. I left for many reasons not least of which was that I did not want to stay on and become part of the problem of the growing population. I feel a great sense of attachment to the islands. I think they nurtured me more than I realised at the time. Even now, I feel I owe them something. I have produced four books on Galapagos, the most important I did with Graham who, as the head of the Charles Darwin Research Station in Puerto Ayora, wrote the text. It was a project for 2009, celebrating 50 years of the Station's operation, 150 years since the publication of Darwin's 'On the Origin of Species', 50 years of Galapagos being declared a national park and Darwin's 200th birthday – quite the year for Galapagos. A little over halfway through the book the reader was invited to flip the book upside-down and start again, this time with text and imagery referring to the vast human impact both negative and positive. I included images of cock fighting, new cars being imported, a dock full of empty beer crates, prostitutes and shots of introduced insects. Balanced by some of the many successful and Herculean conservation efforts that have been pulled off. HRH Prince Philip wrote the foreword and the extremely upmarket watch company, IWC Schaffhausen, printed a boxed edition as their official annual gala-dinner gift. It felt good to get both sides of the coin out there.

I have been fortunate to be able to follow scientists at work in the islands and while developing the book, I was officially able to join many projects which were deeply rewarding to me. To come to know the visitor sites so well through continuous guiding, there manifests a serious yearning to go beyond the familiar. Each time I did so, the archipelago opened herself up to me a little more and pulled me closer into her embrace.

My first experience of being outside the range of visitor sites was when a secondary cone on my favourite island of Fernandina spewed lava into the sea. I ended up as a passenger on a tour boat that was on a western itinerary. Almost all boats at the time had dropped a portion of their itinerary to sail to Cabo Hammond on the southwest corner of the island to witness the fiery display. Red molten rock was flowing down the slopes of the crater, it split into 'fingers' as it reached the ocean and steam hissed as each one poured into the frigid waters of the Cromwell Current upwelling. The guide took us out in a rubber dinghy to the face of the action. It was a pretty crazy ride. As dollops of lava dropped to the water some exploded and 'shrapnel' went whizzing past us. The smell of the steam was strong and boiled fish were floating on the surface. Pelicans had dived in to catch them and badly scolded their pouches. It was the boat driver who called the end to our excursion, I don't blame him, the water-cooled engine was sucking in hot water, it was going to overheat and seize up. That would have been messy. We peeled away and back to the ship where we stayed until nightfall when the darkness imbued the pyroclastic scene with a different aura. Little by little, we watched the island grow.

On one scientific mission, I left with a team for Santiago Island in the central part of the group. We set up camp in the mangroves near a beach and had the pleasure of watching female turtles come up and lay their eggs each night. Shy ghost crabs were common as were the yellow warblers and Darwin's finches that soon accepted their new neighbours. We were to be looking at the endemic Galapagos hawk, a ridiculously tame raptor. So tame that Charles Darwin wrote of them 'A gun is here superfluous; for with the muzzle I pushed a hawk off the branch of a tree'. We made camp in a non-tourist area and set about laying rattraps to catch rats to catch hawks. The idea was to ring those birds not already banded and weigh, sex and measure all birds captured. The rat traps were fitted with running nylon nooses which would entangle the hawk's feet if it landed on the cage. Catching them was easy. Another, even more fun, method was to stake out a chunk of meat, wait for a hawk to land next to it and simply drop a noose over it from a sitting position a couple of metres away. They are beautiful buzzard-like birds (Buteo genus) but have been extirpated in many islands by farmers, blamed for killing poultry, there may be as few as 150 pairs left in the world. For the first time, since beginning as a guide, I was allowed the luxury of watching the comings and goings at a nest as adults arrived with lava lizards to feed their chick.

Another exciting science trip was to help participate in the annual penguin and flightless cormorant survey. This meant visiting every known nest or colony of both species. Many birds had been previously PIT tagged (a sub-dermal tag about the size of a grain of rice) and we checked each individual where possible with an electronic reader to see if it was a known bird. Breeding was noted as was clutch size or chick number. Mostly distributed in the west of the group, we ended up circumnavigating many islands whose 'dark side' I had never previously seen. Our penguins are small, black and white and nest in crevices in the lava. It is strange to find penguins juxtapositioned alongside iguanas and giant tortoises. They are the only tropical penguin in the world and like the flightless cormorant, are endemic to the Galapagos Islands. The cormorants, the largest of the world's twenty-nine species, still have vestigial wings which they have to hang out to dry after a swim. There are perhaps only 1200 breeding pairs of Galapagos penguins, whose population growth is being aided by building artificial nest sites, while only about 800 pairs of cormorants. Both are very fragile populations susceptible to climatic events or disease.

Any chance to head all the way north to Darwin and Wolf Islands on a dive trip is to be grabbed and held on to. The two remote islands offer world-class diving. Not for the feint-hearted, the currents can be horrendous, but the ocean is full of big things. From massive female whale sharks to an abundance of Galapagos sharks, sealions, tuna, turtles and large schools of scalloped hammerhead sharks. Twice I have had the privilege to be up there with scientists, once to attach satellite PAT tags (Pop off Archival Tag) to whale sharks. They are secured to a shark on its back, behind the dorsal fin using a harpoon as the shark swims by. Designed to 'Pop Off' on a programmable date, the tags float and beam up their scientific data to a satellite.

The second trip was to fit hammerhead sharks with satellite tags by actually bolting them on to the dorsal fin. The tags have antennae which beam up the data each time the shark comes to the surface. Bolting the tag on required catching the shark and bringing it onboard. It was first caught on hook and line with a barbless hook, brought alongside the research vessel and manoeuvred into a stretcher before being hauled aboard with the crane. Time was then of the essence and after first inserting a tube of flowing seawater into the mouth to keep the gills flushed; the operation was like a Formula One racing pit. Everyone having a small, precise job to do before it could be released. I went into the water, just before release and had the shark lowered down in front of me to photograph it re-entering the sea. We dived often, aiming to attach ultrasonic tags onto other hammerheads using a traditional Hawaiian sling. I can't recall ever seeing so many larger fish and top predators in such a small area. Sometimes a curtain of large, scalloped hammerheads would cruise lazily by; it was the stuff of legend. During some downtime one morning before lunch, I went into the water just behind the boat to photograph the rainbow runners that I could see below the surface. The chef had no idea that I was there and began cleaning a fish over the side. The effect was instantaneous, and the second the first trickle of blood hit the water I was surrounded by sharks. What amazed me was that they came from every direction, not by following a blood-trail upstream. Their olfactory and electrical sensitivity are truly amazing. I have great difficulty in understanding exactly how they read their environment. Our primary sense is visual, where we are able register very fine gradations of light and colour. By extension, with the incredible degree of a shark's senses do they have the equivalent of a smell 'image' and an electrical 'image'?

Years ago, Reneé and I always included a hike up Alcedo Volcano on every Galapagos itinerary. It is one of five and a half volcanoes that are melded together to form the largest island in Galapagos, Isabela. Climbing Alcedo was always a pre-dawn start from the eastern shore. We would take all the able passengers, guide and two crewmembers for the long slog west to the rim. The path was open, denuded by thousands of feral goats, although steep in the last third. The reward was to be on the rim of a large basaltic volcano, with sulphur fumaroles billowing across the crater to the left and huge giant tortoises resting close by. It was a very special feeling to witness the tortoises, the dominant herbivore of the islands, doing what they seemingly have always done. Some of them may possibly even have been alive when Darwin visited. In preparation for the book, I made arrangements with the national park and set out with a good friend, Tui de Roy, her boyfriend, Alan, and a woman writer, Carol Ann, who was writing a literary nonfiction book about the islands for National Geographic. Goats, along with many other species such as rats, cats, dogs, pigs, horses, cows and donkeys have had a terribly detrimental effect on Galapagos. None of them is native to the islands; all of them run feral. Some were introduced accidentally by pirates and buccaneers while they also left pigs and goats as food for subsequent visits. Horses, cows and donkeys came later with more modern colonisers. North of the lava field known as the Perry Isthmus, the 'waist' of Isabela, where Alcedo lies, there were reputed to be 100,000 goats. Project Isabela addressed the problem. It was a phenomenal success and was able to completely eradicate goats north of the isthmus. A combined effort of the national park, the Charles Darwin Research Station, New Zealand helicopter pilots and marksmen and a slew of other entities, wiped them out in what was the largest goat eradication ever. Tortoises had been virtually starving and some may well have died of overheating in the lack of shade, cooking in their own shell. Tui was born in Galapagos and had hiked Alcedo possibly four-score times in the past 40 years. It was her first time up Alcedo since project Isabela had been completed. Our plan was to go down onto the crater floor and camp. As we began the hike, leaving the arid coastal zone behind us both Tui and I noticed that there was much more vegetation than there used to be. This was a direct result of drastically reduced grazing pressure from the goats whose browse line was simply out of reach of the tortoises. The normally visible path was completely overgrown and we lost our way. All we knew was to continue up but we got into some really thick vegetation and could not even see the rim. Luckily, Tui had brought a machete and between us we had to now hack our way forward. It was tough going, our packs, full with camera gear, camping gear, food and water were heavy. We were being chewed by ticks and mosquitos. Carol Ann was not managing too well and we divided up her load. The heat of the day was brutal, even under the dense vegetation. At least three of us knew that lack of water in Galapagos is the prime killer. We tried to be careful with our supply. We had no choice but to camp about two thirds of the way to the summit and for the first time in four decades and eighty ascents, it was the first time that Tui had never made the rim in a day's hike. We spent a miserable night, with little sleep. At dawn, we decamped and continued hacking our way up the slope. Eventually, the vegetation subsided as we got more into a fern habitat. We pushed through and made the rim by mid-morning. The next leg of the hike was a significant walk along the rim until we were to climb down to the crater floor. Carol Ann had a knee problem and decided that she was in no condition to keep going. On the firm promise of not hiking on her own, or taking any risks, Carol Ann pitched her tent and was to stay on the rim until our return in two days' time. The three of us continued, making good time. We passed many tortoises along the way. It was a magical feeling to be up there, where so few had been before in the company of these six-hundred-pound reptiles. We camped on the crater floor, next to a shallow pool, filled with gloopy mud and about twenty-five wallowing giants. My tiny, borrowed, somewhat broken, tent was precarious, dwarfed by the big male tortoises and in danger of being completely disrespected as they wandered by. The night was punctuated by farting tortoises and the melodic sound of gas bubbles rising through the mud. The images were many and I had so much fun with my subjects. We wandered off in different directions so as to not be in each other's way. After all these years of wanting to be in Galapagos, this was perhaps the culmination of the experience. I found another wallow and was alone with its flatulent denizens. I was my own Darwin, my own Attenborough my own onlooker into the private lives of giant tortoises, far away from any 'civilised' world both in time and space. I was happy.

The last time I camped on Isabela Island, it was also to do with tortoises. This time was on Wolf Volcano, two north of Alcedo and just jutting into the northern hemisphere. There were perhaps forty of us, a group of scientists, national park guards and a couple of photographers who had left Puerto Ayora on the M/V Sierra Negra research vessel. We were divided into groups of four. Each group was to have a specific area in which to work. The volcano was to be covered from sea level to the rim. Our mission was to catch and take blood samples from as many tortoises as we found in our area. The blood was to be analysed and the DNA tested to see if there were any tortoises matching those from Pinta Island. Lonesome George, the world's most famous giant tortoise, was, at the time, the only surviving tortoise of his race. He was found on the island of Pinta and brought into the Galapagos National Park tortoise-rearing centre in Puerto Ayora. Extreme measures were taken to try and find him a breeding companion. In the end, nothing worked and he died. He is now stuffed and on exhibit in Galapagos in a climate-controlled room. One of my images of him in life was purchased by the embalming team to use as reference for their art.

Those groups that were sent to the rim of Wolf Volcano made a major discovery, an unknown, new to science, pink no less, land iguana – a truly incredible find. I was honoured to be partnered with Peter Pritchard, recognised by many as the world authority on all things tortoise and turtle. He was elderly and we were given the low elevation coastal zone. I'd known of Peter for many years and treasured his tome Encyclopaedia of Turtles, which he now modestly told me was best used as a door stop. We were to look for tortoises of any size, the small ones we would bring to the mobile 'processing station' where the park guards took blood samples and recorded biometric data. As a child, I was given a pet tortoise (which was almost certainly taken from the wild in Greece, where the wild-caught tortoise trade should of course be condemned) surprisingly they tame extremely well and become very responsive. Tortoises have much more character and individual personality than most people will ever give them credit for. Now I got to be hands-on and for the first time was legally allowed to touch a Galapagos tortoise. I found many, picked up the manageable ones and carried them to the guards. A number was painted on the rear of their shells and they were subsequently released. They are certainly tough animals. Whalers and co would collect them from the islands and store them upside-down in the holds of their ships where they would stay alive for up to a year without any food or water. For the sailors, fresh tortoise meat was a far superior fare than the traditional rations of salted pork and weevil-ridden biscuits.

Lonesome George was a saddleback tortoise, i.e. his carapace was raised at the front, he had relatively long legs and a long neck. Usually, an area has either domed tortoises, i.e. a closed-down front for bulldozing through thick vegetation or saddlebacks which live in the sparser xeric vegetation. Surprisingly, to all of us, we were finding both morphs in our search area. Of particular interest, we found a large, elderly adult, veritable classic, saddleback which should definitely not have been there according to our knowledge of tortoise ecology (see the front cover). It was later determined, from blood samples that we extracted, that this particular individual was a pure-bred (or with a very high percentage DNA) 'extinct' Floreana tortoise. It was another incredible find. Latterly, in 2015, some 30 plus individuals shown to contain the Floreana DNA have been moved from Wolf to the breeding centre as part of a reintroduction program to re-establish tortoises back on Floreana from where they have been missing since the mid-nineteenth century. The theory goes that Galapagos was a known place for pirates. They would hide in places like Tagus Cove and surprise passing whalers and fur seal hunters. A chase under sail would ensue and in order to out-run the pirates, the whalers would jettison their heavy cargo of tortoises to go faster through the water. The tortoises would then float ashore to a new and different island, hence the present-day mix of tortoise types on Wolf Volcano. It was another rewarding adventure in my portfolio of Galapagos highlights and again I had a visceral sense of being exactly where I wanted to be, in deep connectivity with a wild and untamed speck on the planet. Camaraderie was high and Peter and I shared much in conversation. I celebrated my 50$^{th}$ birthday while camping with the team and our evening meal for the occasion was rice with a topping of warmed-up, canned, cow's intestines! Who the hell would can cow's intestines was all I could think of while trying to get it down.

Galapagos remains perhaps one of the places in the world that I know best. I finally left Ecuador in 2019, after 34 years as a permanent resident and moved with Reneé to her home country of South Africa.

# Sparkling Spirit
# Pacific Ocean

Ecuador had cast her spell but I was reluctant to succumb easily without first testing the waters elsewhere. Jane was in Galapagos; it was too small for both of us so I decided to go around the world making sure that there was nowhere else I would rather be. I managed to hitch a ride heading west on a tiny ten-metre yacht with three permanent crew. The Sparkling Spirit was beautiful, a Sparkman & Stephens, 50 years old, wooden hull bestowing her with lovely lines. I had not sailed before but trusted in the competence of the young English captain and the younger couple; they had already arrived safely to the Galapagos from the UK after all. It took a few days to get to know each other, buy provisions and set up the boat for the trans-Pacific crossing. While in Academy Bay, a single-handed yachtsman dropped anchor a few boats along from us. We held our beers high and invited him to the Spirit. Soon onboard, dripping wet, beer in hand, he was relating stories of his adventures to date. He introduced himself as Rod Newall, an ex-British Army Green Jacket. He was impressive, we became instant friends and over the following days he had a calming influence on any nerves we might have had prior to casting off. James, our captain was a purest, a sailing snob actually. He refused to use the motor at all, even leaving the mooring and once at sea sailed by sextant. He had just finished reading Dougal Robertson's book Survive the Savage Sea, as had I, where a slightly larger, wooden yacht, on its way to the Marquesas, as we were, was holed by killer whales 200 miles out from Galapagos. The crew survived 38 days at sea in the appalling conditions of a tiny raft. I think it was our fourth day since leaving. It was night-time and James was on watch. I was the only one of us that seemed to know much about biology so it was no surprise when James, in total panic, screamed at the top of his lungs, "Pete! Pete!" I jumped from my bunk and scrambled through the hatch. 'Fuckin' killer whales!" he continued. *He was right,* I thought. There were huge cylindrical tubes of phosphorescent light barrelling around the yacht. There were many, maybe ten individuals and their paths were criss-crossing close to our hull. James was apoplectic. Something was awry. I studied them, wracking my brains and suddenly yelled, "They are not breathing!" Indeed, they were not, therefore, they were not whales, air breathing mammals, at all. They were actually huge, oceanic tuna, blue fins, probably with a length of eight feet or so and a girth of the same. Record breakers but not boat breakers.

A few days later, when only Angela was on deck taking her turn at the helm, she shrieked and we all scampered up the ladder. A missile flew past her head at eye-level, then another, she dodged it. There was a fusillade of animated projectiles, flying six to eight feet clear of sea level. Some landed with a splat on the deck, writhing and pulsating colour. They were flying squid! I had no idea that they could come so far out of the water. We had obviously sailed through a large school of them and they took to the air in their natural escape response. James grabbed a bucket and collected enough of Neptune's bounty to satiate all of us on a very welcome plate of fresh calamar.

My mind cleared as we headed deeper into the ocean. Insignificance in our environment became overwhelming. I remembered everything, almost all of which I've long since re-forgotten. Every detail came back to me of my days in the Duke of York's Royal Military School, a boarding school where I was very unhappy. It was all boys and I really needed girls around. I remembered all my classmates and, in particular my best friend Andy Smith. I used to spend my half-terms with him at his parent's house in Southampton. I could picture him clearly. I can't anymore. I could not in fact believe the depth of my memories. I thought the disc had been wiped but all the information had been stored away in some hidden folders, where it must be again now. I thought about Andy a lot. I had not heard from him, or even anything about him in over fifteen years. I wondered what he was up to.

In the middle of our passage, almost the furthest point from land on the globe we hit a storm. It lasted three full days. We took down all the cloth except for a storm jib to give steerage and asked ourselves if we were going to make it. There were huge swells, reaching as high as the spreaders on the main mast, but no breaking waves. There was a full moon. We were forced to surf every swell, to point the bow down the wave and surf it. One mistake by any of the four of us and we each knew it would all be over. We had to trust, in our exhausted sleep, that all was well above deck. I learned to let go and saw my life as finite. They were tense days yet none of us was worried, we each accepted our fate and got on with the job at hand, cooking, eating, sleeping or surfing. The moon saved us, it gave us the chance to see the shape of the swell and aim the boat correctly. We bobbed like a cork, one minute completely surrounded by a mountain of water, the next sucked to the top of everything with views forever – mind blowing!

After 21 days, we spied the magical outline of Fatu Hiva on the horizon. An oceanic shield volcano, it was tall and verdant. The following morning we were already upon the island and had rounded the northern tip when the stunningly beautiful Bay of Virgins opened before us straddled by two gigantic monoliths forming the arms of a welcome embrace. If there was a paradise on Earth then this was it. As we dropped anchor in the transparent blue water and furled our sails, a muscled native pushed his out-rigger canoe off the beach and paddled towards us with a sack on the bow. He reached the Sparkling Spirit in no time and without a word being spoken, hoisted the heavy bundle on to our deck and left. It was full of grapefruit, the perfect gift to anyone arriving from three weeks at sea. We went ashore and sat for a while on the beach. It felt strange to have escaped the reduced confines of wooden decking. A man walked down to us. He entered the water with a mask and spear and spent close to 45 minutes before he came out with an octopus which he promptly began beating on the rocks. When fully dead and tenderised, he offered it to us. As the French speaker in the group, I first thanked him then refused on the grounds that it was the only thing he had caught, how could we possibly take it. With much to and fro. He finally floored our argument by saying, "Why do you think I went fishing in the first place?" The island population was a mere hundred strong and the most surprising yet rewarding thing of all was that the currency was generosity. He who gave the most was the richest. Our arrival was early July, one week before the big Polynesian Bastille celebrations where teams from various islands converge on Papeete to compete in games, dancing and sports, we were the only visitors on the island. The women were gyrating in grass skirts to the rhythmic beat of a plethora of hollow log drums, practice was fervent, the atmosphere electric and our eyes boggled as we pleaded with our inner rationale never to leave. An 11-year-old girl, whose name translated as Princess, had already been passed on by her parents to her grandmother and it became her duty to make sure that frangipani flowers were always behind our ears and to sew, in the correct order, a flower garland for each of us to wear every day. She also gave us royal treatment as a tour guide. From the desert of an expansive ocean to the abrupt verdant lushness and dramatic topography of Fatu Hiva, peopled with exquisite mortals of rare humanity, the experience was surreal and almost overwhelming. It was one of the hardest places I have ever had to leave.

We sailed north to Hiva Oa to officially register our entry to the Marquesas Islands with the port authorities before sailing on to explore Ua Pou and Nuku Hiva. It was our first chance to use a telephone since we left Galapagos and I was anxious to phone home to my folks to tell them that we were safe. They were very pleased to hear from me, congratulated us all and then my mum said, "You will never guess who phoned while you were sailing."

"Who?" I said.

"Andy Smith!"

# Catching Crocodiles
# Australia

We continued onward in our tiny but loveable vessel. Four adults trapped in a space 10 metres by 4 by 1.5 decks. Incredible when you think about it. If you had asked us to remain together on a piece of lawn, staked out to the same dimensions, for three weeks, we would probably have ripped each other's throats out. On the ocean, however, it is everything but boring. There is an intense sense of well-being, purpose and connection. We sailed on to Bora Bora watching the rich, until their shallowness became too much for us and set a course for the Cook Islands. At anchor in Rarotonga James decided to stay for a few days to re-provision. I managed to procure a Cook Islands driving license and we explored the island. My sailing days had come to an end and it was time for me to leave. Those 21 rotations of the planet that we made between Galapagos and Fatu Hiva remain, to this day, one of the most intensely rewarding experiences of my life but, I was on a deadline. I had watched, some years previously, a documentary on TV about a team, headed by the legendary Professor, Grahame Webb, catching crocodiles in the Northern Territory of Australia. I knew I wanted to do it too. A university friend, I discovered, was already working with Grahame and she was willing to help me make the connection. I jumped on a plane and flew the rest of the way to Australia, via Auckland, landing at Melbourne. Darwin, the capital of the Northern Territory, was a long way away but I wanted to go overland. Australia has large double-decker coaches travelling across the continent. I snagged the best seat in the house in the front row at the top of one of them, looking out to a panoramic view of the outback. The journey was three days but spectacularly the great red desert was in full technicoloured bloom. The flowers were amazing, having sprung up simultaneously after some rain. Enormous red kangaroos bounded across our path. I couldn't understand why I was the only one excited. Stopping at Alice Springs and Humpty Doo *en-*

*route,* I eventually arrived, in stifling heat, to Darwin. A quick appraisal of my new town and it seemed that everyone wore a black singlet, had a beard and drove a Harley Davidson – including the women. I was met by Christine Lippai, my college buddy, and driven to the edge of the bush on the outskirts of Howard Springs where I was to set myself up in a demountable (caravan) for the extent of my visa – the next six months. When the Sparkling Spirit caught up to us in Darwin, there was a big reunion and Christine left Australia, continuing on with James and the Sparkling Spirit while I stayed, she has since gone on to become a deputy chair of the IUCN Crocodile Specialist Group.

Where we were located near Howard Springs was a wild area, feral water buffalo were always close by, orange-footed scrub fowl, black kites as abundant as crows, blue-winged kookaburras and my favourites, blue-tongued skinks were all common. Grahame was a true character, the archetypal Aussie and easy to like. He ran a crocodile research facility and was the leader in his field. Crocs are a threat to people in Australia, particularly the massive 'Saltie' or saltwater croc which regularly attacks the unprepared. Grahame's maxim for croc conservation success was two-fold 'Love the People' and 'Use it or Lose it'. It worked.

I was quickly absorbed into the team and issued with my tools of the trade – a Toyota Landcruiser (my favourite vehicle), a one metre length of sprung stainless steel no thicker than a knitting needle and a Magnum .44 handgun, Dirty Harry's 'Most powerful handgun in the world'. The idea of the gun was to shoot feral wild boar to be fed to the crocs back at the facility. It was the beginning of the egg-laying season and my first job was to do a round-circuit, alone, of 200 miles through the bush to visit seven different, drying billabongs, every second day, where 'Freshies' (freshwater crocs) were laying eggs. Following their tracks, I estimated where the crocs had buried the clutch and began poking my steel rod into the sand. One of the main goals was to beat the predatory goannas and wild boars to the clutches before they made a meal of them. At the first sign of a yolky, sand-covered, tip to my steel, I knew I had pierced the 'sacrificial egg' and began digging up the rest by hand. Carefully transporting each clutch back to the lab, they were incubated *ex-situ* for eventual repatriation. At the end of egg-laying, our job was to catch the adults, scute them, weigh them, sex them then release them. My two partners in crime, Stuart and Brett, were hardened croc guys. I took their lead. With nothing more than our swags on the ground, we slept under a huge night sky to the sounds of the bush. For days on end, we visited each billabong in turn until it was fully 'processed'. The first and perhaps single-most important thing was to study the billabong and all its inhabitants to confirm that one or more of the heads was not a Saltie. Salties are game changers that play by a whole different set of rules. Once we knew who we were dealing with nets were strung in a zig-zag pattern from one side of the pond to the other and back again. We were each armed with three sets of screwdrivers, small, medium and large, stuffed into the back of our belts. Then we got in, chest deep and herded the crocs towards the nets. As soon as one hit it had to be disentangled before it drowned, taken ashore, blindfolded and tied off to the capture line. If your mate was bitten during any of this, we first had to check if the croc was small, medium or large, grab the appropriate screwdriver set and use it to prise open the jaws and release the friend. At the end of capture, we had almost 100 crocs tied off on the line at any one billabong. They all had to have their biometric data taken and numbered, if not already done so, by slicing off some tail scutes in a particular order, before release back into the water. I was in my element, improved only by a handful of beers, opened with the foresight of the Magnum and stories shared between mates.

Back in Howard Springs, the back door of my demountable opened into a fenced-off area of bush the size of a tennis court. It was here that Stuart and Brett kept their pack of bull terriers. They were kept mean-and-lean (except when I would let them in and on to my couch for some TLC, until I was caught too many times). For fun, Stu and Brett had a couple of favourite pastimes, either hunting wild boar or wild buffalo. The dogs loved it. With the pigs, they would either grab them physically or bale them up until they could be stabbed by one of the guys. Field surgery was a regular necessity every time the sharp tusks of the pigs opened up the dogs. With buffalo, it was different. First prize was a dog swinging from each buffalo ear and one from the nose until Stu or Brett could get in with a rifle. Great fun they told me – I should try it. No thanks, I told them. If buffalo or pigs became too mundane, there was always the option to drive around (no dogs) and shoot a few brumbies (feral horses) or go lamping, with a rifle, for cats at night.

As things calmed down a little between crocodile seasons, something came up which I volunteered for. The wildlife commission were looking for two guys (they had one already) to be left on Cape Hotham for ten days and cut bushwalking trails zigzagging across the peninsula. Cape Hotham is a remote, uninhabited area east of Darwin, apparently the last habitation was by aborigines fifty years previously. We were to access by speedboat from Darwin, passing the Vernon Islands to port. We were given two days to prepare before setting off. It was very exciting as there were apparently dingoes out there, kangaroos, lots of snakes, crocs and wild pigs. My interest for going was as a naturalist. When I met up with my new buddy, Jack, it was obvious that we were different. He was dressed like an Alabama redneck, full camouflage, baseball cap, sunglasses a huge jagged-edged Bowie knife and the rifle that he had been issued with, over his shoulder. He was Australian; therefore, he got the rifle. We were augmented with machetes, water containers, food, cooking utensils and insect screens to sleep under. Jack wanted to do this because he saw himself as Rambo.

We were dropped off, after a long ride, onto a beach on the western shore of the peninsula. The boat crew were then going to continue up the coast and every few kilometres would flag a tree with red plastic tape and leave a drinking water stash below it. They would pick us up in ten days near the lighthouse in the north. We would see them coming. The boat crews parting words were 'Watch out for the salties!' We had been instructed on how to be safe with the large saltwater crocodiles. It was predicted that they would actually be in the surf close to the beach. To wash dishes, for example, the instruction was to head directly to the water's edge at ninety degrees to the shore, stop about fifteen metres early turn right or left, walk another twenty metres parallel to the shore and then access the water. The crocs will watch your approach, submerge and grab you at the expected point of entry unless these precautions are followed. We did not have tents but individual mosquito nets that we slept under. These could not be pitched in view of the water or the crocs would come up the beach at night to grab us. I believed them. It all sounded like *bona fide* croc tactics to me. The first thing we did after the boat left was lug all our gear over the first ridge of the beach, away from reptilian eyes. Then it was time to wash. Behind our camp, under the forest cover was a shallow tannic billabong. We decided it would be a good place to bathe. Jack handed me the rifle, to keep guard, he stripped off and waded into the water up to his knees. As if commanded, a flotilla of scores of giant, six-inch horse leeches came free-swimming, undulating in a sinusoidal motion, directly towards Jack. It was like something out of a horror movie. He turned and came out of the water very stressed. It was then that I noticed something much more frightening. He had a pierced foreskin with a gold ring running through it. This was more like a scene from a thriller. We were alone for ten days in the Australian bush, crocs, dingoes, wild pigs, anything could dispose of me. He had the jagged knife and the rifle, which he had now reclaimed. This was no ordinary guy. Nobody with a pierced foreskin can claim to be an ordinary guy. I realised how potentially vulnerable I was and decided to watch my back. I tried to ignore the ring and never brought it up in conversation.

The plan was to cut diagonal trails with our machetes from west to east and back again. We would leave our gear and campsite until enough trail was cut before moving camp. Out in the woods, we heard some wild boar. They were close and Jack managed to shoot one for our rations. They are introduced and very destructive. We butchered it and took the hindquarters back with us to camp. Two hams, which we left in a tree. It was not long before a magnificent wedge-tailed eagle, Australia's largest raptor, came down and actually stole one of the legs. I was very impressed. One morning, Jack was up before me and down on the beach when I heard him shouting, "Pete, Pete, there's been a big bloody gnarly bird on the beach," I ran down and sure enough, there were what looked like giant bird tracks. He was the Aussie Rambo. Surely, he must know something about the bush. I was still new in Australia but I was damned sure that there was no bird alive leaving tracks two feet long. I looked hard, he had me confused.

Then it dawned on me. "It's a bloody kangaroo, mate!" I said with perhaps a tinge of scorn. The outside 'toes' were the kangaroo's big flat feet and the centre and hind 'toes' were the tail imprint left as it loped forward. Who *was* this guy? Cutting the trails was much harder work than anticipated and the ground was boggy in places. By day ten, we had done what we could and sat to wait for the rendezvous in the north. We waited for hours, sitting on the beach looking out to sea. The most amazing thing to me was that there was a big croc, pacing up and down in the shallow surf watching us intently, yet it was nearly an hour before we had spotted it. It was hunting us. If I walked up the beach, it followed and back, it turned around, it was an unnerving feeling. The boat came, picked us up and took us home. I had enjoyed it all immensely and tried to put behind me my irrational fear of the ring.

At the end of the 'dry', when crocs were highly concentrated in any remaining water it was time to count the salties. As three of us unloaded the *tinny* (small aluminium skiff) off the *ute* (Aussie for truck) at the water's edge, the reflected light highlighted the horrendous scars of the team leader's mangled leg hinting at the damage a croc can do. The sun set and we pushed off, unstable, into the water. Our job was to count crocs and guesstimate their size by calculating head length and multiplying by a factor of seven. The closer we got, the more accurate our estimates. As we scanned the water with the flashlight, it was like a city of lights. Hundreds of burning red eyes reflected back at us, akin to floating in crocodile soup, except these monsters were alive and hungry. I only ever got one crumb of advice whilst in Australia and it was then. As I was standing in the tiny craft, to get a higher view of the heads, in a thick Aussie drawl, I was advised, "If ya gonna fall in the water anywhere in Australia, don't let it be here!"

Leaving Australia and heading further west on my sojourn Grahame connected the dots with more croc guys along the way. I continued through some of Asia, which was pretty much as to be expected. I used to live in Singapore as a child during one of my dad's army tours. We travelled in the area as a family and once went to the Penang snake temple where two venomous pit vipers were draped around my neck and my dad recorded it with his Kodak camera. I use the image today as my Facebook profile picture. On this trip, I returned to the same temple, I'm not sure why really but I carried the photo of me, as a young boy, posing with the two snakes. I showed the photo to the oldest guard I could find, just for interest. He took the photo and studied it, then looked up at me and said, "Oh yes, those were the days before we used to take the fangs out! Now all the snakes have yellow dots on their heads when they are safe." I left Malaya by train. Dramatically, it derailed between Penang and Bangkok resulting in me landing on top of a guy called John, who turned out to be a great travel buddy. Hiring a motorbike each, we drove from Bangkok to the far north of Thailand where we slept rough, including in a cramped chicken shed, while spending time with the various opium growing hill tribes of the region. After more fascinating days staying in a working camp with the elephants and crew of a logging concession highlights were waning and I pushed on to India. Hosted at the Madras Crocodile Bank in the company of its founder Romulus Whitaker was an untold privilege and I had Grahame to thank for it. India was special for me and a place I would be drawn to frequently in later years.

Subconsciously, Africa was my real target. It was the place I believed I would come closest to nature and to mammals. Of all the natural kingdom mammals move me most, I connect with them best – probably because I am one. Zimbabwe was my first and only call. I started out assigned to a wildlife vet, given jobs like collecting ticks from warthog burrows or cutting the heads off moribund bats in caves for rabies studies. This led me to join a game capture team where we caught hundreds of wild antelope in thrilling encounters. There is a lot of movement, commercial or otherwise, of game animals in southern Africa as most of the parks are artificially fenced and an exact balance is hard to meet. Some areas need antelope, others need to get rid of some. Being the Africa virgin, I was likeably abused. It was to me that Mike La Grange said each time, "Go and pull out the males," as he shoved me into the wooden 'crush' area at the end of the fabric capture tunnel. Alone, inside, I might have been with up to fifty crazed impala, a mix of males and females, driven into the confined space by a noisy chopper. They were in three dimensions, clipping my head with their sharp hooves as they leapt over me. It was like watching meat in Brownian motion. Peering through narrow slits the guys thought my efforts were hilarious. Grabbing, one-handed, a single horn (the first time) the animal bucked high and away from me almost wrenching my arm from its socket. The trick was both horns, with both hands and wrangle each male to a standstill before calling for the escape hatch to be opened.

Other capture methods included chasing, on foot from a camouflaged position, larger antelope into a net as the chopper drove them past you. As the buck (which was always bigger close up) hit the net, you had to be there and jump on it, an animal immensely stronger than you, and try to pin it down, screaming a Mayday to the runners for help. At the end of a day, nursing my tired and bruised body, while soaking in a tin bath, heated by a donkey boiler, I dutifully pulled the 100+ ticks from my skin, which had worked their way into places I never knew I had, before I could finally crash into the relative luxury of an old army cot. I saw my first aardwolf from the chopper and watched in awe as a Tsessebe bull had to be shoved with the skid of the imposing helicopter as it stood in defiance on an anthill – tough cookie I thought, but that was Africa.

My Zimbo croc contact panned out well and I had fabulous first-hand experience of working in a commercial croc farm. I slept in the owner's house who was an ex-member of the British South Africa Police force. After first getting to know me over several days, he asked a favour. Would I mind if he and his wife both went out for the evening, as they had not been out together for a very long time. "Of course," I replied, not fully understanding their request. He took me to their bedroom where I was to sleep until they returned. Against one whole wall was an armoury. Before they were content to leave, he gave me full weapons training on a variety of automatic weapons, told me to lock myself in, left a loaded shotgun under my pillow and the two, large, Rhodesian ridgebacks in guard mode. White-farmer murders were a real thing.

I was extremely happy in Africa, where, after 34 years living in Ecuador, I am now back and writing this book. At the time, though, I was broke and desperately needed a cash injection. Somewhere I had seen an insignificant advertisement for a job vacancy in the Falkland Islands, looking for a qualified marine biologist to work in the Falklands Islands Fisheries Department.

# Jigging for Squid
# Falkland Islands

The Falkland Islands lie off the southeast of the Southern Cone of South America, perhaps three hundred miles from Argentina. They are sub-Antarctic islands. Sovereignty has, of course, been hotly disputed but I can tell you first-hand that the few thousand inhabitants that live throughout the archipelago of more than 700 islands are British. In fact, they are even more British than their namesakes in the north. Sheep and wool farming was the mainstay of the economy which has now become superseded by revenue from licensing fishing rights within the 200-mile Exclusive Economic Zone. The discovery of offshore oil might very well soon be the top earner.

From a biological standpoint, the islands are spectacular. I have travelled widely in the archipelago, including some photographic overflights in a British forces helicopter. Reneé and I have even managed to spend several days with researchers way up on Steeple Jason Island, an absolute wildlife jewel and home to the largest black-browed albatross colony in the world. I have spent several nights totally alone on Kidney Island, camping in the ten-foot-high tussock grass trying to avoid the big, territorial, Southern Sealions bulls who I swear were out to get me and really, really wanted to kill me. I was there to photograph the nightly spectacle of the thousands of sooty shearwaters that return to their underground nests at dusk. The Falklands are like the Galapagos, sure they don't have endemic marine iguanas or giant tortoises but they have a very high biomass. Thousands and thousands of five penguin species (including the largest gentoo penguin colony in the world), tons (literally) of elephant seals, fur seals, sealions, geese, hawks, caracaras and so it goes on. What makes them better than Galapagos is that you are able to be totally alone at a colony for as long as you like. No guide is necessary (it assumes good behaviour) and no itinerary to follow. You can't go absolutely everywhere of course and certain areas are definitely out of bounds. They are demarcated by red, metal signs on fences emblazoned with bold, white, skull and crossbones and the words 'Danger Mines'. The cool thing about these no-go areas, I have been reliably told, is that the Ministry of Defence soldier in charge of demarcating the minefields was a keen birder. He wrapped a few fences a little wider than necessary to include some penguin nesting colonies or in some cases around colonies where there were never even any mines in the first place. Conservation in action!

Arriving in Stanley, the capital of the Falklands, I was met by the fisheries boss who turned out to have been one year ahead of me at Bangor University studying the same course. Things looked good. I was to work as an observer at sea for stints of several weeks at a time on foreign fishing vessels, working in some of the roughest seas in the world, recording catches, fishing effort and seabird data. I longed to be back on the ocean.

Lodged in a communal house on Squid Row, after initial training, I was sent off with an unfamiliar laptop computer and a sailors duffle bag worth of gear. My assignments were varied. On an old and dilapidated, rust bucket of a Polish stern trawler I was anonymous and went about my business without much social interaction. My closest friendship was with the doctor who had a smattering of English. Together we imbibed the medicinal alcohol from the first aid supplies, by way of festive distraction. The target fish species for the vessel was blue whiting and I spent much of my time in the factory below decks, measuring and sexing fish as well as collecting cysts of the heavy parasite load. Especially when the trawl was fishing, the ship rolled, pitched and yawed 'like a bitch on heat', as the expression went. A plethora of birds were regularly trapped by their feet in the trawl net as the trawl was stretched when it hit the surface, from albatross, penguins and petrels to dozens of diminutive storm petrels. They mostly ended up in my care, either in my shower or the smaller ones rolled in towels in my drawers overnight if they needed to recover enough before being released.

On the Spanish trawler, the target species was a more upmarket hake with the occasional toothfish as bycatch. I was designated officer status on board and consequently plied with wine at every raucous meal. Likewise, on a Japanese squid jigger, I was treated with respect. The captain relinquished his cabin for me and every crewmember gave a welcome present, be it as mundane as a pair of slippers or a set of chopsticks. Food was abundant and delicious. I could even help myself 24/7 to cook up a storm from any of the pre-prepared foods in the refrigerator. The one weird aspect was the *ofuro* bath. It was a voluminous stainless-steel tub, large enough to fit a dozen naked Japanese men standing. Filled with seawater, in the tub stood an oversized, bare, kettle element to heat the liquid to scorching point. The only sign in English to be found on the entire vessel was above the tub warning 'Danger! High voltage!'. I chose discretion over valour and bathed early – on my own.

A squid jigger is a highly specialised fishing vessel. There are some 20 alternating long and short arms on either beam, each with an elliptical collection drum at the base from which a nylon line is played out over a revolving spool at the distal end once the arms are lowered outboard into a near horizontal position. Attached to each line is a series of brightly coloured lures equipped with a double crown of multi-pronged, barbless hooks. The key is the lighting. Some 200, two-kilowatt lightbulbs are suspended above the ship's rails, lighting the vessel like a city and throwing light into the depths below. Often a 5kw red or blue lightbulb is also lowered into the water to create an 'angry' response in the squid. The captain and fishing master watch on the fish finder as the squid gather below the hull, attracted by the lights. The ship is static in the water, held by a sea anchor, or drogue, akin to a submerged parachute that causes drag. Once a ball of squid is gathered the lines are dropped overboard and 'jig' erratically with the elliptical collection drum repeatedly up and down through the school. The squid grab the lures in a frenzy, are dragged to the surface and flicked over the spool, whizzing past our heads to land with a wet splat onto the deck. Chromatophores still flashing, I learned to decapitate them, slice the mantle into strips and gorge myself. We also dried them on the exposed hot water pipes and ate them as squid jerky for a pre-bedtime snack at dawn. The efficiency was wicked and one single night I recorded a catch of 75 tons. Although the licensed fishery in the Falkland Islands is one of the best managed in the world, beyond the FOCZ (Falkland Islands Outer Conservation Zone), its 200-mile exclusive economic zone, the high seas are a no man's land and the realm of pirates. Anything goes. Life is cheap and profit is king. Once, while jigging on the inside limit of the FOCZ, the squid had gathered, we were fixed in position by our drogue, when a Russian pelagic stern trawler came full speed on a collision course with our starboard side. Everyone was screaming while the captain repeatedly blasted the foghorn. It was a very tense moment. At the last possible millisecond, the Russian dramatically turned to port. Our hulls nearly crashed together and, as his trawl swept under the jigger, it stole our squid and disappeared into the night.

I had obviously done well enough in my job, in the eyes of the powers that be, when, with a certain tact and discretion, they asked if I might consider being seconded to a Taiwanese flagged vessel. Although licensed to operate in Falklands waters no observer had ever been placed on a Taiwanese vessel so far, they told me – they were too rough. When they came into Stanley harbour the Taiwanese crew would scramble to the West Store on Ross Road and buy out all the cans of dog and cat food. Because there was a picture of a dog or a cat on the label, they thought that it was what the can contained and bought it for food. I agreed to go.

After some days R&R with my colleagues up in the Squid Row house, I was mentally preparing for my new trial. They had been rewarding days off. When I returned to shore my good friend and colleague, Jo, was excited for me to meet her new boyfriend. He was a single-handed yachtsman, that had pulled into Stanley, on his way around the world and chosen to stay. We met and instantly recognised each other. It was Rod Newall who I had last met in the Galapagos Islands before we set sail across the Pacific in the Sparkling Spirit. The coincidence was too much and accentuated our friendship. For days, we were like a family of fisheries staff, Falkland Islanders and Rod. We spent time on the blindingly white, stunning beaches, cooked communally, visited the penguins in 'camp', went out sailing on his yacht and partied at night in the bay on the Black Pig, which was an Argentine tug captured as a prize during the Falklands conflict. Rod was well spoken, good looking, dashing almost and virtually celebrated by the community. Jo was giddy. Finally, to much dismay, he sailed away from the archipelago leaving a hollow sensation behind him. When passing the Straits of Gibraltar, heading north, the British Navy deployed from 'The Rock' and arrested him. On a previous call to his uncle, which had been recorded by the British intelligence services, Rod had as good as admitted that he had brutally murdered both his mother and father, with his younger brother as an accomplice, in their home on the Channel Island of Jersey. Five years previously, he had bludgeoned his parents to death and the brothers had then buried them both in the woods. The motive was said to be money and could have been the perfect murder if he had not been racked with guilt and privately confessed to his uncle. Jo was addled and became undone. Rod is now free.

Before boarding the treacherous Taiwanese jigger, I was called in for a briefing, the gist of which, in high English, was that if I should have any problem that should require urgent recovery, I should say Bravo, Bravo, Bravo, during my radio schedule. The message will be understood and the Fisheries Protection vessel will pick me up at her earliest convenience. Should the situation be even more pressing, such as rape, I was to say Tango, Tango, Tango somewhere in the message and all haste would be made for my extraction. It was not a briefing that inspired confidence. Although required, under terms of the fishing license, to accept a government observer on board when asked, to a Taiwanese captain I would not be popular. I had no powers of arrest but became the eyes of illegal activity and the under-declaration of catch tonnage. I boarded the Fisheries vessel and we head out to the quadrant in which the Taiwanese jigger was fishing. It was blowing at least a force eight and we hunkered down through the night. The day saw flocks of albatross, following boats and dancing nonchalantly on the high winds. That night, with little moon, winds having dropped to a blustery force five we reached our ship. An agreement was struck and I was snatched from the comfort of little England, whisked, in an inflatable, at high speed, from wave crest to wave crest on an angry, inky-black sea, by a crew whose movie had been interrupted when they were told to take me to a place I didn't want to go. We craned our necks to look up at the skeleton crewmen leaning over the rails. A rope ladder was thrown down. In a serious roll, I had to grab the ladder, duffle bag on my back, and scurry up the side before the next roll dunked me under. It was treacherous but for the fisheries captain, it was now or never. He had places to be. I climbed over the rail, the ladder was pulled aboard and the RIB peeled away back to sanctuary. Language was the first and most crucial barrier. I was shown to a cabin. A basic shell with not even a mattress. Adopting an air of authority and standing tall, lest I make the mistake allowing them to exploit any weakness on my part, I argued for a mattress. Barging into another cabin, I began removing one until my message was understood. A mattress was delivered. It bowed like a banana in the bed-well being too long at head and foot – no sheets or bedding but a mattress, nevertheless. Not only was the boat rough but it was dangerous. Rats running over the deck were prevalent and accepted, the food was awful and the only thing I was ever given to eat was rice with chopped, yellow intestines. Of what I will never know, nor do I want to find out. Rat maybe? Theft was obviously a problem and everything was locked in my duffle at all times. Crew safety was abysmal, life was inconsequential. During foul, stormy weather, the lines of the jigging arms would tangle and the Filipino crew were made to crawl four or five metres outboard on the arms, untethered in any way, to disentangle the fishing lines. Crew are regularly lost overboard every year with no hope of recovery. Being Filipinos, they were considered expendable and treated very badly. They did however speak Spanish and I could converse with them which I did with relish. The cook was the largest man on the ship. He was rampantly gay and carried a big carving knife. Scarily, he would come searching for me on the boat and invariably I took refuge, cloistered in a Filipino cabin. In an effort to 'know thy enemy and keep him close', the captain mellowed towards me. We 'spoke' with difficulty, by means of a two-way electronic translator, it was tedious and not much was said. One night, however, he invited me to his cabin. We sat on two chairs, separated by a metal waste bucket on the floor, in front of a large TV screen close to our faces. He produced a bottle of a potent spirit alcohol awash with suspended particles that turned out to be crushed deer velvet – considered a powerful aphrodisiac. I understood the potential power of the drink when, accompanied by a crescendoing 'Whoooa!' He unfurled his index finger from a clenched fist until it pointed rigidly upwards into my face. Drinks were poured, a cheers was made and he turned on the TV to indulge me in hard-core, triple 'X' porn. The bucket was a spittoon, which, after each offensive rasp of the throat, he regularly used. I was an unwilling and captive audience and it felt like an eternity before I could finally, politely, bow my way out of his cabin to navigate my way back to my own whilst evading the cook. How close I was to ever raising the Tango, Tango, Tango alarm I will never know but I did understand that it would all have been over long before the fisheries protection vessel Falklands Protector ever broke the horizon to bring me home. My four months in the islands flew by and I have returned many times since, having spent about a year of my life in the archipelago. Without doubt, the Falkland Islands remain one of my top wildlife destinations anywhere in the world.

# Jungle Days
# Ecuador

With more money in my pocket than when I left Galapagos almost three years earlier, I returned to Ecuador to live. This small, jewel of a country, perhaps the most biodiverse per unit area of any on Earth, had won my heart – I was back! Zimbabwe was a close second. This time however, I figured I would head into the jungle to live and guide, somewhere less predictable than Galapagos. The best and most prestigious lodge at the time was La Selva, it had, after all, featured in Playboy Magazine and it was Eric Swartz, the owner, to whom I made my pitch to become a guide. Eric was a small man and heavily burdened by all the attendant attributes. He made it abundantly clear that he was king of the jungle and that should I ever be deemed appropriate guide material, not only would I be forever in his debt, but his word was gospel and if I wanted monkeys, he would pay me peanuts. I got the job. For all his faults, through clever marketing, a unique position in the marketplace and a touch of vision, La Selva was a success. It was also a fabulous place to work (except for the odd weekend when Eric would travel down the Napo River, with his Sony Walkman shutting out the world, to descend on the Lodge and begin banging out messages to the guides, in red ink, in his drunken stupor, on his typewriter starting with 'Shut the Fuck Up!').

There was simply so much information to soak up and working with fellow guides, we would bounce our observations off each other to try to make sense of the new things we had seen. A sense of camaraderie was high and indeed I am forever grateful to Eric for the opportunity even though I may never have got around to actually telling him.

It was here in La Selva that I met Reneé. She had come as a tourist and we hit it off immediately. There was obviously a significant mutual attraction but the actual pickup was as cheesy as it is possible to imagine. She was allocated to my group, along with others, twice her age and half her agility and so became the obvious choice for my dastardly trickery, without drawing any attention. I took her by the hand and walked her up a 45-degree fallen log until she was two metres above the ground when I told her to stay. Walking back some 30 metres along the open, straight path, I reached behind a tree and grabbed the end of my pre-cut vine which hung 40 metres from the canopy (every self-respecting guide should have one). Taking hold with both hands, yodelling like Tarzan, I ran fast and hard directly at Reneé. Leaving the ground with the pendulum motion, I snatched her off her perch in my tightly gripping legs and we swung freely to and fro until finally falling in the mud. At the edge of a lake, I proposed we go for a quick dip to clean off but felt it my duty to warn her of the electric eels, caimen, anaconda and piranhas. She was free to stay close or hold on to me if she was at all apprehensive, I reminded her. Glued to me like a limpet, it was a *fait accompli*. Six weeks later, from a job as a leading designer for Bob Mackie in the haute couture fashion industry on 7$^{th}$ Avenue, New York, she swapped her plush apartment for a jungle hut which we shared with six others. There was Tom, who remains one of our best friends, famous for his mess and undies so stiff they held the shape of his body when he took them off. There was Jason the young jock from Idaho with the hottest body and who got the biggest tips because of it, which drove us all mad. There was Matieu a Count from France who was crazy about butterflies, which there were many more of in the rainforest than the gardens of his bankrupt chateaux at home. Josh was tall, lanky and the great grandson of Joseph Hooker, Charles Darwin's closest friend. There was Bill, a member of Alcoholics Anonymous who was just the all-round nicest guy you ever met and then there was Efrain – an Ecuadorian who used to spy on Reneé and I at night through the many gaps in the bamboo structure. There was not hot water in our hut and we would have to ship out, a couple at a time, to Quito for a week every month or two, to dry out the fungus which grew on our bodies, but all in all, living in the Amazon rainforest for several years has to be one of my most rewarding experiences. Reneé was the only female member of the staff and naturally her underwear stood out on the clothesline amid a cluster of stained boxers, 'Y fronts' and Jason's all-too-smalls. We were pretty much all dirt poor. I earned US $25.00 per day – the days that I worked – which was supplemented by my tips. These, however, I donated to Reneé who earned no wage but had set up a sewing centre in the local Quichua community downstream. Surprisingly, many of the split palm and bamboo households were already proud owners of a

Singer treadle sewing machine, aspired to by the women, while the men dreamed of chainsaws and shotguns. By begging old clothes (a typical large American T-shirt could make a whole outfit for a kid), she successfully transmuted her skills and taught the women to sew properly. So successful was the venture that donations of whole sewing machines were made for communal use and a permanent structure was built for the women. Living on a shoestring was ultimately fulfilling and meant that we had little to steal but, on the other hand, any luxury was given great value. And so, it was that one day the lodge had its first robbery – a disaster for an establishment attracting foreigners with a lot to lose. Reneé's Victoria Secret underwear went missing. Not only were they expensive but they were my favourites! Admittedly, I went ballistic, part of it was to nip stealing in the bud and protect our expensive binoculars but a lot of it I guess was macho pride. I was sure none of the guys were wearing them – not even Efrain but guessed that one of the local staff had nicked them to woo a girlfriend. In a way, it was funny and reminded me of the time we had a court visit as a school outing when I was 10 and the case being tried was a man from Totness in Devon with the nickname of Dick-the-knicker-picker for his alleged repeat offences of stealing women's underwear. I meanwhile confronted the entire staff during their dinner and fumed at them. I posted a hard-earned $100.00 bill on the noticeboard as reward and in grand finale, with feathers puffed in a dramatic display, punched the table. Crack! I broke my hand. As sore as a bear with a hangover, I retired from the dining hall and whimpered back to my communal hut to great mirth from my colleagues. Reneé had the grace at least (as reward for my valiant efforts to protect her honour), to splint my hand using an old paintbrush. Next morning I was in a canoe to the sleezy oil boomtown of Coca, where crude oil was sprayed on the dirt tracks and called a road and where prostitutes and wildlife traders made a good living. I went to the clinic where a woman, built like a Russian shot-putter, recognised only as a nurse for her white uniform, came to my aid. She held my arm in a vice-like grip while the unsure and unconfident doctor did the deed. Hands are complex and full of bones and by the way he would first look at his hand for comparison and then tugged at my fingers causing me to double over in pain I figured he'd missed out on the hand anatomy lesson. He gave me a wad of gauze which I was made to grip tightly as my whole fist disappeared in a swath of bandages. I returned to the Lodge – 'cured' and continued guiding.

Three days later, there was a doctor in the next group whose curiosity eventually got the better of him. He asked what I had done and we unwrapped the mummified hand for inspection, "Ah ha! Typical boxer's fracture! If you want a club for a hand the rest of your life…" I got the message and we went back to the paintbrush which pleased him greatly.

Still no Victoria Secrets! Things were bad now as the thief was getting away with his booty. A new approach was needed. I went to Pedro Charco, the lodge manager, and we made a plan. Pedro was a large man; a Serrano from the Andes, who ruled with a rod of iron. Harsh but fair I think would sum up his long reign. He was the reason for Eric's success. Difficult to approach sometimes but I liked and respected Pedro. It saddens me to think about him as I write this. One afternoon, many years later, long after we had left, there was yet another, armed, robbery at the lodge and Pedro was forced at gunpoint to open the strong-room. He was deliberately shot in the stomach, in front of the guests and not allowed any assistance as everyone watched him slowly die.

Our plan for the secret, victorious Victoria Secret picker was to call in the Shaman. Shaman's have great power among the local communities and because everyone believes in their power, it seems that he who sweats the most did it! He took the hallucinogen ayahuasca and went into a trance. The 40+ staff were lined up and two sweaty culprits were identified and fired! I was never let in on their identities as my actions could not be trusted but to this day, I wonder what intimate secrets Victoria has to tell?

# Two Weddings
# Ecuador

Reneé and I decided to get married. Yes, we were in love but there were more practical things to think about, she needed a visa to stay, or be thrown out of the country!

The problem was that I myself was between visas and wouldn't qualify to secure her residency. My friend, Andy Watkins, was in the process of forming a company with a somewhat etiolated lawyer in the bustling and (then) majorly corrupt seaport of Guayaquil. He was in the shrimp growing business dealing in broodstock, his company's name was an acronym, it was called SPERM. We travelled to Guayaquil and consulted with his lawyer to try to come up with a solution. Not to worry, he had the answer. All Reneé had to do was to marry the lawyer's office boy! The marriage would be annulled after a year and did not even have to be consummated he exclaimed triumphantly. He ignored the fact that the office boy was half Reneé's age and size and omitted to mention that on annulment, fifty percent of Reneé's possessions were to become his, of which, no doubt, half of that would kick back to the lawyer. We left and Reneé cried.

Finally, Andy annexed me to his company and now, with SPERM stamped boldly in my passport, I was fit to be married. Reneé, with a certain trepidation of not being quite sure what she was getting into, was delighted. An obstacle, however, still remained.

I had managed to get a document declaring my proof of bachelorhood from the British consulate – a requirement under Ecuadorian law even though no such certificate exists in the UK. However, since there was no South African embassy or consulate in Ecuador, Reneé could not get the equivalent document that she needed.

So, for three days, in one set of clothes, in the humid tropical city, we trudged the sleezy backstreets looking for a public notary or anyone, who could marry us, do the paperwork (for a bribe of course) and solve all our problems.

It was to no avail as none would legalise our intent. We desperately needed to sign a registry book and produce a marriage certificate. Andy's lawyer had a friend, 100 miles west along the Santa Elena peninsula, who worked for a registry office. The friend lived in a small village called Atahualpa, in which neither Reneé nor I have ever been. For a small sum (according to our lawyer, a large sum according to us), the friend was persuaded to 'borrow' the registry book after the office was closed for the day, jump on a bus to Guayaquil, meet us in the lawyer's office at midnight, get us to sign his book, type out a certificate (full of spelling mistakes but what the hell!) and jump back on the early morning bus to secrete the book back into the office, miraculously recording a foreigner's wedding that no one in the village ever knew happened! Our vows were stated in the office with me having to elbow Reneé every time she was required to say, "*Si, Señor*!" as her Spanish was as yet non-existent. It all went according to plan and we, in our very grimy attire, also caught an overnight bus and headed up to Quito as Man and Wife – we think!

Dissatisfied with our wedding from a romantic point of view, we decided to stage a more traditional ceremony – in the jungle. Back at La Selva with a group of guests in tow, we made an announcement that today, if it did not rain, we would get married. Of course, there were walks planned but as an optional activity, everyone was cordially invited to attend. Arrangements were frantically made. Tour leaders for the group were Shirley Metz, who claims the shared honour of the first women to ski to the South Pole, and her husband, Peter Harrison, an eminent ornithologist. I borrowed a white shirt from Shirley and pair of white shorts from a guest. Reneé had a loose skirt and blouse quickly made by the local Indian women at her sewing centre, decorated with seeds and print designs from a sectioned liana fruit. We began decorating the lodge. Cut palm fronds, tied at the top, were arranged in arches down the small wooden dock leading into the blackwater lake. I arranged our chauffeur and limo – a beautifully honed Quichua Indian called Patricio Jippa and his dugout. Patricio stripped to the waist decorated his body and canoe and looked great. (Tom made a garter belt for Reneé – decorated with seeds – but did not have elastic so used Velcro which in order to stay up was cutting off the circulation and making her foot tingle) Tom and Jason carved out the words 'Just Married' into banana leaves and Bill was prepped as official photographer with my camera. Lastly, I explained to the chef how to construct a three-tier wedding cake. No rain, so the wedding was on. With zero dissention in the ranks of the commandeered congregation, no walks were needed. As Patricio hid around the corner for the drama of surprise, the congregation sat in dugouts pointing at the dock. Numbers swelled as the local Quichua Indians arrived with a large vat of alcoholic *chicha* to get the party going. Potentially unpleasant to a western palate, *chicha* in the rainforest is a mainstay for the local communities. For us, hardened *sacha runas* however, it was the most refreshing thing we could imagine and more than a welcome addition to the fun. Pepe the barman, a Quichua from the Andes as opposed to the Amazon, had a bamboo flute and led Reneé and I down the 'aisle' under the arch of palm fronds playing the first line of 'Here comes the bride' repeatedly on his homemade instrument. Our entry had been delayed by the misadventure of two of the guest canoes which had capsized, dunking the majority of the throng. Bill used most of the film I had given to him recording the calamity but luckily, our guests, in due course, sent us images they had taken. Meanwhile Reneé, who had earlier gone to the forest to pick flowers with the Indian women, had walked into a big nest of chiggers and had now broken out all over her body in a cloak of red, itchy, polka dot bites. Furthermore, the garland of flowers, that was made for her head was too large and obscured her vision. Hence, the need for me to call stop at the end of the dock where Peter the 'priest' was waiting clutching his sermon. Waxing lyrical, as is his want, the speech came to an abrupt stoppage as he yelled 'Toucan!' and a large gawdy bird with an oversized beak, like a flying banana, undulated overhead. Our necks craned skyward until the toucan perched and began yelping incessantly like a whelping puppy for the rest of the ceremony.

The speech over, fresh vows declared and tears in people's eyes the happy couple boarded our flamboyant floating carriage and we were serenely paddled across the lake in a symbolic gesture of going on honeymoon – actually returning to guiding a few hours later. After a few minutes absence, we returned to the dock and led once again by Pepe blowing his singular tune were ushered to the main lounge. The infrastructure at La Selva was rustic and buildings were built in the traditional manner using bamboo for walls, palm leaves for thatch and long lengths of the straight-grained, very strong and flexible, split chonta palm wood for flooring. As we reached the top of the walkway and the open lounge, there, in the far corner stood our magnificent cake. The bride was carved from a turnip and the groom a carrot. They both stood proudly with their feet sunk into the icing of the top tier which balanced precariously a clear 2½ feet above the bottom tier. Three supporting poles of one-inch bamboo held each tier aloft separating it from the next. It was magnificent indeed – but unstable. The wobble factor of the floor immediately became obvious as we attempted to approach the cake in which the wobble was magnified. Like the movement of a skyscraper in an earthquake. The cake became animate and we had to creep up on it. The wobble intensified as more people made it into the lounge and a desperate lunge to save it was ineffective as each layer careened across the table. The damage done, it was rebuilt and really didn't matter. We cut the cake with a machete and passed it around, the food colouring used by the chef had caused everyone's mouth to turn blue but after a little *chicha* that didn't matter either. Our honeymoon was a guest cabin for the night with no neighbours and romance was secured. It was a $60.00 wedding, which was gratifying, as we did not have any more money anyway. Twenty years later, we had to legally reaffirm our marriage which was acknowledged by the British Embassy.

# Beny and Sacha
# Ecuador

It was inevitable that with so much animosity between Eric, the owner of La Selva lodge at the time and the staff that there would be a lot of tension built up between the two factions. As much as we wanted to remain in the jungle, it was not pleasant to stay with Eric.

Most of our guests were keen on natural history and very nice people. The most frustrating guest proclivity that we had to endure was apathy, jadedness or sheer disinterest. Some were just so out of place that, by mutual consent, should simply never have come in the first place. There was a time when a group arrived including a woman with a shock of orange hair, garish red fingernails and high-heeled shoes. In the dugout, being paddled across the beautiful lake, they arrived at the lodge perched alluringly on the embankment. Staff were proudly standing with a tray full of welcome cocktails and it was always at this moment that I would sneak a look at all of their faces to share in the smiles that crept into the corners of their mouths. We disembarked the group and staff unloaded their luggage including the oversized rigid Samsonite suitcase of the redhead. The palm roof thatch of the lodge reflected a bright straw colour in the sunlight while the dark split-palm wood frontage hinted at the promise of shade. We climbed the rustic stairs and stepped inside. The inquisitive group looked around pleased with the sense of harmony and rustic luxury that the lodge offered. The redhead stood silent. She asked, "Where is the reception?"

We said, "This is it." She cried. She quickly became frantic, panicked and distraught. I blame her travel agent for misrepresenting the product but she had been convinced that the pictures she had seen of the 'junglesque' lodge was simply a façade, behind which lay the plush marble, hair salons and elevators of a Hilton Hotel. She never left her cabin until it was time for the group to leave. Some people just don't get it and I have even suffered comments from lodge clients, while being serenely paddled in a dug-out canoe through a gorgeous narrow creak under a full interlocking canopy.

"Wow, this is just like Disney World!"

Another, particularly dull, group, was returning one afternoon from the morning hike. Clad in their rubber boots and still in protective ponchos (as we had had a hint of rain earlier in the morning), they were all tired and drenched with sweat under their garb. Maintenance in a jungle lodge is continuous, as rot and termites are quick to render any wooden structure to dust. To arrive at the lake, for the final leg homeward, we had to walk on a slightly raised boardwalk, a kilometre long, over the marshy surrounds. Every $100^{th}$ slat or so was broken and the head of the passenger contingent would diligently call "Broken board!" at each one. This revelation was verbally passed down the line advising all on-comers of the imminent danger. "Broken board!" "Broken board!" "Broken board!" went the monotonous peal. So utterly unadventurous, I thought and it got to be very waring until I found the funny side and muttered, "So am I! So am I!" with each exclamation. Feeling poor, overworked and underappreciated, it was with some curiosity that shortly afterwards, I was assigned to a small group of a mother, her young son and an armed bodyguard. With our native guide in the lead, the five of us traipsed for days alone through the forest, the son, John Jr, was not much more than a toddler, bedecked in a very expensive pair of hand-made leather cowboy boots, which looked to me, in the words of Toby Keith, like 'The meanest boots on the boulevard'. I had always defended my lack of liquid assets by declaring I was rich in experience. The mother was the lovely Patricia Kluge, socialite and once 'the wealthiest heiress in history' after recently divorcing her media baron husband, John Kluge. Every time I had to pass little John Jr over the creeks or muddy patches to the bodyguard, saving his boots from getting wet, I secretly thought to myself, *Who'd have thought? Here I am, holding a hundred million dollars!*

On one of our dry-out breaks in Quito, where we hoped to desiccate our body fungus and weeping sores in the stringent Andean climate, Reneé and I received a message from a Swiss man to meet him at the café in the Swiss Hotel. Intrigued, we made the meeting and sat down over a coffee with Beny Ammeter. Immediately likable, he told us that he was building a jungle lodge close to La Selva. 180 degree opposite to Eric Swartz in character, Beny's intro was "I need your help, I don't have any money and I don't know how I can pay you." It was an offer we could not refuse. We were desperately keen on the forest but could not stand working for Eric any longer. We immediately went to La Selva's office – quit, made arrangements for Tom to bring out what was left of our possessions and joined forces with Beny. We returned to the jungle to discover Sacha Lodge (Sacha is Quichua for Jungle), set on another stunning blackwater lake, in the early stages of construction – it was awesome. We were shown to our quarters, constructed of wooden planks, roughly hewn with a chainsaw, and told essentially, to take charge. A large two-storey structure, to serve as dining room, lounge, kitchen and bar was already in place, supported by an ingenious latticework structure which sat on the swamp. Experts said it would sink but Beny was good at construction, had vision and, most importantly, balls! It is still there today. A dividing wall, like a septum, separated the kitchen from the public area in the main building. A while later, Reneé and I were alone at a dining table. It was evening, already dark and we were illuminated by candles. They were hungry days, in the beginning, our food supplies were irregular, we sometimes ate large palm beetle grubs with the construction staff by way of alleviating hunger. We were mostly vegetarian as there was only a tiny freezer compartment in our gas fridge. In it were a couple of chicken breasts which we were saving as a special treat. Looking out across the lake we saw a flashlight. Realising that it was a dugout canoe being paddled towards us, we wondered who it could be. It was a guest. Totally unexpected but a guest, nevertheless. Running around like headless chickens, we warned the staff and tried to make everything look professional. He was a German, travelling alone. His luggage was sent to a cabin as we ushered him directly to our table to join us for supper, allowing the cabin to be made up. There was no meat but our precious chicken. We ate together and he commented on our stalwart vegetarianism as he tucked in. Our eyes widened in dismay as we watched each juicy morsel disappear. I looked up. On the second half-floor was a rat. Not a black or brown city rat, but a native, spiny tree rat. They are very cute but to a client a rat is a rat. I discreetly alerted the kitchen staff behind the wooden divide. The chef and his assistant came running out and instinctively grabbed the 'loaded' Huaorani blowguns that were adorning the walls. Now, chasing the rat around, they were firing off the darts at it. It was chaos but the German said nothing. I believe his stoic thought process was, "I have come to see ze jungle. I am in ze jungle. Zis must be vat jungle people do." The chef ran to the open second floor, where the rat was running all over the place, he was wearing his white chef's hat, a white chef's coat and thumping around in rubber boots. He managed to make contact with the rat and kicked it, flying through the air, to land with a thud against the corner of our table. The assistant ran over, and with *his* rubber boots squashed the poor thing underfoot, right below the German, who still said nothing except, "Zat vas delicious chicken."

The lodge was missing cabins, roofing and critically, a trail system. Velisario was a native Quichua Indian from the neighbouring Pilche community. Although Beny had bought his land outright, Velisario ignored that fact and would hunt regularly in the area. He knew it better than anyone. I hired Velisario and we sat down to make a plan. Unable to grasp a written map, he had one in his head already. I explained my criteria and, over a period of many weeks, we carved out our trails. I wanted a system where several groups could be out at any one time and never see or hear each other, to arrive at points of interest every 20 minutes or so be they a stream edge, a giant kapok tree or stranger fig. I wanted to vary the trails between walking and being paddled and that the trails be looped with options of short or long versions. Velisario got the idea very quickly and we joined the dots with our machetes. He knew the extent of the swampy areas (which are harbingers of different species and need to be accessed) but, with no boardwalks as there are today, we waded chest deep or deeper on boundless occasions to access the successive patch of *terra firme* often hundreds of metres away. I always wondered on such a crossing if it was best to have brusque actions to scare the electric eels or would it further attract the anacondas, caimen and piranhas? We thoroughly explored the area and opened up beautiful creeks, previously totally impassable with overgrowth and fallen trees. We even had to build dams to retain the water in the lake once the creeks were opened. We found a lake that not even Velisario knew existed, climbed trees as close to the edge as we could get and saw it to be crammed with caiman. We named it Lagarto Cocha – caiman lake. We named everything and I felt like a true explorer. It was a totally fulfilling and rewarding time. Velisario became my *compadre* as we were honoured with Godparent status of their beautiful daughter Helena. As pseudo managers of Sacha, we had to talk regularly with the Pilche community, with whom we had several agreements in place, of traversing rights over their land, the designation of no hunting areas and a guaranteed supply of raw materials. A meeting was held the first Sunday of every month at the large community structure. The venue quickly filled up, many of the women sporting a tiny pygmy marmoset, the world's smallest monkey, clinging on to their heads. After much convoluted, back and forth discussions, where they would regularly break out in

Quichua, leaving me none the wiser as to their thoughts, we would always end in some kind of agreement. As everyone had made the effort to come, often walking many miles through the forest or paddling for hours up the Napo River, the gathering quickly restructured into pleasure – not business. First was always a football match. Men or women playing with a heavy, sodden, leather ball, often in debilitating heat and humidity they would run around like crazy things leaving us exhausted just spectating. They are a tough forest people and I was amazed to watch women nine months pregnant out on the field running as hard as the rest. One, a friend of ours called Rosio, received a high pass, checked the ball with a thud on her belly and kept running. She gave birth two days later. Next came the feast. The large communal hut possessed one small table and a bench which is where Reneé and I were customarily sat while the remainder of the community were on the floor in two rows facing us. A line of banana leaves was spread out in front of each row. The serving ladies then followed each other dolloping out, onto the leaves in front of each person, whatever they had on offer in their huge aluminium cooking pots. Basically boiled rice, boiled yuca and boiled meat. Reneé, who pleaded vegetarianism on these occasions, was fine with the rice and yuca, but only one of us could get away with that argument so I was given meat. It was bushmeat and could have been anything unlucky enough to be shot but was almost invariably a fine blend of peccary and monkey. Whatever it was would first be singed on the open fire, indiscriminately hacked into chunks and boiled into a big stew. While the 'commoners' at our feet were issued non-descript pieces, I was always given the tastier morsel – the monkey's hands, while the president of the community, also at our table, would get the head. A woolly monkey's hand, charred and boiled, looks very human and not unlike that of the recently severed limb of a child. Under severe public scrutiny, there was no way even to accidentally drop anything on the floor and so with apparent relish, I picked the meat off the bones, left the fingernails on the side and grinned convincingly. The main course was swiftly followed by *chicha*. In this area, the *chicha* is made from yuca (aka manioc or cassava) a cultivar. It is first dug, scraped and boiled (to remove toxic cyanide). The pieces are chewed by the women, from young to old, whereupon, after sufficient mastication, they are spat into a bowl, water added to the mix and left to ferment for three to five days depending on the strength of the alcohol required. The pink liquid, full of stringy and lumpy bits, both looks and smells very much like vomit! It was hard to voluntarily put in my mouth in the early days but by now, I loved it. Hard to refuse, with no shame, the ruthless, toothless old women would literally grab my hair pull my head back and pour! With blaring music from a rented mobile disco unit and generator, the deafening, distorted, rhythmic beat would soon get the dancing going. More of a lazy shuffle than anything else such that it was always hard for me to imagine they were actually having fun. One lady did though and I remember dancing more animatedly with her, both of us in rubber boots, she, reaching no more than my nipple height, continually biting mouthfuls off the whole, boiled peccary head she held aloft in her hand. What if we were somehow magically beamed over to a London nightclub, exactly as we were. Would we be hailed as the vanguard of a new style – or locked up?

Somehow, before it became too late and everyone had fallen over, we would harness our driver and slip away into the night, on our motorised canoe, upstream, back to the lodge. We often saw night monkeys, kinkajous and owls in our spotlights from the long, raised boardwalk leading to the lake while the eyes of caimen would reflect back at us like burning coals as we paddled silently before reaching the comfort of our musty bed.

Building was fun but hard work and the two-score crew squeezed long hours out of the day. Beny was a compassionate patron and understood what it took to keep the workers happy. One day, he took a trip to Coca (aka Francisco de Orellana) looking to contract the services of two brace of the local working girls. On learning of the huge, captive, untapped client base, however, the first girl he approached vehemently refused to work with any other girl. She wanted all the business for herself. A deal was struck and she accompanied Beny back downriver where she set up shop in a makeshift hut.

Peter and Shirley returned to the Ecuadorian Amazon, this time to Sacha Lodge. We were headhunted and asked if we would like to join a trip as staff in Antarctica the coming November. My answer was an immediate and resounding yes whereas Reneé was more hesitant. Come November, we were however driving zodiacs and lecturing in one of the most beautiful landscapes imaginable. It was a new chapter and one which lasted almost a decade. The work was punishing and we only managed an average of a month leave at home per year, being told that our intercontinental flights were the time to rest. The trips generated a lot of client-related stories along the way…

# The Crush
# Madagascar

Poor Bob was totally hen-pecked. You could almost see the thumbprint on his forehead where Molly kept him subservient. She was larger than him in nearly every way – not least of which physically and intellectually. Reneé and I had led them on innumerable trips around the world. She was intense, while Bob was meek and merged into his surroundings as effectively as a leaf-tailed gecko on a tree trunk. She was a sexual psychologist of some kind or other; it was too dangerous a territory to enquire into to any depth. She had a habit of possessively stealing me away from the rest of the group, and, with chin supported by the tips of the first three digits of her right hand, rested by a crooked elbow, she would stare, from within my personal space, as deeply as she could, to probe my psyche. She was paying. I was her guide, so I guess she felt she owned my soul. However, I also think that she had developed a crush. A realisation that I do not admit to lightly. In the order of thirty years, my senior I had only ever known Molly as an old lady. My first indication of her amorous inclination was when she became very clingy after depriving her over-active brain of oxygen and she erupted into fits of uncontrollable, very silly, giggles on the snowline of Ecuador's Cotopaxi Volcano. Whilst in Peru, she insisted on needing to hold my hand walking up a slight incline despite admitting to negotiating the staircase perfectly easily in her home. A further clue came in the Seychelles while walking through the Vallée de Mai on Praslin Island. The world heritage site is famous for the fabulous coco-de-mer palm trees. The female tree produces a huge double-coconut shaped husk, highly reminiscent of a woman's *mons pubis* with even a remarkable hairiness in the appropriate region. The male tree produces a gigantic catkin. It was on this slow, tropical forest, walk that Molly muscled up to the front of the group, physically stopped me and leant hard into my ear to say, "Don't you think it a tease that the magnificent phallus never actually gets to penetrate the voluptuous vulva?" She got me that time, the words phallus, vulva and voluptuous kept ringing in my ear from the proximity and the megaphonic effect of her cupped hands. I flustered but managed to explain that in essence it does as the fluorescent green day-geckos, covered in pollen, visit both male and female flowers pollinating in the process and so the palm does indeed get to have sex.

Despite her misgivings and misdirected attentions (I think that husband Bob had simply been all used up – fried), I had to hand it to Molly that she had an indomitable spirit and would have a go at anything even if she knew that she really shouldn't. Once, while trying out scuba diving in Polynesia with a colleague of ours, Jack, she felt a little unsure of herself in the water and told him she needed special assistance. He let her hold the anchor rope of the dinghy. Jack has a booming voice. He is a fabulous fish guide and I swear can even talk underwater. With his divers tanked up and treading water-awaiting instructions, Jack repeated maximum depth, maximum bottom time and began the countdown to duck dive simultaneously to begin the descent. Molly was still holding to the anchor rope. "Regulators in your mouth," boomed Jack, "deflate your BCs," he added, "dive!" Well, poor Molly, as she had put the regulator in her mouth, while still clinging tightly to the rope, had wrapped the reg around the rope before gripping the mouthpiece tightly between her teeth. Dutifully, she dived on command.

Gripping that mouthpiece meant air and her ability to breathe underwater – she was not letting it go. But she was now interwoven with the rope. The weight of her body, against the obstruction, had to give somewhere and ripped out both plates of dentures, that were biting hard into the mouthpiece, which went merrily chattering down to the bottom, unseen by anyone. The entire expedition ship of 100 passengers remained two days at the site while the staff diligently searched the area to no avail. The teeth were lost. Molly then spent the rest of the trip, I am told, a gummy mess but not quite as intense as usual.

We were in Madagascar, one of our favourite countries, in the north, in Montagne D'Ambre National Park, near Diego Suarez. The last time we had visited, while guiding a small group through the forest one of the ladies came to me with 'something in her eye'. I took a look for her and was horrified to find an arboreal leech attached to her eyeball. It was pretty freaky. Dangling from low-hanging leaves, these small leeches wait for a passing vertebrate and latch on. I asked her to hold still and managed to grab the mollusc by the rear end and pulled it off. The reaction was grotesque and instantaneous. The whole eyeball gorged with blood and the white of the eye was totally red, not just red-from-being-sore-red but red-red. It remained like that for the rest of the trip. She was hard to look at but said her vision was not at all impaired.

It was now another expedition-ship trip and the 100 passengers were being talked through the options for the visit. There was something for everybody from specialist birding groups, to slow, general-nature walks, medium hikes, long hikes or, for the really brave, the 'Survival of the Fittest'. I, for my sins, was to lead the latter. Sign-up sheets were passed around and the staff gathered to organise logistics. I was horrified, despite the harshest sell, that Molly and Bob were on the Survival of the Fittest walk. No amount of discussion would get them to change their mind. Our objective was to reach the bottom of the stunningly pretty Grand Cascade (Big Waterfall) which tumbled over an 80-metre cliff through pristine rainforest to a pool below. My local guide, Louis, was timid, of little help and had the body of what I considered should be that of an average eight-year-old, but he did know the way. Things, surprisingly, had been going fine, despite a few slips in the wet mud. We had spotted crowned lemurs, ring-tailed mongoose, blue vangas, vasa parrots, a leaf tailed gecko and even the much rarer Sandford's brown lemurs high in the canopy. I love the smell of true tropical rainforest, the peaty smell of rotting wood, the verdant greens and Montagne D'Ambre's amazing bird's nest ferns, the freshness, the shade, the grandeur and the unexpected.

Abruptly, a clearing opened up in front of us. A big sky poured into an unnatural and tortured space. A major landslide had taken trees and everything in its path to the valley floor. It had also taken our path, leaving only an extremely steep, unstable slope of loose scree, which disappeared into oblivion. Our hearts sank but bravado rose and it was figured that with extreme caution, we could cross the bare landslide along a precarious goat path to the security of the forest beyond. Yes, we could I agreed but turned to look at Molly and Bob. "Anything you can do, I can do too!" was written all over her face. I went for the transparent pow wow approach and with careful steerage of the conversation got the rest of the gung-ho group to agree that it might just be too much for the 'elderly', already-somewhat-tired and rather-muddy-from-several-slips Molly and Bob to negotiate. I was forced to agree and made Molly, Bob and Louis promise faithfully and in Louis' case, in the name of his ancestors, that they would stay put while the rest of us made our descent to the falls. The pace quickened markedly and we sprang, light-footed, down the steep muddy path. I did not ever like to split a group and about halfway down I stopped, gathered everyone and explained how well I knew Molly and that I had an uneasy feeling about leaving them. They agreed to carry on as one, reach the pool and come straight back up. I did an about face and virtually sprinted up the hill harbouring the panic of an ugly premonition.

Cresting the final rise before the landslide, I felt that I had been hit by a brick wall as my eyes and ears took in the scene. It was Molly – she had tried to cross. Bob had gone first and Louis last. She had obviously slipped and was now spread-eagled on the loose face, with nowhere to go but down while Bob clung desperately to one arm and Louis the other. They had their heels dug in but their grip was slipping. The first words that assailed me were from Molly. "I don't know if I can hang on any longer, Bob."

"If you go, I'm going too!" he answered heroically.

I felt like the cavalry in a John Wayne movie, as I blustered, "Hang on, guys – it's me!" Grips visibly tightened and a new resolve set in. Louis looked pale with worry and Bob simply resigned to do anything for Molly. I took in the situation more carefully and determined that at best this was a disaster, at worst life-threatening. In the slide, her loose shirt had been dragged up to her armpits and her bra was in complete disarray as were her 'grandmotherly' shorts. She was face down on the slope. A few broken roots poked out from the scree and I used them for purchase as I also lay face down on the slope, kicking footholds and crabbing my way to Molly. I reached her and saw that a sturdy root crossed under her chest from left to right. I had no choice and despite any fears of repercussion or misdirected hope on her part, I explained my plan. "Molly, I'm going to lie on top of you and put my hand between your legs," I said. I did just that and could feel the clamminess of her pink, sweaty, exposed belly. My hand and bare arm slid up to between her voluminous breasts, I grappled the root and held tight. Molly was now straddling my right bicep. I was able to take some of her weight and Bob and Louis were able to change grip and dig in. My left hand reached for another root higher up. After several minutes, I decided we should make a move and, "On three," I said, "you should both heave while I push." Molly was frightened and nothing more than dead weight. "Three!" And we heaved and pushed. The root snapped and instead of Molly erupting miraculously to safety, we both slid down a little more. Suddenly, I felt that the situation had tipped. I figured it was now me and Molly going to oblivion and wondered if Bob would still follow of his own volition. As my life was flashing past and I wished I had been leading the slow nature walk, the sounds of true cavalry jolted me to the present.

It was Michael Mars, heir to the Mars chocolate empire, one of my intrepid survivors of the fittest who came over the rise to unassumingly exclaim, "Need a hand there, Pete?" Soon a second hero was over the crest and a third. They had felt my preoccupation and done the round trip in record time. With strong, eager helpers cloaked in wry grins (the situation after all did look rather comical if the deathly fall was ignored), we were all swiftly yanked to safety.

Back on board, a big deal was made of the adventure with Molly taking it upon herself to personally commandeer the pre-dinner recap session and tell it publicly. She told how she worshipped the ground I walked on and left letters expressing similar undying emotions pinned to the notice board which I removed as soon as they were posted. She signed up for every trip that Reneé and I were scheduled to lead into the distant future. I almost resigned as a result and contemplated the fact that she may have even deliberately courted the accident for the sake of being rescued. But my final clue to her crush came when after returning home she decided to write up the story for her local paper. She sent me an email asking for a short bio as the one in the company brochure described me as a 'passionate naturalist' which 'sends her heart a flutter!' I never did write back and have had no further contact. She was subsequently advised, by the company we worked for, that all those trips she had signed up for were already full.

# Drips and Diapers
# India

There were many times when Reneé's nursing skills were put to good use in India. Delhi belly, Gandhi's revenge, the squits, the runs or the shits seem at one point or another, to hit even the most iron-cladded-stomach traveller to transgress the exotic boundaries of India.

In fact, shit is pretty much everywhere, the sacred Ganges is full of it. Human turds float past bathers who are there to cleanse themselves, while those that drink the water partake of the holy river as purification. In India, faith (and perpetual exposure) is more powerful than e-coli.

In Rajasthan, at least one of the forts has 'potty holes' high up in the walls through which to defecate so that, in days of old, it ran down the outside sliming the surface to create a wall too slippery to be climbed by an enemy. Although things have improved greatly recently (India has now been declared 'Open Defecation Free' after having built 110 million toilets). On long bus journeys, to relieve the monotony, (after a few days of acculturation to the very un-western spectacle) we would actually call out every time we passed someone blatantly having a crap at the side of the road and see how many we could rack up in an hour. Often we would watch two or more heterosexual men, holding hands, walking together merrily across a field, each holding a small brass jug of water, to have a pleasant social interlude while communally defecating.

Before re-boarding our bus after each and every frequent roadside stop at anything of interest, we would rotate through shit patrol duty where you would have to individually flip back the soles of your shoes exposing them for inspection of anything the pigs or dogs had not yet got to. It is true that it was omnipresent, hardly surprising when travelling through a vast countryside with very little infrastructure, where there is often still no sewerage system, where a toilet is anything green and when water is manually carried home from a village well. It is the ubiquitous nature of faeces that was often laid blame by our clients for their runs. However, we usually knew better. Perhaps the single biggest culprit on our trips almost anywhere in the world, for diarrhoea, vomiting, nausea and the like has been dehydration. In India, it is common. Many of our clients – not all – are too shy to want to pee in public and would rather simply not drink. The hot muggy climate soon sucks out their fluids and they dehydrate. Such was the case while in Bandhavgarh National Park in the centre of northern India. We were there for tigers which, if we had no luck, we hoped to pick up at our next stop in Kanha National Park – a ten-hour bus journey away. Having been close to lion, leopard and jaguars in the wild on many occasions it is without hesitation when I tell you that a tiger 'out cats' all other cats. Face to face with the black, white and orange, boldly marked cat, whose parallel stares from each of its eyes seem to look inside of you rather than at you is a haunting experience. Its gaze feels like it could slice you into pieces with the efficiency of two of Luke Skywalker's lightsabres. A tiger sees you – a lion thinks that you are part of a big noisy, smelly vehicle. Tigers are truly iconic and both parks are phenomenal areas with fantastic wildlife, including tigers. By the end of our stay, even though we had to work hard for it, everyone had been successful in their personal quest.

Of course we had encouraged everyone to drink liberally (we did discover that Jean and Ingrid's camel-packs were filled with vodka and tonic which was not what we meant!) but for Charlie and his wife, Sherry, an elderly couple from Kansas, they were the shy type. Most of our clients were known in the industry as high-end, many fabulously rich, some very important and all with a sense of adventure. Some were 'HM' or high maintenance but 90% or more were very nice people. The huge majority were repeat passengers and those that were not were usually direct recommendations from past travellers who knew the ropes. It was almost like one large extended family. For Charlie and Sherry, this was their first time with the American company that we worked for and they had come straight through the front door to get here. They were unknowns and as such, we usually tried to break them in easy. The last night at Bandhavgarh had been rough on them, they had both been losing fluids in every way possible and by morning, with a long bus ride ahead, were nowhere to be seen. We went looking for them in their room and could in fact have found them by smell had it been dark. They were in a bad way.

There was nothing for it but we had to pay for several towels from the lodge, codger up some large plastic bin liners, and make a giant diaper for each of them.

They were sat at the front of the bus, closest to the door. Frequent stops were made where Charlie and Sherry would have to jump out and do what they had to do on the side of the road. At the next village, Reneé purchased two sets of saline intra venous drips – medical supplies and prescription drugs are incredibly cheap in India and seem readily available and everyone else took the opportunity to stock up on anything they needed! The bags Reneé summarily suspended from the overhead luggage rack and plugged the needles into Charlie and Sherry's veins where they remained for the following nine hours of the bumpy road. Meanwhile, so as to include everyone in their misery and make light of the situation which could have happened to anyone, we requested that Charlie and Sherry pee into a glass bottle and held up the amber liquid every hour or so to group scrutiny to check it was becoming paler and paler as their IVs began to rehydrate them. It all may sound rather perverse, I suppose, read in the wrong light, but I can assure you that back home nothing could be further from the minds of any of our clients than to want to watch strangers crap or inspect a fellow traveller's urine, yet it seems that India is a great leveller, a place where necessity and practicality rank higher than bashfulness or a sense of image, or self-consciousness.

We saw tiger again in Kanha and were even lucky enough to watch a pretty relaxed sloth bear for a while.

I think that for Charlie and Sherry, who recovered rapidly with Reneé's intervention, the whole thing was a bit too much, even though we had grown accustomed to a closer than usual association with human faeces, when it was their own a sense of ingrained shame kicked in. They'd had some incredible sightings and were very lucky but we never saw them again, even though we were polite enough never to have included them in our hourly score to boost numbers.

# Muslim Uprising
# Assam, India

I have previously enjoyed relating to friends how I have just returned from an incredible safari. I tell them I saw wild elephant, lion, leopard, rhinoceros, buffalo, crocodile and antelope. I then continue with hyena, jackal, vultures, cobra, mongoose, eagles, storks and cranes. They listen in awe as my bragging moves on to include monkeys, hornbills, wild dog, python and civet. Finally, they relent and tell me how much they too want to go to Africa, then stand in shock and disbelief when I tell them that I wasn't within a thousand miles of Africa but that my safari was in India.

Apart from the classic images of the Taj Mahal, poverty and crowded cities India is indeed host to a fabulous gamut of species. A list which goes on to include another whole range of birds and animals not known from Africa. These include an incongruous blend of beasts such as red panda, bears, deer, gibbons, giant squirrels and peacocks culminating in, of course, the tiger! Wildlife in India, apart from tiger, is still a relative secret. For us, what makes it even more special is that a large portion of the human population is vegetarian and they treat wildlife with respect. Because there is no threat from people, fantastic wildlife can even be seen close to villages. The day we leave India is always the day we begin to miss it.

It was a good group. We had travelled with all of the participants previously, indeed about half of them many times before. Our first issue was that Charmaine's luggage had not arrived in Delhi, despite her first-class ticket. The worry was that she always brought a suitcase worth of sweets to share with the group. How were we going to get through the long bus rides without jellybeans? Charmaine was the largest client that we travelled with and she already had about ten trips with us under her very long belt. She complained of bad knees, which was understandable, always flew first class to have extra space and paid a single supplement. She was quite a character, knew what she wanted and very direct. She was 'new' money. One of five siblings and the only one who inherited from her rich uncle. Apparently, the others were not up to much. The stipulation of the inheritance was that she uses it on trips abroad, the uncle believing correctly that it would vastly broaden her mind. She took it to heart and even once treated her entire office staff to a white-glove safari in Kenya, before we got to know her. She now chose us as her vehicle to travel. Our last, more recent, trip together was to Mongolia. On returning to the States, the police were waiting for her and she was arrested. She had a high-powered job as PA to the boss and vice president of a big institution that I will not name. She was completely trusted and had used that confidence to embezzle six million dollars directly from the CEO. No charges were laid as embarrassment would have been too damaging. Instead, rather like Al Capone, she was sent to jail for five years on tax evasion, for not paying taxes on her illegally gotten gains! She is out of jail now, in a new town, with a new name. There never was a rich uncle.

Phil and Ellen became friends long ago, so much so that Reneé and I were virtually integrated into the family as two extra kids. They were from Chattanooga, in the USA and Ellen was the epitome of a classic southern belle. To emphasise the point on how close we had become, I remember once, while they were with us on a trip in Botswana, I left the public area of the lodge to go to the loo. A simple rope barrier was either hooked across the pathway (occupied) or not. Ellen came a short while later and not only entering the gents but she absentmindedly breezed past the rope, opening it and closing it behind her. She walked straight in on me sitting on the toilet. "Oh my, oh my," she blurted and rushed back to tell everyone what she had done adding, "Thank God it wasn't one of the grown-ups!" Phil was always a trooper and on this India trip, he had come with a broken collar bone sustained only a week previously when he fell in the bath.

The luggage arrived, Phil was strapped up and we left for Bharatpur by road from Delhi. At the entrance gate, the rickshaw drivers formed a scrum around me seven or eight deep. As the tour leader, I was the one that would either pick them to work or not. We had not been to Bharatpur for quite a few years but I heard my name being called. It was my driver from our last visit. I chose him for myself and others for the group. There was mutual recognition and I ushered him to come forward through the ranks. From my inside jacket pocket, I pulled out a photo of him that I had taken on the previous occasion. Everyone was floored. I took another, to present next time, of him holding a plastified photo of himself.

We often take photos, that we have first covered in durable plastic, back from one year to the next, to gift to the subjects if we can find them. In Calcutta, there is a viewpoint where we would habitually stop. An 'untouchable' shoe-shiner sat across the road. While the group took photos of the Hooghly River below, Reneé and I had our shoes shined. We had watched him before and noted that higher caste Indians would simply stretch down, use his brush and polish and drop them at his feet with no payment. He was not even 'allowed' to make eye contact with them. We crossed the road, sat at his level and gradually engaged him in conversation. I took his photo. A whole year later, we were back with the image and I handed it to him. I can tell you that it was a truly heart-rending moment to see his astonished gratitude. In Calcutta itself, we would naturally visit the bustling flower market, a labyrinth of chaotic activity and vibrant colour. It was classic India. I would gather the group, make sure that they fully understood where we were in our *rendezvous* point, give them a return time, pull out a stack of 40 or so plastified photos of market vendors, divide them up and let loose our guests to find and deliver them to the appropriate people. It was a riot. Of course the vendors knew each other and would literally tug our guests as far as was necessary to find their friends, then the next one and the next. It was a pretty good icebreaker to get through culture shock as all foreignness was lost, being replaced by beaming smiles of gratitude that were easy to relate to.

After an obligatory stay in Agra to visit the magnificent Taj Mahal, we were expecting to fly to Khajuraho. The pilots were on strike however so we crammed on to a train for a hectic ride. In Khajuraho stands a group of stone temples famed for the expansiveness and intricacy of their highly erotic carvings. It feels quite odd to be looking in detail at sexually explicit art with clients, some of whom were really into it. Herbert, for example, was so engrossed that he failed to notice that he was about to be censored by a cow that butted him, ripping a gaping hole in his trousers. Due to our delayed arrival, our bus for the next day was gone. Someone else had used it. Telling folks not to set their alarms for the morning, it took us time to gather enough of India's beautiful classic cars, Ambassadors, for the long journey to Bandhavgarh. The first car hit a goat which was deflected past the second but other than that everything else was avoided.

We love Bandhavgarh, it is one of India's top parks to spot tigers. A good friend of ours, Pradeep Sankhala, whose father founded the well-known Project

Tiger in India, was our ground agent for the trip. He also owned the lodge where we were now. It was rustic and the beds were traditional Indian cots. The nights were frosty and we went to bed fully clothed including our hats and gloves. Typically, we would have an early rise, cloaked in blankets to leave for a morning game drive, downtime, then lunch followed by an afternoon safari. What we call 'tiger tension' seems to be a real phenomenon, where there is so much pressure to see a tiger that the clients are unable to enjoy anything else until they have done so. Bandhavgarh has so much more to offer, apart from the 250 bird species, there are jackals, spotted deer, sambar, nilgai, wild boar, jungle cat to name but a few. We in fact did see a lot but only one tiger, which one couple missed altogether. It was however no ordinary tiger. It was Sitar's mate, a big male called Charger. He earned his name for charging tourist elephants and safari vehicles. We met him as he came out of the bush on our left. We were parked. I was with Charmaine in the back of the open vehicle. Charger lived perfectly up to his name and burst at us broadside in a full charge, snarling. He came to a dramatic dead stop, paws spreading in the sand, dust flying, about two metres from us. It was extremely impressive and a real honour to have been charged by Charger. Charmaine was sitting on the left side nearest him as he flew in and what was almost as incredible to watch was how quickly, measured in milliseconds, that her entire human mass was launched from one side of the jeep to the other.

After our second morning drive, we wandered down to the river to help bathe the working elephants with the mahouts. Many friends, or people that we know, who understand wildlife, claim elephants as their favourite animal. Personally, I have too many favourites to narrow it down to a single species but elephants are always hovering near the top of my list too. It is an animal with which one can have a very clear mutual understanding. An elephant is a 'who' not an 'it'. On the way down to the river, doing a little birdwatching as we went, we passed our group's laundry hanging out to dry. Mostly, it was underwear and Phil was delighted to confidently point out Ellen's knickers which we were all able to study with our binoculars. Ellen's were no surprise, we already knew what they looked like, as she usually had her pants down way before she ever found a tree to pee behind. The fun part was trying to match up the rest with their owners. In the river, we got down-and-dirty with brooms and stiff brushes scrubbing hard the elephant's tough skin, which they clearly enjoyed. I noticed one on the bank with its leg chain tied to a tree. It had an itch on its belly that it was trying to scratch with the soft tip of its trunk. It was obviously not very satisfactory. I looked around and found a short, stout stick, out of the elephant's reach. I gave it to him, which he took in his trunk and without even an instant of hesitation, understanding why I had done so, used it to scratch his itch.

Our next tiger park, Kanha, was another long drive away. Here, for a while, it all came together. We more than neutralised everyone's tiger tension and were able to enjoy an impressive wild dog chase (dhole), as they went hell for leather after a sambar deer. The real cherry on the top however was sighting an unprecedented four individual leopards.

We left Kanha and hit the long road to get to a hotel for the night before flying up to Assam. For the last few hours of the journey, I took a bucket and was throwing up violently in the back of the bus. We had several doctors in the group, each with a different strategy, one said to get me out of India ASAP, one get me back to Delhi and the other to treat local. I usually advocate the latter. We disembarked the bus at the hotel where porters arrived with a wheelchair. I had to be tied into it as I would fall out otherwise, not even being able to hold my body up. The decision was to treat local and they lay me down. The disturbing thing were the headlines of the complimentary Indian daily newspaper. In big bold type, they stated, "If you get sick in an Indian hospital, only God can help you!" The article went on to describe how a stray dog had gone into a hospital recently and made off with easy prey – a baby! It was about here that the trip started falling apart.

I miraculously got better however and we made it to Guwahati from where we drove to the Wild Grass Lodge outside of Kaziranga National Park. There was wind of trouble in the air which we had no choice at the moment but to ignore. Our first morning, we went to the furthest section of the park, a forest area to specifically look for hoolock gibbons. It was a hike and beautiful but no gibbons were seen. We heard them though. A piercing, haunting sound, amplified by an enlarged throat sac, somewhat reminiscent of the call of an indri in Madagascar but not so complex. We sloshed about in the damp forest wondering why our feet were getting so wet. All was revealed when we eventually took off our shoes to find our feet swimming in our own blood from the dozens of terrestrial leeches in our socks.

That afternoon, we left for a drive in the park, which from a wildlife perspective was fabulous as usual. Anne, however, who wasn't getting the attention she desired, when she made a call to stop to look at a bird, gave the driver a hard thwack over the head with her umbrella. The effect was an instantaneous halt, we all lurched forward and the bird flew off. The second, rather more worrying incident, was that the engine of another of our jeeps actually caught fire. Everyone jumped out, the park guard burnt his hand trying to open the bonnet and the driver threw spades full of sand on the flames over the engine. The guests were transhipped and we carried on. We received a message over the park guard's walkie-talkie that we were to immediately vacate the park and return to the hotel. There was a militant Muslim uprising and it was not safe. We were to make a dash back to Guwahati and get on the last plane out that would be leaving for a while. It was complete upheaval but we made it despite the group's high stress level. Our guide, Arun and driver were continuously dipping into and chewing the contents of little blue bags. We didn't need to know what it was and instead passed around copious amounts of Old Nun Indian rum to help get us through. It was late at night by the time we arrived at the Guwahati hotel where our nine rooms had been reserved. We were a shock to the management. As we had taken so long to arrive, the rooms had been given up for other guests. We caused quite a fuss resulting quite literally in guests being woken in their sleep and forcibly removed from three rooms which were given to us. It was all they would do. Reneé in her indomitable fashion was able to allocate people to rooms with almost no dissent. We had come a long way together and by this time, the group was thoroughly gelled. Arun was a nervous wreck and dipped frequently into the blue bags. He was Hindu and deathly afraid of militant Muslims. Reneé and I were in a room with Charmaine, Phil, Ellen and Arun, who I made sleep on the floor at the door, in case any Muslims came to get him in the night, in the hope that they would not disturb us. There was one bed, it had only three legs, we propped it up with our Samsonite suitcases. As Charmaine was the only one who had paid single supplement, we gave it to her. The rest of us were on the floor using what we could scrounge from the hotel for bedding with extra padding for Phil with his broken collarbone. It was a short night of sleep. The following morning the streets were an eerie quiet. No cars were on the road and we were refused transport. We walked 2 km to the airport, pulling our suitcases along the road. In relative safety, within the confines of the heavily guarded building, we waited. After a long delay, we finally made it on to the old aircraft, strapped in only to be told to disembark. There was a bomb threat on the plane and we had to get off. Back indoors, while security forces were thoroughly checking for any evidence of a bomb, one of our ladies, of a couple we thought we knew, began sobbing. She dug into her bra and pulled out a photograph of her cats that she held close to her chest. She was crying that if we were blown up she would never get to see them again. I remember thinking that she probably wouldn't care either. The story was that these two cats were adopted from the cat pound where they were immediately socially elevated from regular street moggies to self-centred lords of a multi-million-dollar mansion. They had connived to win their owner's hearts and now featured in their will, such that, in the event of the husband and wife dying simultaneously, like being blown up on a plane. Then the two cats must continue to live in the fully functioning household, in the manner to which they have become accustomed for the rest of their natural lives. Wow!

# The Scalping
# India

A few weeks later, we were back in India – a whole new group with a whole new set of expectations, each client looking for an experience of a lifetime, a story to tell back home in the game of one-upmanship. So, in that regard, Paul was no different from anyone else and we found ourselves back in Assam, back in the same 'Wild Grass Lodge' as in 'Muslim Uprising'.

At this point, it has to be stated, so as not to give the wrong impression, that if anyone asked either Reneé or I to name our four favourite destinations, not only would they be the same but we could list them in five seconds flat – namely Antarctica, Botswana, India and Madagascar (in no particular order) and within India, I daresay Assam would rank favourite. Enough said. Whereas the majority of the populous in 'mainland' India are Hindu and look very 'Indian', Assam is geographically removed from the bulk of the country connected only by a thin and tenuous political corridor (as narrow as 21km). With the remaining six 'Sister States' for neighbours, the Assamese look very 'Asian'. The area around Kaziranga National Park is quite refreshing, the people are wonderfully friendly with small, neat, fenced gardens, often with a hand dug earthen pond growing carp below and ducks on top. Many grow silkworms and harvest silk, which is fascinating to watch as they unravel the delicate silk thread directly from the cocoon. The children quickly learned my name and every subsequent visit would run out of their homes sounding like day-old-chicks calling Peet, Peet, Peet as they fell in behind and joined our throng on a walk through the village. Despite a total language barrier, they seem like a people with whom one could have an easy and quick understanding.

Our drivers are 'Indian' Indians. We set off in a procession from the hotel in our safari vehicles to the gate of Kaziranga National Park. For those who may have been to Africa on safari, you have probably already conjured up a mental image of a romantic sojourn in luxurious open-topped Land Rovers, each guest with an outside, padded seat and expert guide effervescing with his willingness to impart his unfathomable depth of knowledge. Ignore that image. We were a group of 16 people plus Reneé and I, our mounts, in those days, were tiny open-backed Gypsy jeeps – omnipresent in India and very uncomfortable. The seats were a pressed metal, parallel to the direction of travel so that we faced each other with interlocking knees. The driver remained mute or unintelligible and if he spoke at all, it was only to remark in Hindi to his co-pilot, a surly park guard touting a .303 number 8, bolt action rifle of about WWII vintage. Reneé and I were therefore diluted between the six vehicles we needed for our safari. She took the front and I brought up the rear. Nobody wants to eat anyone else's dust so each maintained a significant distance from the vehicle in front. Despite the discomforts, our high-end clients were willing enough to suffer, sensibly understanding that our aim is always to put people in front of the best wildlife before looking for luxury.

Kaziranga has phenomenal fauna including herds of wild Indian elephants, tigers, wild water buffalo, gibbons, hornbills and chickens. Just as wild peacocks in India are hard to take seriously because we are so familiar with them, yet to see them in their natural state, being shy, alarming at predators and just doing their thing being wild is really quite extraordinary – they are truly one of the world's most spectacular birds. So too is the chicken. I wonder how many of you out there even know that the humble chicken is a 'real' bird not some man-made thing that walks around farmyards put on this earth to give us 'buffalo wings' and eggs. The jungle-fowl (or chicken) in its wild, untainted, free-of-the-hand-of-man state is another truly spectacular bird and actually rather hard to see – one of the best places being Kaziranga. So not only were we thoroughly satisfied with all of the above-mentioned wildlife, including chicken (we dipped on tigers) but it was also a day we counted 72 of the Jurassic looking Greater Indian One-horned Rhinoceros, (capitalised to give due respect, not only to the number we saw in one day, but to the animal itself). Nowhere in Africa can match that number of wild rhinos in one day. The heavy plates of armour cladding, apparently bolted on to the backside with large studs, proffer the beast a truly formidable air of an animal not to mess with or be messed by – hence the rifles.

The park is divided into different areas requiring accessing the main road to connect from one to the other. To stop unwanted, large vehicles entering the park a sturdy, height-restricting structure, of rough-hewn, square cut, hardwood timber, standing like a Japanese Tori gate straddles the road a few hundred metres before the entrance. It was always our policy to reconvene at each convenient point to read the mood of the group, recap our sightings and see what we might want to do next. We exited the park towards the end of the day, Reneé stopped her vehicle and we all pulled up tight behind her. "One, two, three, four, five…"

"Who's missing?"

"Where's Paul's vehicle?"

One of the drivers was a bit sheepish and had got wind of a situation. Swaying his head from side to side describing a figure '8' in the air he told me, "I am not the one to want to be telling you this, sir, but it seems that there was a slight problem in one of the vehicles, sir."

"I think, sir, he may have been taking the patient to the doctor, sir?" he added. We said to the group that it would be better for them to go back to the hotel while Reneé and I raced off in two jeeps commandeering the driver who at least seemed to know something.

We found Paul, with his vehicle at the side of the dusty road next to a small shack – he looked sickeningly bad! As his vehicle had passed under the height restrictor, he had, at precisely the wrong moment, stood up. The impact scalped him, literally peeling back his scalp from his forehead. He is a doctor and his wife a nurse, he collapsed into a completely bloody heap into the tray of the jeep, his wife Betty panicked thinking he was dead, the driver took one look at the mess behind him and the untold retribution in the back of his vehicle and raced to the shack. In the shack was the man who had now just sewn Paul up. He was a man who repaired elephants during the course of their hard workday. He was an old man, semi-clad, with no finesse – none was needed for an elephant. The tools of his trade were grotesque, elephants have very tough skin and his sense of hygiene and sterility was absent – elephants are resilient. We looked at Paul through parted fingers and counted the eight ferocious stitches that pinched together the leading ledge of his scalp to his face, Frankenstein had nothing on our Paul. We privately declared a state of National Emergency but it was Republic Day and while the rest of India was publicly flexing its military muscle through the streets of Delhi, it meant we were left with no escape out of Assam, as there were no commercial flights.

Renee is an excellent field nurse. Qualified in the profession, her father was a doctor and her mother a nurse. While growing up in South Africa, her father would always stop at motor accidents where they would have to crawl through a minibus load of bodies to find the live ones; she has witnessed the savage results of dog, crocodile and shark attacks. Her medical kit comprises three basic items: sutures, mercurochrome and hydrogen peroxide.

Betty should have been in control but admitted a complete ignorance of how to act outside of a clinical, USA emergency room. Reneé took charge and gave the first order. "Do not let Paul anywhere near a mirror!"

We rushed them back to Wild Grass Lodge, removing anything reflective *en route* and Reneé set to work. Removing the Frankenstein stitches, she folded back the scalp scrubbing thoroughly with $H_2O_2$ before applying generous quantities of mercurochrome, which stains red very badly, making him look even worse. She re-sutured and the wound was taken care of twice a day for the three days before we could leave. Paul was very cool about the whole thing saying that many of his friends were plastic surgeons and could fix it when he got home; he was even excited that he might get a free face lift out of the treatment on his insurance. He was worried about HIV though from unsterilised needles. Betty came around too and took the nurse's role leaving Reneé and I to pay more attention to the group.

Several months passed and we received a mail from Paul who told us that he had not contracted HIV but that he was a little disappointed not to have needed plastic surgery as Reneé's suturing healed perfectly.

Maybe not quite what he expected but he did get his story to tell.

# At Night with the Holy Grail
# Brazil

We brought the jeep to an abrupt stop in the soft sand. I was fully aware that Reneé and I were in a special place but as six blue-and-yellow macaws squawked raucously, taking flight from the top of a solitary palm, flying in three tight pairs, describing a spiral overhead, my feelings were confirmed. Four red-legged seriemas meanwhile, like diminutive secretary birds, strutted haughtily, barely fifty metres away. The adult's coral-red legs and bills just a touch more saturated in colour than their two offspring. To complete the scene, a Toco toucan with oversized, yellow bill drove a wedge-shaped path through the dry hot air in a lazy, undulating flight. Even I had to admit to myself that it was a little strange to ignore everything around me and instead focus on a fresh pile of scaly looking dung – the reason for our stopping. Yet this particular dung was much more interesting to me than all other things put together. I knelt in the warm sand and with a dry twig teased the dung apart, revealing several large, hard seeds and infinite snake-like scales of the Buruti palm fruit. Dog-like tracks led away from the scat towards a dense mat of low, gnarly trees and trunkless palms.

We guessed that in the thicket, deep under cover, our quarry would sleep out the heat of the day that was already building even though we hadn't yet had our first morning coffee. Thus far, this was the closest I had ever been to the highest-ranking South American mammal still on my 'wish list' – the maned wolf.

We were on private land in the Brazilian Cerrado, Brazil's largest ecosystem, even more threatened than its Amazon. A foreign NGO had bought the extensive property aiming to preserve the wildlife, particularly the large macaw populations. Ecotourism was to pay the way – nothing, after all is *de graça*. Today even wildlife has to *earn* its freedom. Bird diversity is high in the area as are the 'herps', vipers, rattlesnakes and even, unexpectedly, large anacondas. Stoic iguanas, spritely lizards and steadfast terrapins were also common. Toads abounded, fabulously humongous, the size of dinner plates – mouse-eaters! Mammals too were relatively visible in the sparse and stunted vegetation, monkeys, marmosets, tamanduas, armadillos and cavies. The real draw card, the Holy Grail, trophy-mammal of the would-be ecotourist to the region however was the maned wolf. A definite money-spinner. More money to the NGO means more land, which in turn means more conservation and buying more time. The maned wolf's 'umbrella' would therefore protect the freedom of all lesser mortals under its umbra. Easy? No! Wolves are shy, secretive and nocturnal, at best crepuscular. In an effort to improve predictability of sightings, it was decided by the NGO to regularly bait an area to attract and habituate an animal normally spooked, having learned to fear human persecution. We were there to photograph, to raise awareness of this long-legged one-of-a-kind canid. More of a fox than a wolf but it is neither and falls in a monotypic genus. Truly one-of-a-kind. Its main colour is rufous with dark 'socks' fore and aft. The tail is bushy with a white tip, ears are large and there really is a short, black mane on its neck. It stands nearly three feet at the shoulder but is not at all dangerous, feeding largely on fruits, insects and smaller animals. It is a very handsome animal.

We arrived at the edge of the property. There on a spike of the barbed wire fence was a tuft of maned wolf fur. I was struck by the powerful contrast of the sharp, hard wire having clawed at the soft fur of the animal. I thought it highly symbolic of Man's encroachment in the Cerrado where the tough reality of human society is slowly tugging away at the wildlife. In this case, the habitat's flagship animal. We spent the day at rest in a rundown concrete building and moved to our place of night-time vigil in another small brick-built space of low walls and huge glassless open spaces where windows were once dreamed of.

Night fell sharply at ten degrees south. A fingernail of moon arose quickly, laying on its back, in an inky, star-studded sky. We were quiet. Our ears strained in the noisy silence. Mosquitos deafened our senses. We waited. Midnight left us tired as we passed into the predawn. A soft padding in the sand? Real or imagined? Adrenaline spiked and alertness flooded our beings. Little though it was, the ghostly silver sheen of the moon gave life to the sound. Not more than five metres in front of us stood the lanky shape of a large-eared dog. We sat at eye level to the trusting soul, fragile, alone, precious – precarious. Elated by its presence, saddened by its predicament of persecution and harassment, yet to me (not a chicken owner) one of the most electrifyingly beautiful animals I had ever seen. We stayed a week, every night a vigil. One night four wolves came. Two were regulars. We watched, observed, memorised. We came to know them. We watched them interact, express their characters, become individuals. We became thoroughly enamoured and they unquestionably came to trust us. A rare privilege. They curled up to sleep only a few metres from where we sat. Our last morning, when packing to leave, I realised my shirt was missing from the clothesline. There were tracks; I followed them. I eventually found my shirt, a hundred metres away. A wolf had taken it, apparently slept with it and left it under a bush.

# The Machine
# Peru

My freezer bag was full of urine. It had been a long wait, crouched, alone, in the thick of the Peruvian rainforest. In an effort to minimise human scent, I had taken no food and even peed in an airtight bag. Although the sun was still high enough to bathe the nearby Madre de Dios River, the light was quickly being sapped from beneath the closed canopy.

In front of me, a quagmire of gloopy mud, studded with footprints of myriad mammals lay testament to their penchant for eating the mineral-rich clay. I had come to photograph. Although far from disheartened, my first three days had been quiet. As consolation, my solitary hour and a half return walk in darkness, at the end of each day, gave me a buzz like no other. I knew I was being watched, inspected and evaluated; I could feel the intensity of nocturnal vision burning into my back. Who was watching? That was the question! Deer and paca were common – but so was jaguar. I only hoped it was not puma.

The rain had stopped an hour earlier and a warm smell of mustiness now pervaded my senses. Ants were once again marching in a double highway at my feet. One lane carried larger-than-life pieces of leaf, in a gesture of incredulous strength, while the other, carrying nothing, was single-mindedly bent on fetching another load. Chachalacas fed sloppily on clusters of small fruit in the canopy which rained noisily, bouncing from leaf to leaf, onto the distant forest floor. Not sloppily enough however for the opportunistic, earthbound, acouchi that gorged surreptitiously on the heaven-sent bonanza. Parrotlets were once again active. Unaware of my presence, they dangled acrobatically in front of the small cliff to my right, nibbling deafeningly on the clay. Sitting, solitarily in the presence of abundance, filled me with a sense of companionship. I found myself talking silently to the birds, even the ants, in fact to almost everything. Not a sound was made that I didn't hear and I began to feel a part of it all. I began to commune. With a deep sense of contentment, that only nature has ever inspired, I waited.

Unconsciously, I registered the dull thumping of the heavy machinery. An oil platform perhaps? I paid it no heed. I was tired and cramped after ten hours in my tiny cloth hide – four posts, in a square, set one metre apart in the ground and wrapped by a thin bolt of material, no roof, just a thin viewing slit for me and another for my lens. The rumbling grew louder and I casually wondered who was out there. Suddenly, I was gripped in suspense. There was *nobody* out there – what *was* that noise? My heart quickened with indecision. It was moving towards me, slowly, steadily, but surely. I could run. What from? It's only a machine. A big machine! The cacophony was changing. Sounds grew from the noise. The sounds of clicking, loud, pure clicking. The once muffled thumping was given voice. Individual grunts and snorts grew louder, unseen, from the dense understory. From fifty yards, a scream seared my heightened awareness, another and I knew a child had been brutally murdered. My senses were pinging. The machine was alive; it was coming for me too. Twenty yards and the first glimpse of coarse grey hair caught my sight. Again a movement, then the smell. Pungent and acrid, it hit me like a freight train, leaving me reeling in momentary nausea. The odour of weeping scent glands. From the slit in my much-too-flimsy structure, I peered, unseen, into the piggy eyes of a nervous, prime male white-lipped peccary. The vanguard of the troop, two hundred strong, he violently, clacked his ferocious canines, gnashing repeatedly at the frightened smell behind the pathetically vulnerable green cloth. A threat to me, a command to his following. Something was wrong, he knew it but he wanted his clay. It was the clicking I had heard. Another young pig screamed hideously – the murdered child – as it was reprimanded by porcine authority. The sound was chilling, the proximity intense. Beasts of legend, stories are rife of how natives have been ripped to shreds by menacing tusks. The herd swelled around me. Some I could have touched. Photography was not an option. As my knuckles whitened around a stout stick, a morbid fascination kept my pupil glued to the minute viewing slit. There were no trees to climb and nowhere to run. Quelling my fear, I was ecstatic at such an intimate encounter. As a wildlife biologist, I was humbled by the grandeur of their presence. For twenty minutes, I watched perhaps the last great, all too rare, of rainforest spectacles – alone with my stick. Calmly, after forgiving my intrusive scent, noisily and covered in mud the herd passed on through. I stayed a while not wanting to break their entrancing spell.

# Huaorani, Missionaries and Self-Determination Amazon Rainforest

The Huaorani Indians (pronounced WOW-raan-ee) have lived for at least a thousand years, deep in Ecuador's Amazon rainforest, in complete harmony with their environment. Since their first contact with the outside world, they have, unfortunately, held an unenviable position within Ecuadorian society: as Indians, they are automatically relegated to the lowest social strata, and within that strata, they come in a resounding last.

When I came to live in Ecuador in 1985, through a mutual acquaintance, one of the first people I met in this diverse country was a Huaorani Indian, Samuel Padilla. He was the son of Dayuma, a famous Huaorani woman who had fled from her territory, during inter-tribal conflict, as a young girl in 1943, to become one of the first of her Stone Age tribe, in modern times, to reach the 'outside'. She had subsequently been befriended in 1955 by a missionary called Rachel Saint. Saint, immediately realising the value of a 'tame' Huaorani, set about meticulously learning the Huaorani language from her. Dayuma, in turn, was toured around the United States and paraded in front of millions of television viewers as a savage from the jungle. Dayuma was converted to Christianity with great zeal, and eventually led back to her people to spearhead their religious conversion.

Some half a century ago, in 1956, five North American missionaries on a crusade to prepare the Huaorani for heaven were speared on an Amazon riverbank. These men, knowing of the Huaorani's formidable reputation for defending their territory against outsiders, were nevertheless prepared to risk all in an effort to impose their personal beliefs on the 'heathens' and 'save their savage souls' from darkness. For one reason or another, the Huaorani killed the missionaries, destroyed their light aircraft and left the bodies in the river punctured by spears, a common practice for a tribe living within the laws of

Nature and, from their point of view, a totally understandable reaction to the missionaries' presence. Today, to their detriment, the Huaorani remain notorious for that act. The public reaction at the time around the world was phenomenal. Headlines abounded along the lines of 'Savages massacre missionaries deep in Ecuadorian jungle'. Images of the dead in *Time* magazine further stirred civilised emotions. Indeed a great deal of fuss was made of the missionaries' deaths, one of whom happened to be Rachel's brother. Headline-makers were once again kept busy when she later returned with Dayuma to the same area and Christianised the 'savages' involved in the killings – even forgiving them completely in a further heart-warming gesture. Public interest in the story ran high and continues to this day with Hollywood producing a documentary about the killings as recently as 2005, followed by a feature film released in 2006. The Huaorani seem to evoke fearful echoes of our distant past, of our primordial inner fears of predators in the forest. An editor's dream indeed – particularly when the perpetrators of the spearings are sensationalised and totally misrepresented. These headlines and controversy remain the legacy that shapes the image of the Huaorani in the eyes of the vast majority of Ecuadorians and the public in general today.

So they were missionaries – was that important? Did that make them special? They were after all still trespassers whose purpose was to impose their foreign culture on the Huaorani – perhaps there in itself lies the true crime. Eventually, however, the objective of the five dead 'martyrs' was realised. Having watched original footage of the missionaries' initial efforts to make contact, one certainly has to admire their pioneering spirit, their conviction and their tenacity. They worked hard for their goal. They used cunning methods such as circling overhead in a light aircraft while jettisoning parachute guided baskets of presents, such as machetes and talking to the flabbergasted Huaorani on the ground in the Huaorani language (via a transmitter relaying to speakers hidden in the baskets) that Rachel had learned from Dayuma. The unfortunate Indians could not help but be impressed by this huge, benevolent, talking 'wood bee'. Their instinctive mistrust evaporated, and the naïve Huaorani were catapulted into the twentieth century and changed forever.

Once accepted by the Huaorani, the missionaries' first act was to create an impractical sense of shame about the tribe's nakedness as well as converting them from their semi-nomadic, hunting lifestyle by persuading them to grow crops. They encouraged the Indians to cluster in more permanent groups where the Bible could be more effectively read to them and they could be better supervised. However, polio, previously unknown to the Huaorani, soon broke out, due in part to their unusually high population densities. Many Huaorani lost their lives. Even though far more than five Huaorani died, there were of course no reciprocal headlines screaming 'Missionaries massacre savages deep in Ecuadorian jungle'.

The abnormally high numbers in the settlements also quickly caused the nearby forests to be depleted of protein through over hunting. Thus, these naturally self-reliant people soon became dependent on the Christians, on foreigners from another continent. The egalitarian social doctrines of the Huaorani soon floundered and, as resources became more and more scarce, the previously unknown Western concepts of greed, possession and social stratification were introduced, thereby finally and convincingly 'civilising' them.

On whose authority I ask were westerners allowed to impose their beliefs in the first place. The Christian God? I wonder what Buddha or Allah or the gods of the Dulong people from northern China would think about this premise. Is the rule that any crusader who arrives first on the scene is allowed exclusive rights over heathen souls, free to peddle whatever foreign beliefs their conviction dictates? Shouldn't the Huaorani have simply been left alone?

I have been using the word 'civilised' somewhat sarcastically up until now. Having spent so much time in the presence of Huaorani, I have come to question my preconceptions of what civilised means. They are a rich and resilient culture. Their language, *Huao Terero*, is not related to any other. Women have an equal voice within the community. The Huaorani understand the value of a healthy forest. They live in an egalitarian society. Their leaders are transient, elevated to overcome crises. Decisions are made on the basis of what will best benefit the community as a whole. That sounds very civilised to me.

Over the past, nearly three, decades I have had frequent contact with various Huaorani communities and individuals. I have never failed to enjoy their company, although the happiness I have felt is tinged by the sadness of what I have witnessed become of their world. Reneé and I once hiked for three strenuous days through the forest to reach a contacted Huaorani community to photograph for our first book on the Ecuadorian Amazon in 1995. On our next visit to the same community some ten years later, we drove on a new road built by the oil industry that dropped us at their doorstep. The relentless pressure upon their tribal territories means they are unable to move on to new pristine areas, leaving fallow the vacated land in their traditional way. This would previously have caused situations of potential starvation within communities. However, the Huaorani, with typical lucidity and adaptability, have come to consider the intractable and imposed presence of the oil companies in their areas as simply another forest resource. Many now 'forage' at the oil camps within their tribal territories, thereby creating the unfortunate negative image of begging Indians. The Huaorani feel no debt to the oil companies. In their eyes, they remain, without a shadow of a doubt, the true owners of their territory.

Samuel, Dayuma's son whose Huaorani name is Caento, was no ordinary Huaorani. He had been sent to Bible school in Florida, spoke perfect English, Spanish and Huao and, when I met him, was a techno-music junkie who owned a bar in Quito. I was living in Quito and it was my favourite bar in town. Being recently separated from Jane, I was on the dating circuit and had met an attractive Ecuadorian woman. Our first date was 'You show me your favourite bar and I'll show you mine'. We went to hers, had a great time, then I took her to Sam's place, called, naturally, 'Caento's'. We sat at the bar and chatted. Being a regular and having certain special privileges, I left her for a moment to use the telephone in the back. Returning there were two large, ugly Ecuadorians pressed up to her. I wedged myself between them and sat down. A while later, one of the men returned to the bar next to us and got locked into a nasty argument with Sam about paying the bill. The man was very drunk. Then I heard Sam say, "If you had of told me at the beginning that you were policemen, of course I wouldn't have charged you!" At that same instant, the other two cops stood up, waving their pistols in the air and ceremoniously marched everyone out the door onto the street. The guy at the bar then turned to my date and stuffed the muzzle of his gun in my girlfriend's kidney. He made her get off the barstool. Then he moved closer to me and pushed the muzzle in my temple, hard enough to leave a red dent in my skin, as he continued his argument with Samuel. Forcing my eyes to glance sideways, I could see his drunken finger on the trigger! Calmly, I got off the stool and let him walk us both out to the street as well. The rest of the patrons were on the other side of the road shielding themselves behind parked cars. He returned inside, slamming the door. Samuel was now alone with the thugs. Bang! A shot rang out and we figured they had killed him. The three of them came out, brandishing their weapons at us. One of our friends followed them to a strip club. Another friend and I literally kicked the locked door open. The walls were covered in blood and Sam had been shot. Miraculously and certainly by sheer fluke, after pistol-whipping him with the butt of a handgun, the shot had creased the top of his head. His scalp was bleeding profusely but he was going to be OK. There was no retribution. Yes, the three cops were arrested after we alerted others but they were not jailed. In fact, they threatened Sam against him deciding to prosecute. They were suspended for a while.

Caento had married Jeanne, an American nurse. They had a son called Shane, whose 'tush' Jeanne asked me to wipe the first time I met him as a baby. The last news on Shane was that he was now a US Air Force fighter pilot! Despite his city lifestyle, Sam still regularly 'went native' in his tribal community unable to resist the call of the forest. I, meanwhile, remained deeply captivated by the breadth and pace of change that Dayuma's family had undergone over a period of some 50 years and three generations – from uncontacted Stone Age to US fighter pilot. Obviously, the culture was rapidly dying out – and we, the industrial world, were the catalyst of that extinction.

I have been fascinated by the tribe ever since. Not to mention that there are at least two uncontacted tribes, living in self-isolation, still today, in the Ecuadorian rainforest. One, the Tagaeri, are direct blood relatives of the missionarised, 'contacted' Huaorani. The other, the Taromenane, are a mystery.

I decided to produce a book, not an anthropological one, but rather what I hoped would be a sensitive photographic vision of the Huaorani's human qualities, their charisma, their sense of humour, their incessant laughter and their simple *joie de vivre*. Targeting the Ecuadorian public the aim was to raise their social status and reframe them as a truly incredible people. I arranged for Sting and Trudie Styler to do the foreword to give the subject more gravitas.

And, I venture, if you too were to find yourself amongst them in their own environment, an open mind would soon pierce the thin veneer of the T-shirts, boots and shorts they mostly now wear. The fabricated shroud of the developed world would melt away and their true spirit would come alive before you, just as it does for me every time.

Mist rose and crouched on the canopy like a puffy white snake sinuously mirroring the course of the lazy Amazon tributary below. The pilot and I raced low over the treetops at 120 miles-per-hour (200kph) leaving vast tracts of pristine rainforest in our wake. Our helicopter gained altitude to help us find our goal: a clearing, half the size of a football field, somewhere 'down there'. The canopy was majestic, a carpet of myriad greens, it stretched as far as the horizon in every direction. Beneath the roar of the rotors, I couldn't help but wonder about the mysteries hidden in the half-light below the dense layers of leafy tree crowns, and yet I was simultaneously struck by the idea that if we continued on our flight for just a short while longer, it would all be over. We would have flown out of the airspace of the planet's most biodiverse assemblage of life while crossing the entire ancestral home of one of South America's oldest and most traditional cultures.

Only three hours before, I had left my home in Quito, nearly 3,000 metres (10,000 feet) above sea level in the heart of the Andes Mountains. I had taken a cab through the chaotic traffic of morning rush hour, been whisked into the comfortable lounge of a private air charter company and had soon been gazing down at the dry, brown, craggy mountain scenery below. A patchwork of smallholdings disappeared behind us as we raced downhill, eastwards towards the Amazon, on our 30-minute flight. The crumpled eastern cordillera began to smooth out while the browns turned to greens. As large plantations of regularly spaced African palms began to dominate the view, I knew we were close to Coca, a bustling oil industry hub on the western edge of Ecuador's lowland Amazon basin.

I had been a regular visitor to Coca since 1991 when, as I have already told you, I had worked as a professional tour guide in the rainforest. In those days, it had been truly repugnant to me. Law was the whim of the top official. I had even been put in jail there and since then liked it even less. It was with something of a sense of relief that the chopper took off and left Coca behind.

Cocooned in the front seat of the helicopter, the comfort of my familiar world was stripped away. My concentration now focused on riverbanks and clearings, in case of engine failure, in the event we needed to autorotate to relative safety. Even if we were to survive an impact, could we survive for much longer, I wondered? I had already spent a total of two-and-a-half years living in the Amazon. I was certainly no jungle novice, yet what skills did I really possess? How long would it take me to construct a rudimentary shelter, something I had watched Meñewa build absent-mindedly in a few minutes on a previous visit? Could I really climb the forty-metre (130 feet) *chonta* palm to harvest its fruits? Were they even in season now? Fishing would seem like the easiest source of protein. But I would have to identify the fish poison vine *barbasco* first. Maybe I could spear a fish through the murky waters. I could try… Even finding a river in which to fish wasn't at all obvious. With little or no reference to the sun beneath the canopy, especially hard on the equator, direction was more guesswork than science. Perhaps my questions were academic anyway.

Within half an hour, we were already flying over an area inhabited by fearsome Tagaeri and Taromenane groups. The incongruity of the juxtaposition of my high-tech flight and their Stone Age existence was both compelling and saddening. I couldn't help asking myself what they thought about the frequent drone of oil industry helicopters overhead, or what possible hope these last free spirits could have of halting the disintegration of their traditional culture when confronted by the march of the insatiable machine of the industrialised world? How could they ever not be drawn into it and eventually consumed by it? I was even a part of their change. The helicopter ran on fuel derived from the forest after all.

I was flying in for my second visit to the Gabaro Huaorani community. The Huaorani today provide an 'example', if you will, of the intermediary stage of the process of contact and acculturation. For untold generations, they had lived in the forest virtually unchanged. Only half a century ago, they themselves had come face to face with the machine. Today, they wear its clothes, eat oceanic fish from small tin cans and are read to from a two-thousand-year-old book. Change has come, thick and fast. Their once true course is swiftly and inexorably being altered.

We arrive at Gabaro. The coarse dust buffets the inclined bodies of the welcoming committee who have braved the downdraught of our fearsome helicopter at the edge of the small clearing. I recognise the familiar faces of old friends. Making friends among the Huaorani people is easy: you are either welcome or you are not. If accepted, you are truly taken in and treated as part of the family. The sense of generosity abounds. What meagre amounts of food, shelter or possessions a person might call their own are yours to share. I had brought a small tent to sleep in but because of the expected mutual sharing, I had to keep it secured with a small padlock. I had brought a computer, solar panels and downloader for my images. The problem was that something as strong as a computer cable was perfect to hog-tie a dead peccary.

Once known as 'Aucas', a derogatory term meaning savage, the Huaorani who greet me with beaming smiles are no more hostile than the memories of my grandmother. The helicopter pilot however was very nervous of their formidable reputation as killers. He left the rotors turning idly. As I stepped out, I walked towards the crowd and embraced an old man, Gewa, who had stepped forward to greet me. He took off his feather crown and sat it atop my much larger head. Only then did the chopper pilot shut down the engine to unload my gear before taking off back to Coca, with the promise that he would return in three weeks. I was now alone with them. Meanwhile, children gathered around, rubbing my forearms and pulling at the unfamiliar hairiness, likening me to a woolly monkey.

My entry to Gabaro had been cleared by a Huaorani called Ima Nenquimo. Although I had had plenty of previous Huaorani contact while living in Ecuador, this particular project jelled when, by good fortune and coincidence, I met Ima who had been brought up and educated in Quito. Whilst I was preparing for this book, he was looking for a photographer to illustrate a book of Huaorani mythology which he had just finished writing. In order to complete my work, I had wanted to spend more time in fewer places, staying at the most traditional communities I could find. I thought it would be better to spend longer with a smaller number of people, accepting the likely repetition of characters, while hoping that the group would become as relaxed as possible in front of the camera, until, to all intents and purposes, I disappeared entirely.

I have always loved the Amazon rainforest. As a biologist, I consider it one of my favourite places on Earth. The eminent naturalist Charles Darwin exclaimed of rainforest that 'Epithet after epithet was found too weak to convey to those who have not visited the intertropical regions, the sensation of delight which the mind experiences [...]. The land is one great wild, untidy, luxuriant hothouse, made by nature for herself'. I remember my first visit to Nature's hothouse. My initial impressions were not dissimilar to Darwin's. With time, I also came to realise how benign this 'wild, untidy' world really was. Hollywood had it all wrong, as usual. Wasps, ants and hairy caterpillars were the most troublesome creatures I encountered. Poisonous snakes? Anacondas? Jaguars? They were all pretty much impossible to find, despite hours and days of diligent searching. One thing that struck me on long walks was the sensation of neither progressing towards, nor leaving behind, a particular place. Points of reference deep in the forest were non-existent, or, as I later came to understand, very subtle. There were no mountains to leave behind or ridges to approach. I felt like an ocean fish swimming in deep blue water.

Everything in the rainforest seemed accelerated. Coming from the temperate regions of my youth, it was as if the senescence of winter, the rotting of autumn, the new life of spring and the luxuriance of summer were all compressed into just one day. Four seasons affected the same tree at the same time. Organisms either seemed to be eating or being eaten, foraging or waiting, warning or hiding. The forest also eventually revealed order. Layers could be discerned. While familiar houseplants abounded in the dim, warm and humid understory in similar conditions in which we like to maintain our homes, epiphytic cacti grew on the canopy top, a harsh environment beneath the rays of the equatorial sun where rain and nutrient capture-and-retention is the limiting factor in survival. The rainforest for me is always a surprising, complex, contradictory and disorientating habitat.

I understood how much of a foreigner I was in this environment while walking with Tage. He had been wearing a cheap plastic watch. I was never sure why he needed to know the time, or indeed if he even knew how to tell it. I asked him to remove the watch for my photographs, so he kindly took it off and placed it under a leaf at the side of the trail. Returning the same way several featureless hours later, he leant down and picked it up from under one of hundreds of thousands of leaves we had walked past. He just *knew* the place – unlike me, who was trying to recognise the leaf.

Staying with the Huaorani, I am amazed by how quickly my life's woes and worries inevitably fall away. By sheer osmosis, values rearrange inside me, my worldview changes and I begin to question many of the mores I hold dear. I did not have to hunt to feed myself, nor did I feed from the Huaorani. I had arrived self-sufficient. But it was obvious that my friends' vision of food and food acquisition was completely different to mine. One hardly noticed a man reaching up for his blowgun and untying the quiver of darts from the string suspended above the fire (the driest place in the hut) or slipping quietly out of the slit in the hut's palm fronds to disappear into the forest. It was as if any one of us had just left the house to pop down to the local shops. Imagine our lifestyle makeover if calling for a take-out meant stealthily creeping up on a troop of wily monkeys and shooting them silently with a three-metre (10 feet) blowgun from 40 metres (130 feet) with poison-tipped darts we had previously crafted. Or if getting a bite to eat meant sprinting at full pelt, losing all one's bearings, after an angry herd of some 200 dangerous wild pigs in order to get close enough to spear one to death, with a weapon hewn from a felled palm tree, running the risk that the spear might miss and the herd turn on their aggressor. Or we could simply trip and break a bone on the uneven terrain. Or even – and most of us would do this convincingly within two minutes of leaving a trail – simply getting lost. Can you imagine buying a week's worth of groceries and carrying them home for three or four hours on a jungle trail? A mature peccary, weighing 45kg or 100lb, is heavier than a large German Shepherd. It's hard enough to lift one off the ground, let alone lug it home for your dinner. Despite the prowess and skill involved in hunting, there was little or no ceremony associated with it. When a hunter returned to the community with his prey, a peccary usually caused a stir, but monkeys or birds were taken for granted, expected. I compared this with the images of hunters posing with their 'trophies' in my culture. Did my Huaorani friends realise how macho they were? I was included in everything yet never made to feel 'special' or different. Conviviality was the order of the day.

Many of the Huaorani men have muscles that ripple as if they have just stepped off Venice Beach in California, (a crazy place where I have watched an old lady, with purple hair, on a skateboard being towed around by a small dog, a guy juggling live chainsaws and a woman lying on broken glass while furniture was being placed on top of her). I couldn't resist comparing the two. At first, they would appear complete opposites. The Venice Beach men spend hours every day pumping iron in order to impress the girls with their muscles, despite never putting their hard-earned physiques to any real use. Shopping trolleys have wheels, after all. The Huaorani's muscles are testament to his proficiency as a provider: he has to be as fit as the wild herds in order to run with them, catch his prey, kill it and bring it home. Could a Huaorani understand how California girls could be impressed by the mere aesthetic of muscles, without them actually producing anything at the end of the day? I think not. He would be pleased to think that his muscles could have an impact on California girls, to be sure. I did notice that Huaorani women seemed impressed and attracted to a hunter's skill and his ability to bring meat to his family's table. So, I came to the conclusion that when a California girl swoons over a steroid boy's biceps and washboard stomach, she is actually, subconsciously, attracted to his potential as a hunter. I was also interested to note that the Huaorani had a different criteria for attractiveness. An individual with no teeth, for example, seemed no less appealing to a woman than anyone else as long as he could hunt.

During my stays in the communities, new experiences and sensations filled my days. During breakfast, a captive harpy eagle cries plaintively, laughter echoes from all around, white smoke curls upward from singeing monkey fur being roasted on the fire, slowly filling the hut. I watch, captivated, as the lips of a severed coati head, put on the same fire to cook, contract into a snarl and the prehensile nose curls up bit by bit. Later, the guts are removed from a white-lipped peccary. The stench is overwhelming. I sit in silent admiration as a young child, oblivious to the stomach-churning odour, crawls over the animal and plays a game of looking for ticks to pull off. Other children are also at play. One challenge seems to consist in finding the poison dart tips broken off inside the bodies of hunted monkeys and birds. I cringe with my 'health and safety' values as a five-year-old, razor-sharp knife in hand, leans over the fire to slice a piece of meat off the carcass when feeling peckish. Another sound makes me turn. The old man Megatowe leans contentedly out of his hammock to hammer the femur of a howler monkey. The banging is followed by a sharp suck, as he gets to the precious marrow inside.

Hammocks play a fundamental role in Huaorani life. No matter what the activity, everything it seems can be achieved from its cradling embrace. It is primarily a bed, often shared by more than one family member. It is laboriously made from the dried and woven fibres of the *chambira* palm. It serves as the main seat of the hut. Because of its pendulum suspension, it can be swung to reach a large radius without ever having to get up – ideal for the sapping heat of the tropics. It can serve as a platform from which to eat, construct a feather crown, fashion a clay bowl, weave a split-cane basket, play, make love, cook, feed the pets, prepare poison for the blow gun darts, even make the blow gun itself, sharpen knives or chant. And, when it's time to move on, it can be disassembled in a flash, is lightweight and resilient.

Preparing food with Huaorani is always an education. First, the fire is moved to a particular spot, determined by the prey to be cooked. Be it macaw, parrot, peccary, fish or monkey, everyone, from the smallest child upwards, knows exactly how the animal should be prepared. There are no tribulations from the chef regarding the menu. The meal is food, fuel. The Huaorani favour some meats, such as peccary, tapir and monkey, above others, but everything is relished as if tasted for the first time. There are no sauces, salads, desserts or presentation involved. The choice is simple: roast or boiled.

Mealtimes are always animated. Everyone shares plates and eating utensils if available. Stories of the hunt are often recounted with much gusto. Sounds – the dart flying through the air, the squelch of mud or the multifarious animal noises – are sewn into sentences like words. The cadence of conversation might only be occasionally interrupted by the dull thuds of an old woman chopping more wood to keep the fire stoked. Evening meals continue well into the night, long past the time that bellies are full. Stories are told and retold, kids staying awake with the adults until, lulled by the voices, they finally fall asleep in their parents' arms.

Late evenings, I eventually retire to my tent, pitched amongst the huts. I lie down, exhausted, drifting in and out of sleep, allowing myself to be enveloped slowly by the cacophony of forest sounds that emanate from every point of the compass. As I lie with my eyes closed, the grunts, chirps and croaking of frogs, the chirrups of crickets and a million-and-one noises multiply, colours flashing on the lids of my eyes in a synesthetic dance. One sound stands out. At first, it could be an animal. But then, it becomes more distinct in my mind. I realise it is the old men of each household, beginning their night-time calling on the spirit of the jaguar to enter their bodies. It sounds like the chanting of Buddhist monks: a low, monotonous intonation, repetitive and mesmerising. On and on it goes, the river of syllables echoing around the village, off into the night air. They are communing with the spirits, asking them where the peccaries will be in the morning, how to cure an ailing relative, what messages they are to communicate. The elder men of the Huaorani always chant late into the night, just as their fathers and grandfathers and forebears did before them. The rhythmic singing of words stretches back through their bloodline to the origins of Man. In the huts of the Tagaeri and Taromenane, somewhere off in the forests of Yasuní, the elders will also be evoking the spirits to help them, to come to their aid, to tell them what to do as the outside world closes in around them. I wonder how soon their chant will become a lament.

# The Brute
# Peru

We'd been to the Peruvian Amazon before. In fact, I'd lost count of the times and hours I'd spent crouched in small, dank photographic hides, rustic assemblages of bent and woven vegetation. Ants, ubiquitous in the rain forest, become like family. Intently, I have watched their comings-and-goings, searching, finding and carrying any scrumptious morsels out of my hide, along a trail somewhere and back to their nest. If I was ant sized, I'm sure I'd get lost in such a thick tangle of debris and rotting leaves. I know they follow chemical trails but that doesn't fully explain how they go out on their own to find food and still get home, especially after it rains. I know they are strong too and can carry huge loads relative to their body size. I learnt that at school. I didn't care about that though, because if it looked like it was too much hard work for them I'd always move the obstacle or try to help. That's what it is like when you're alone in a hide in the forest you seem to get sucked in. It's not scary – why should it be? Cities are scary but not rain forests. Anyway, I digress. Here I was back again. This trip though was different. I was in a canoe with a team of helpers. Ishmael was the motorist – he was very young but very competent. All of us trusted his judgement – even through the rapids that most people walk around – including through the infamously dangerous Pongo de Maniche. Close to him, near the back of the long, narrow craft were two of his kinfolk, girls and also Machiguenga Indians, rainforest people. They were the cooks. Reneé and I only needed one but they won't go alone into the forest. It struck me as a bit ridiculous for people born and living their whole lives in the forest but they are scared, even though there's really nothing out there. Actually, they are even scared of giant earthworms it turns out and toads as well. Personally, I love toads. Anyway, I digress again. In the middle of the canoe I sat, discussing plans with Oscar Mujica next to me. A tiny frame, but a bright, sparkling personality seemed to sum up Oscar. He was a biologist, familiar with where we were now – somewhere along the Lower Urubamba River – a place we had never been. At the bow was 'Anaconda' another Machiguenga and Ishmael's assistant and soul mate. A macaw conservationist friend, Charlie Munn, had asked us to go. The mission, if I chose to accept it, was to get me and my cameras into a position that I could photograph the rare blue-headed macaw. That meant constructing a tower, using the scaffolding that separated Oscar and I from Anaconda and making another hide on top of the tower. I was hoping that the ants would find me perched on my steel castle, so that we could while away the hours together. The first ant to leave a trail would have to be a courageous explorer braving the 20 metres of cold steel before he found me. That bothered me a little.

We'd stopped once too often I guess (my fault as usual) and now we were running late and all of us wanted to make camp before it got dark, especially Lucmilla and Regina the girls. Simple darkness was what seemed to scare them the most.

The rain had been hard recently and the river beaches had all but disappeared. Our camping options didn't really look that good. In the interest of keeping up morale, we decided to stop where we were and make the best of it. There was a beach but it was small and plagued by tiny biting flies. There were nice fresh tracks of a large tapir however coming out of the water and up the beach into the tall 'pindo' grass where we decided to camp. That was exciting. Even if we didn't see the animal, it was very satisfying just to know that one was close. I even joked that Oscar should be careful where he pitched his tent as he might get a visitor in the night. That of course was unlikely as tapirs are very shy and almost never seen, even though they are the largest wild terrestrial animals on the whole South American continent. Stockily built, somewhere between a horse and a rhinoceros, I had known many as pets, they actually become very tame and attached to their owners.

The Machiguenga quickly set about clearing a small area in the pindo grass. The grass was six-metres tall, so I guessed it was something like what an ant feels walking through the lawn in your garden. Or being in the movie 'Honey, I Shrunk the Kids'. From the stalks of the pindo, which was rather like a bamboo, they built tables, a kitchen, clotheslines and even a fish drying rack where they put out the filleted catfish they had caught from the river. It was evening now but in the daytime, any fish on the drying racks would quickly go black with a covering of sweat bees. Nobody minded, we let them have their feed before we had ours.

At our base camp a couple of days down river, I had asked them repeatedly to please save me the catfish heads as I wanted to use them on riverbanks to try and bring down the spectacular king vulture close enough to photograph. They would leave the heads in the canoe but claimed that caimen had climbed in during the night and stolen them. Then, one morning in the pre-dawn, I heard the very subtle noise of our wooden canoe clunking against a fallen tree trunk. Looking up, I was gobsmacked to see a jaguar, standing IN the canoe, with a big catfish head in its mouth! The Machiguenga panicked and spooked it. I do believe though that it was the same individual young male that I later met, face to face on the trail standing a few metres apart, as I walked between my two photographic blinds. Alone together, we stared curiously at each other for a while. As we were so remote, I could very possibly have been the first human he had seen. Curiosity satisfied, it gave a little spring off the trail and disappeared. I was, of course elated. I do not fear jaguars at all in the forest. Pumas on the other hand are a different ball game.

While camp was being set up, Oscar erected the antenna on a particularly tall Pindo stalk and took out the radio from its large, rigid, waterproof Pelican case and attached it to the antenna cable. We called back to our guardians in civilisation, just to let them know we were OK. I don't really know what they could have done if we weren't as we were literally in the middle of nowhere.

Now it was nighttime and we were all in bed. Reneé and I were on a mat with a large, tarpaulin-covered, mesh cover improvising as a tent. I liked the intimacy with the forest. Oscar was alone in his tiny pup tent and the Machiguenga were huddled in a tent together in a separate clearing that they had made for themselves.

I think I heard it first, the gentle crushing of vegetation underfoot with the soft squelch of mud. I woke Reneé. Oscar awoke next. He said he could hear it breathing it was so close. Finally, the Machinguenga heard it. They thought the sound was bandits creeping up on them and ran, semi-naked out of the tent to the canoe, clutching the fuel pipe (removed as security out of habit). I think they were going to leave us and make their escape. The tapir – for that's what it was – was seriously startled. It went crashing through the pindo out onto the cobble beach, met the freaked out Machiguenga turned 180 degrees and came blundering back like a bulldozer until it stopped abruptly at the 'kitchen'. I put my powerful spotlight on it, more excited than I can even put down in words. It was, after all, a tapir, four metres from me at eye level – in the wild! With all the bedlam, Oscar poked his head out of his tent and he saw it too. The Machiguenga were still screaming, not knowing what was going on. I swear I could actually see the tapir thinking! "Machiguenga behind – not good, big mesh thing and bright light to my right – not as bad, but still not good, small pup tent with tiny biologist – not too bad." I could see Oscar thinking too. Tiny biologist, big, heavy tapir. He, from somewhere, procured the presence of mind to hide behind his oversized Pelican case. You guessed the rest. The 250 kg tapir galloped, nought to sixty, in whatever a juggernaught can do, straight over Oscar's tent leaving muddy footprints on the fabric, knocking the Pelican case for six (thereby saving Oscar's life), collapsing the tent and disappearing in a tumultuous display of hitherto unthinkable (for me anyway, knowing all those placid pets) display of brute power. I thought Oscar was dead – crushed, but he wasn't. We heard him groaning. He was lucky. Lucky because he was a biologist and his friends were biologists and this was a story he could dine out on for a long time to come. I was awestruck, having seen the whole thing, the Machiguenga were ambivalent because they knew that the rain forest is always full of surprises.

# Wild Dogs, Lions and Valium
## Botswana

Botswana is one of our very favourite destinations. Only thrice have Reneé and I been there without paying guests, but all 50+ trips we have done to date have been exceptional. We have seen the many iterations of some of the lodges, from their humble beginnings of tented ex-hunting camps to the over-the-top opulence that many of them are today. Regardless of which camp you stay in, though, the wildlife sightings are remarkable. Mombo Camp is one of our favourites and the pillar of most of our trips. Set on Chief's Island in the middle of the fabulous Okavango Delta the area is crammed with predators and there is lots of action. We always place the younger, most gung-ho, types in one of the two end tents. It's further to walk in the dark and usually the most exciting. One trip, for example, a single, young male, tax exile from the UK, perfect for an end tent, had brought with him a pair of night-vision binoculars. After dinner, he went out onto his deck and was watching the green impalas through the optics. Happy with his experience, he pulled them away from his eyes, turned to go back inside when he saw a leopard sitting erect, sphinx-like on the deck next to him. He froze and had to wait until she slunk off to try and nab one of the impala they had both been watching.

Another client, Brian, that we took to Mombo was a rather odd, highly intelligent, depressive, introvert. Even he would agree. He really wanted to have been a physicist but, in his opinion, everyone hates their jobs and he never wanted to hate physics, he became a mathematician. He always took a Valium before every light aircraft flight we made between camps and had a very nervous disposition. Nevertheless, he was young and we put him in the end tent. Somewhat of a social pygmy, Brian was not missed in the pre-dinner get-together. Back in his tent, it was dark outside and he knew that he should have met up in the social area by now. He was nervous and so decided to go to the toilet first. It was the best place for him. As he sat there, suddenly and very dramatically, the entire set of wardrobe, shelving, water jug, drinking glasses and thermos flask came crashing down in front of him. The noise was deafening but worse was the sounds of extreme excitement and bone crunching. It lasted a full five minutes followed by diabolical laughter. He waited and when all was quiet made his move to join us. A hyena walked straight up to him and Brian, to his credit, did not run but stood his ground. He arrived, shaken and we all went to check out the details of his story. It turned out that a pack of wild dogs had chased an impala which hit his tent and collided with the wardrobe on the other side of the canvas. They devoured the carcass in five minutes, by which time the spotted hyenas had arrived cackling and calling each other. We all wished we had been there and told him how lucky he was.

Arriving back for dinner, the tradition was that the meal was always introduced. Tonight it was Flo's turn. She was short, very rotund, African and had a beautiful personality with a very high-pitched, melodic voice. She illuminated herself by holding up a kerosene lamp. "Gooood evening, ladies and gentlemen. My name is Flo. I am the lady of the lamp. Tonight, for starters we have tomato soup with…with…with…umm…with yesterday's bread," as she could not remember the word for croutons. It was enough to relieve some of Brian's tensions.

Up in Savuti Elephant Camp, Reneé and I were walking to the dining tent pre-dawn one morning, using a flashlight to see what eyes might be around. We saw a mongoose on a large, grey termite mound partially hidden by some bushes, it did not move as we approached. Our flashlights were not very effective and as we got way too close, the mongoose eyeshine turned out to be a reflective elephant's eye and the termite mound was the elephant. It bellowed at the discourtesy of a rude awakening and charged. Me screaming in vain to Reneé. "Don't run!" I had no option but to follow in her dust. We made it to safety by about a metre as the elephant crashed through the handrail which snapped like a matchstick. Later that afternoon, one of our clients showed me a full-frame image he had taken of an elephant's eye. "Nice shot," I complimented him and asked what lens he had used.

"This one," he said and showed me the standard 50mm.

I said, "Wow, you must have been really close."

He said, "Yeah, and their skin is so soft too."

In the same general area, at another camp, whose name I will not mention, our group had sole use and we had gone to bed in our tents. The staff were a little ways away in a separate area. Only one staff member remained on our side, she was a lovely woman and slightly autistic. In the middle of the night, we heard shouting from one of our clients right outside of our tent. We awoke in a start, jumped out of bed, ran out of the tent to see others, already having been woken up, outside as well. It was quite an education to witness the various examples of nightwear and even curlers that were on display. More importantly, there was a fire! It turned out that a hyena had picked up one of the kerosene lamps, used to illuminate the path, but dropped it because it was hot. The fire was getting large. The grass and bush was burning between the main lodge and the kitchen, a separate building. It was heading towards the main lodge with its low hanging thatch. We had to act quickly. The side issue was that two dominant male lions were fiercely disputing their territory, easily outdoing the Hollywood lion, with some very impressive roars. They had chosen the lodge as the territorial boundary. One at our end and one at staff quarters. As a result, we could not risk walking over there or sending the staff member that was with us. Instead, I asked her to just beat the drum as loudly as possible. Our shouting was in vain, as we tried to raise staff hoping that they would show up with the fire bowser. Out of options, we literally broke down the kitchen door and grabbed anything we could. This particular group were elderly Americans and we now had a cluster of sixteen of us in a bizarre scene. Dressed in nighties, or not much else, filling saucepans with water, beating flames with frying pans and brooms, using a spade we found to shovel sand, in the dead of night, African drums beating like crazy, all covered in soot with two magnificent, way-too-close-lions determined to out-roar each other was really quite surreal. Eventually, after a heroic group effort, we got the fire under control. The lions had wandered off and a staff member finally rocked up wondering why the drums were thumping. We have not been back since but understand that a little brass plaque was erected in our group's honour for saving the lodge.

A quality wild dog encounter often becomes the highlight of any Botswana trip. They are wonderful animals to be around. With a very tight-knit family and matriarchal social structure, they really take care of each group member. Often they leave a pack member to guard the puppies in the den, but then come back to feed her by regurgitating some of the meat they have killed. They hunt cooperatively, fanning out in a line to flush game when one or more dogs then gets a chance to run it down. All members of the hunting party feed communally. Tall, lean and with big ears, they are built for endurance running to wear down their prey if necessary. Uniquely patterned with a mix of black, white and tan, they are easily recognised as individuals, each has a white tail tip. I have, on several occasions, been very close to wild dogs, with no protection at all whilst on foot. I have never felt threatened by them but delighted in their curiosity of me. Due to their incredibly efficient hunting technique, where they might disembowel an animal to bring it down, they have been regarded as cruel killers, persecuted as a result and now are Africa's most endangered large predator. I guess the critics have never watched lions killing which may take hours for prey such as a hippo, sometimes days to kill an elephant.

My finest wild dog moment was with a pack of five animals. We found them asleep in the shade of a jackalberry tree. Parking under the same tree ourselves, we waited almost an hour for them to wake up, which, once they did, was followed by the highly affectionate and excitable meet-and-greet ceremony as if they haven't seen each other for eons. They trotted as a unit towards the water but noticed a group of lechwe already drinking. Deciding whether to slake their thirst and blow their cover or give chase, they went for it. Lechwe scattered in all directions explosively and four of the five dogs ran out of sight in hot pursuit. The fifth pulled down a big buck and killed it. Thirty seconds later, a large spotted hyena loped onto the scene and stole the kill (without too much resistance from the single dog). We were after dogs, so followed in our cruiser to behind the palm island. Incredulously, there was another dog, with another lechwe it had pulled down at the water's edge, but was now in a tug of war with a large Nile crocodile which was half exposed and pulling both animals back into the water with it. The dog let go and we continued. The three remaining dogs had killed an impala, wherever that had come from and were already a good way through devouring it when the remaining two members of the pack found them and joined in the feast. It was all over in about eight minutes.

When you get wrapped up in a dog chase, it can be incredibly exciting. It is impossible to keep up with them without a wee bit of serious bush-bashing and bouncy driving. It's often hard to get a vehicle through a gap where a dog has no trouble and kudos to the amazing drivers we have had that have done so.

We have been privileged by many colourful characters on our trips. One stands out in particular. She was a black lady from Johannesburg and extremely large, in personality, lung capacity and physical size. She was a gospel singer and had once sung in Cape Town stadium, to a full house, without a microphone. Usually, at least once per camp, we have a bush braai where camp staff set up a full-service lunch a mile or so from the lodge. It is always a surprise to guests when we come around another insignificant bend in the road to find a very comfortable, luxurious setup in the middle of the bush. Once we had arrived at the braai with our singer and had a chance to freshen up, I asked a favour of her. Would she please sing for us Amazing Grace? The result was absolutely electrifying. Most of us were teary eyed. The power and resonance was incredible. I can only imagine what the animals thought. It was not a frightening sound to them but they were surely rigid with curiosity. Back at camp, they heard it too.

The Land Cruisers are fitted with three rows of seats behind the driver. The last row protrudes behind the back of the vehicle. It was where our singer was sitting when we got into a dog chase. With her flowing robes, following behind her, she looked like a Spanish galleon in full sail. The vehicle, with its soft suspension was actually bouncing clear of the ground and pitching wildly as it tore after the dogs. Everyone was in hysterics, herself included, as she screamed with delight on every bounce. Quite a character.

We would always lead several trips over a season in Botswana which made it very interesting to have continuity over certain individuals such as the leopards and lions. One lioness in particular was 'good value' to be with. Curiously, she was not part of a pride but a loner in her prime and strong. Exceptionally muscular, her shoulders and forearms greater than Mike Tyson's, made her that much stronger than he. She had three young cubs that she was teaching to hunt and trying to feed. We watched as she spotted an impala, the cubs were told to 'stay', as she slunk forward in a stalk. There were two Californians with us, a young couple that had recently converted to Sikhism, dressed in white robes, with white turbans and white skin they begged us to move on, as they did not want to witness a kill. I explained that we would stay, this was raw nature, it was what we all came for and they should cover their eyes. At the critical moment, after the tremendous build-up of tension, one of the cubs sprang up and raced to the mother. The impala spooked and it was all over, the lioness gathered her family and she carried on, head low, looking for the next meal. Two days later, we were with them again. She was tense, very still and one hundred percent focused on a male warthog 20 metres in front of her. The cubs were behaving and obviously hiding somewhere close by. We could not see them. We parked our vehicle in the predicted path of the chase and waited. A full 15 minutes later after inching forward as only a cat can, the lioness sprang and gave chase. Both animals were hurtling straight towards us in a cloud of dust, until, not ten metres away, she grabbed the warthog, it screamed violently, they skidded to a dramatic halt and she killed it. Panting at the carcass, she called the cubs who came bounding out of the grass and joined the mother to feed. Success! I couldn't help but notice that the Sikhs were totally hypnotised by the drama and were staring fixatedly between open fingers.

Perhaps a month later, same place, different group, we were on our afternoon game drive and I had assured our one hard-core birder that we would look for a Verreaux's eagle owl, Africa's largest owl with famously bright pink eyelids. Towards the end of daylight, we spotted our lioness still with her three, slightly larger, cubs in tow. Some distance away, she was being trailed by spotted hyena, perhaps my favourite animal in Africa. The cubs were vulnerable to more than one hyena working cooperatively and she had to be constantly on guard. She turned off the dirt road and into a palm island thicket. We followed her in, pushing through the low palms and into the calcrete centre of the island (note; these slightly raised palm islands do become true islands during seasonal flooding). She was nowhere to be seen so we sat, waited and listened. It was a beautiful evening and from our Land Cruiser's totally open seats we enjoyed watching the stars begin to appear. Without warning, a doe impala burst from cover and slammed into the starboard side of our vehicle with the drama of a motorway accident. Less than two seconds later, in full charge, our lioness caught up with her. We were all completely taken aback and peered directly down, a metre away, into the bulging eyes of the impala that were looking up at us in shock. Meanwhile, the lioness began eating her alive from the rump. It would definitely have been too much for the Sikhs and was verging on being too frightening for half of our vehicle. Never had any of us been so close to a top predator in full feeding frenzy. It felt like only two minutes later that the clan of five hyenas arrived announced by their heinous, demonic 'laughter'. Their heads were at elbow level with us. As the hyenas circled, inches away, everyone on the port side slid more into the centre. We all had flashlights illuminating the scene. We were literally stuck in the middle of one of Africa's iconic battles between eternal enemies, numbed by the commotion, like our poor, hapless, impala who was fading away. The scene was blood-curdling and the hyenas vociferous calls, from so close, raised the hairs on the backs of our necks in a primordial sensation of abomination. The hyenas made their move and came for our brave heroine *en-masse*. She snarled and hissed loudly, which from so close was a chilling experience. She struck at them and they parried. Holding them at bay for a little longer she was eating the prime meat as fast as she could. The hyenas came in harder but she slapped one so hard, chased it and bit it solidly such that it whimpered out of the circle of light. She strutted back to us and the impala, whose head had now collapsed under the vehicle. She had bought herself a couple of minutes grace and fed voraciously. Two of the cubs were nowhere to be seen through all this but the third had been visible throughout. Somehow, it had managed to climb a palm tree and was still clinging on for dear life, its constant screaming adding to the overall pandemonium. Regrouping, the hyenas attacked again and unwilling to risk personal injury, she succumbed and relinquished the carcass to them. They grabbed it and carried it away as if it was nothing, whooping as they left. It was without question one of the most thrilling and intimate action encounters we have ever witnessed in Africa. The cub reversed down the palm tree, the other two reappeared and their mother left with them, once again, looking for another meal. Nobody spoke for a few minutes as our adrenaline levels tailed off. The engine came to life and the driver took us back to the road. On our way home, emotions were high and the birder was in tears. In an effort to comfort her, I asked what was wrong and she sobbed back at me, "You promised to show me an owl!"

# Kidnapped Russia

I often casually ask North Americans, as if I've forgotten their names, which countries border the USA. They usually say Canada and Mexico and stop (some add Alaska) but almost none of them mention Russia. The fact is that Little Diomede Island is USA and Big Diomede Island is Russia; they are less than 2 ½ miles apart, the border runs between them and in the winter when the sea freezes, you could easily walk from one to the other. In fact, the people of Little Diomede, which is not much more than a rock of less than three square miles, look out at Big Diomede every day and probably say, "I can see Russia from my house!" The International Date Line also happens to pass between the islands so in that respect the Little Diomedeans are always looking into the future, which, for them, doesn't look too rosy.

We have been lucky enough to travel the length of the Aleutian Islands, visit Kamchatka on several occasions and have visited the entire length of the disputed Russian and Japanese Kuril Islands. They all had their highlights but Little Diomede has always stuck in my mind. Its sibling, Big Diomede, is currently occupied by Russian military. The islands lie in the Bering Straits, named after the explorer Vitus Bering who was exploring in the area in 1728.

When we visited the village, we were welcomed by the Inupiat natives who live there. Indeed, they were happy to see some fresh faces in their small community of 100 or so folks. The island is a steep-sided rock, on which are perched a small cluster of houses, built on stilts, facing west towards Russia. The scree slopes of the rock provide nesting crevices for hundreds of thousands of tiny crested and least auklets among other species of seabird. These birds are hunted *en-masse* and their thoraxes were threaded on strings suspended between posts to dry. Walrus-gut bags, used for fishing floats, were at doorways. Yes, they were the Inupiat people, but they were also Americans, from the US of A.

Traditionally they would hunt birds, as mentioned, but also the seals, walrus and whales which migrated ahead of the ice edge as it pushed south freezing the straits and *vice versa* as it receded. Deemed underprivileged by the US government (probably belying a need to have more of a presence during the Cold War with Russia). It was decided that the community needed help. They were built a gym and basketball court up on the rock, a water storage tank, given access to provisions from mainland Alaska via helicopter, such as guns, ammunition and GPS, worst of all, cable TV was brought in. On our first visit, we spent a lot of time talking to the locals, especially the youths who shadowed us as we explored their home. They showed us the gym and we noticed the walls covered in posters warning of drug abuse and heroin addiction. Drugs were smuggled in on the chopper they told us. Cable TV was driving them mad. Stuck on a remote rock with 100 family members for company, on a meat diet of dried birds, pinnipeds and whales, suddenly they were watching the rich and famous, dressed to the nines, in expensive restaurants, every week, over and over on Dallas, Dynasty and anything else that was beamed down on them. They were hit by the realisation of where they were and began committing suicide. If I asked one of them what he might do when he grew up, his answer was likely to be, "Oh, jump off a cliff like my brother." Tempered by the warmth of their welcome was the heartbreak to watch them struggle with self-identity. We left, to return later.

We headed north through the Bering Straits, into the Chukchi Sea and turned left along the Chukota Peninsula, the easternmost point of Eurasia. We were aboard the beautiful, 100 passenger ship, the World Discoverer – a legend in her own lifetime. I was the Expedition Leader and Reneé the Cruise Director in charge of the hotel comings and goings. Cruising for a while through the otherworldly pack-ice and bergy-bits we had been looking for polar bears. I was desperate to see one. It would be my first ever bear! I held on to a short stick which had a grip to hold my binoculars to my eyes, reminiscent of Japanese whalers. Deep into the night I spotted our first bear, it drifted in and out of the sea mist and we eventually lost it. The following day however we found a mother and cub and even managed to follow it at eye level from our zodiacs. I always marvel at the enormous 'pulling power' of such iconic animals, tigers, elephants, emperor penguins, polar bears. For the sight of even one bear, people are prepared to work hard, earn lots of money to pay for an expensive trip, travel for long hours on an intercontinental aircraft, converge from all points of the compass, to board a ship and spend days on end searching for just the chance to see one.

Our plan now was to visit some of the coastal villages such as Uelen and Inchoun. Apparently, we were to be the first white, non-Russians, to visit the area in half a century. It was certainly a privilege and I felt a great sense of responsibility. In preparation for the visit to Inchoun, (we did it in reverse order) I gathered all staff and passengers for a briefing. Most of the guests were from the States, who, as a community, are very generous at heart and they had brought many donations for the local Chuckchi and Yupik natives. I asked everyone to please hand them all into reception, we would collate them, sort them, parcel them and donate them at a ship level to the relevant authorities. For example, medicines to the clinic and school supplies to the headmaster. On no account, I pleaded, were we to be randomly handing out gifts, like Father Christmas, and potentially 'ruining' the culture as has happened in many other parts of the world where begging from tourists has become the norm. *Not on my watch,* I thought. After having gone ashore myself and first met with the authorities, we disembarked all our guests ashore in the zodiacs. The ten rubber boats lined up next to each other on the beach and the staff, drivers, Reneé and I ambled into the village with the guests. The reaction from the locals was incredible. We were literally grabbed by our clothing and nothing short of physically dragged into their wooden houses. The entire boatload of people was now randomly spread throughout the village, sequestered in people's homes, all suffering the same 'fate'. The houses were much more 'western' than we had imagined they would be, both in build and content. In our case, Reneé and I were offered a plate of diced *muktuk* a delicacy of dark whale skin with a section of white blubber still attached. Looking like a plate of Liquorice Allsorts, the bite-sized morsels had a texture of crunchy coconut with their own peculiar taste. The windows were clad with chintz curtains and the whole effect indoors was very homely. We were offered tea which we drank from delicate floral pottery, delicate enough to point the little finger skyward at each sip. Next, we were showered with presents. As a woman, Reneé was given soap, a tea towel and some sewing thread. My presents, in turn, were directly from the man of the house who gave me some coins, fishing line, fishhooks and more *muktuk*. We had nothing to give back in return, our pockets were empty! Boy, did I get hell when we were all back on board! Making my excuses, I left earlier than Reneé and made my way back down to the shore to check on the boats. There was a big crowd of kids and we had a lot of fun together as I let them all bounce on the big black inflatable tubes of the zodiacs. I was dressed in full neoprene waders to help load and unload the passengers. An *umiak* came in at full speed, through the channel from the ocean and into the bay. A traditional hunting boat it has in inboard outboard motor passing through the hull. It is a wooden-framed, open craft, perhaps eight metres long and capable of carrying 10–15 people. The hull is of walrus skin. Carrying men and women, it approached me on the shore but because of its greater draft was unable to properly beach itself. I realised that the occupants would have to get wet to go ashore. I waded out and in fluent sign language got my message across that I would offer to carry the women ashore. This was considered a hilarious idea and certainly not one to be missed. One at a time, I put the women over my shoulder and beached them on dry land. Yep, hilarious! I wanted an *oosik* – a walrus penis bone, or *baculum*. Many placental mammals have such a thing, including some primates. In the case of a walrus, it is an incredibly dense bone and more than 50cm long. They are often carved for tourists but, as a biologist, I wanted a 'natural' one to go with my large skull collection. I made the necessary gesticulations and signage and was given permission to lean over the side of the *umiak* and rummage in the bilge where it looked promising that I might find one. Being a little too far out of reach, I asked to jump in and have a better look. By now, we were all best buddies and 'No problem!' was written in the air with a single hand gesture. In I climbed and in full concentration, head down, was unaware that my new friends had pushed off from shore. The engine roared to life and I looked up with a start. In a flurry of sign language, slightly misspelt due to a certain level of intoxication, it was explained, with excessive warmth, back-slapping and joviality that, because we were now such good friends, they had decided to take me reindeer hunting for two days! I clawed a sentence unintelligibly that I was in charge of the ship and all the people and, thank you, but could not possibly be away for two days. It all sounds fun but pleeease turn around. Nope! Everything was even funnier now than before. I grabbed my two-way radio and repeatedly called for Reneé. She crackled back an acknowledgment. "Reneé, run to the beach. There is an *umiak* running parallel to the sandbar heading for the channel out to sea. Grab a boat and chase it urgently! They want to kidnap me!" She detected the urgency and mild panic in my voice and responded well. Just before we breached the channel, she had caught up. At full speed, gently nestling alongside the *umiak*, walrus skin on rubber, I had to jump across. Reneé peeled off and all was good. With everyone safely back on the World Discoverer, there were lots of stories to share. One house visited even had a butchered ringed seal on the kitchen floor!

Our next stop was Uelen several miles back eastwards along the coast. Our first visit was to the workshops of the local artisans famous for their intricate ivory carvings and scrimshaw which were indeed of a striking quality. There was a commotion some way down the dark beach and I encouraged everyone to get there a quickly as possible – the rule being that where there is a crowd there is always something going on. Two *umiaks* were coming ashore. One of them had three adult walrus, still in the water strapped alongside the vessel, the other left unburdened to chase for more. A crowd had gathered. As different as we all were it was unnoticed, our focus was the same. The *umiak* grounded. The hunters jumped out and the supine animals, in turn, had ropes attached to their tusks whereupon they were hauled up the beach by the crowd as if they were on the losing end of a tug-of-war team. The three animals lay next to each other. Their tusks were massive, highly polished and wonderfully tactile. The animals themselves were huge. I was fascinated by the carcasses. I felt the unbelievably stiff bristles and studied the mouth. The lips were extremely muscular but when closed, left a slight gap in their centre. Walruses are like overgrown vacuum cleaners who feed on bivalve clams. The clams bury themselves in the muddy seabed but to feed and to 'breathe' a long siphon protrudes above the mud. By sucking, very hard, over a clam siphon the shell is blocked by the lips while the negative pressure pulls out the meat from the shell, through the gap and into the stomach. The women jumped into action in a well-practiced ritual. Armed with their *ulus*, an all-purpose knife with a semi-circular blade, one woman per animal, they slit open the body cavity, stretched out the digestive tract and then slit open the stomach. Out poured freshly sucked clam siphons. The kids were unable to contain themselves and pounced on the treats, stuffing them into their mouths like candy.

Suddenly, the hunter boat took off again and sped away after another walrus, we could see in the distance a man standing in the bow with a sturdy harpoon raised in the air. It was getting late and we returned back to our home aboard, to a fancy meal cooked by Austrian chefs and more in tune with our palate.

We repeated the trip and back in Little Diomede we told the 'Father Christmas' story, they loved it, reminiscing that those on the Russian side were relatives, separated by politics. The Little Diomedeans were over-abundant in their generosity and made up care packages of everything that they thought their 'cousins' might need including things like GPS units and fishing gear. They were duly delivered on our return to the east, which was actually west of us, to the astonishment and delight of the locals. It was very rewarding to actually *be* like Father Christmas, even if I was only the middleman.

# Siberian Surprise
# Russia

The following season, we were back in the area. I was on a beach in Teller Alaska; it was the middle of the night, cold and miserable. The World Discoverer sat, at anchor, several miles offshore. My staff and I were dressed in full cold-weather gear. I was standing knee deep in the Bering Sea and Suzana, a Brazilian phenomenon and the defecting expedition leader, left me holding the reins of the incumbent with a curt. "See ya!"

There were 100 passengers, cold and tired, behind me who now had to board the ship. We should have all boarded from a regular dock hours ago at Nome, home of the Iditarod, but the weather was too severe to come alongside. Teller was the closest next-best option. The logistical nightmare of now loading 100 passengers, in their city clothes, fuel for the outboard engines, food and supplies, by zodiac from a very shallow, shelving mudflat, in inclement weather, at night was about to begin and the reason Suzana had forsaken me. It set the whole itinerary back by one day.

We crossed to the Russian side and visited Arakamchechen Island, a well-known haulout of the Pacific walrus. On our way, we were surprised to find the Yamal at anchor in one of the labyrinth of passages around the coastline. She was black and red with a big set of hungry looking teeth painted on the bow. An impressive ship the Yamal, at the time, was the largest nuclear-powered icebreaker in the world and was famous in the industry for carrying passengers to the North Pole. She had an impressive 75,000hp capability and one of her claims to fame was that she could change her propellers anywhere in the world in less than 24 hours.

The first season that we had visited Arakamchechen Mike was the expedition leader on board and I was the marine mammal lecturer, general naturalist and zodiac driver, it was a great job and much less stressful than the heavy responsibility of expedition leader. At that time, we had first gone ashore and talked to Anatoly the solitary Russian park ranger in charge of the island. It was a pretty remote outpost and we were happy to give him a care package of vodka and potatoes. From his lonely hut, we then all walked across the headland, with Anatoly as guide, to peer over the cliff edge and look down on the tightly packed walrus turning pink on the beach below. It was actually a pretty awesome sight and one of our highlights. With each successive visit, Anatoly had come to expect our gifts but always demanded a lot more on top. Increasing through a crate of vodka and sacks of potatoes, to this visit, while I was now expedition leader, where he had 'pre-ordered' a small inflatable zodiac and outboard engine! The threat was that if we did not come up with the goods he would go ahead of our visit to the cliff edge, throw stones at the walrus, they would all take fright, disappear and leave us with nothing. Pre-dawn, I had to sneakily lower one of our fleet of Mk V industrial zodiacs, with his 'present' strapped on top and secretly, and quietly, go about five miles out of my way, hugging the coastline in an effort to avoid the scrutiny of our obligate contingent of KGB on board. If they had of got wind of the act of bribery, it would have become very messy. Once Anatoly's new boat and engine were carefully covered by a large tarpaulin I was able to take the much shorter route across open water back to the 'Disco', as she was affectionately known, and declare the island open. After a successful visit, we went to Yttygran Island nearby, the site of the ancient Whale Bone Alley where a series of bowhead whale jaw bones protruded from the tundra and skulls and vertebrae marked meat storage areas of ancient generations long past. Still in the area, we had once again passed the Yamal, stuck at her anchorage which we thought was odd. Later that evening, after an early dinner we made another landing on a beautiful island. It was to be a nature walk and was well appreciated. I had called a meeting prior to the excursion however to explain the seriousness of fog. It looked like it might come in later and my plan was to use the foghorn repeatedly such that everyone should immediately drop what they were doing and turn back to the landing point. I stayed on the bridge. The fog came rolling in, dense and very low; it was not a very deep fog bank at all and was as if someone was rolling a carpet over us and the ocean. We sounded the alarm. To my surprise, everyone complied and we had a full complement of guests back on board very efficiently. As the ship's passengers and crew retired for an early night, after a long day, I was on the bridge with Captain Lampe, an adored captain who was as much a part of the ship as the ship itself. We were discussing the itinerary and how best to catch up on our delayed start. We heard a helicopter overhead which was extremely usual, it was now dark with night and we were still covered in a blanket of low fog. It must have come from the Yamal we reasoned, as there could not be any other choppers nearby. The aircraft seemed to be using our ship as a navigation beacon as our antennas and radar we presumed were protruding above the fog. The VHF radio was alive with chatter. We sent for one of the KGB officers and asked him to come to the bridge to translate. It seemed that the Yamal was truly stuck, they were carrying passengers who had been ranging from the vessel on day excursions whilst she was under repair but now these passengers were lost. The lifeboat sent to look for them had broken down and they were now using the helicopter which was returning, fog-bound, to the ship. In my experience, Russians are the last people in the world to admit a mistake and also the last to admit to needing assistance, especially from a villainous foreign power – us! We offered help, from captain to captain, as we were in the area (which was not planned due to being a day late) our offer was refused and it was furthermore summarily denied that there was a problem. We kept steaming down the channel away from the icebreaker. The helicopter had stopped and the night was inky black outside. As we advanced, there was a small blip on our radar screen that was uncharted. "That's odd," said Lampe, as he pulled the ship's telegraph to the 'half ahead' position. We slowed down and zoomed in on the display. 'Slow ahead' and we slowed further. 'Dead slow ahead' and we stared desperately through the binoculars from each bridge wing vainly trying pierce the blackness and determine what lay in our path as we crept forward. We were getting very close and the radar pinged a collision warning. "It's moving!" Lampe exclaimed loudly. "And it's coming towards us!" The telegraph moved to 'Stop'. Peering directly down from the port bridge wing, I saw a zodiac below, then another came into the faint arc of light followed by a third.

"Zodiacs," I yelled into the bridge. I studied them and then another realisation hit me. "They've got red parkas on!" The red parkers were a sure sign that the three boatloads, probably 30 souls at least, were tourists. Red parkers were standard issue in the polar regions. We had no idea who they were but logically presumed that they were the Yamal's missing contingent. A voice called up from the lead zodiac, who shall remain nameless, except to say that he later had an expedition vessel named after him.

"We are from the Yamal. How far are we from the mother ship?" he yelled. Why he referred to it as the mother ship I'm not sure but it sounded slightly Sovietic to me. Lampe looked at the charts and calculated the distance.

"Twelve point two miles," I announced down to him. It was a long way. The passengers were scared; they had been in the zodiacs now for many hours and were freezing cold. It was the dead of night. Many wanted to pee but were not taken ashore during their venture due to the threat of polar bears. The two-way radios had no more battery power and the outboard engines were dangerously close to running out of fuel. The guests were hungry and apart from knowing that they were in the middle of the Chukotka Autonomous Okrug, which is in the middle of nowhere, they were lost. I told him that we would lift up his boats on our cranes, give them all hot soup and access to the toilets and that we would take them home. I then asked them to move down to the side gate, which was where we boarded our zodiacs. I ran down. The KGB and some crew were now awake and aware of what was going on. As we opened the side gate, I gripped both edges and leaned out into the night to study the sea of anxious faces. We must have seemed like a monstrous guardian angel looming out of the darkness to their salvation. I was still peering out at them when from one of the zodiacs I heard "Pete!" It was a man's voice, then another, "Pete!" a woman and a third exclamation of recognition. It was shocking to me. Then the first voice added, "Do you remember the photograph I took of you with the sealion on your back in Galapagos?" The situation was tense out there, I was baffled by the question and struggled to find any relevance to the situation. I cocked my head as if not hearing him correctly.

"Yes," I said.

"Well, it made a double page in the book One Earth!" he countered. He was Galen Rowell, the woman, his wife, Barbara Cushman Rowell, the third a client who had once travelled with us. Galen was recognised as one of the top landscape and mountain photographers in the world. It was a classic comment, where, despite any possible danger, photography came first. The couple and I were friends until, in 2002, they died tragically in a chartered light aircraft that crashed while taking them home. It was deeply saddening and ironic as Barbara was a very accomplished pilot in her own right having flown Galen down the spine of South America, the length of the Andes. They were accomplished explorers and adventurers and are greatly missed. To this day, I treasure one of his books that he autographed to me with 'To Pete, a kindred spirit of the wild parts of the Earth that still remain…' The group were Americans, on a trip to the North Pole when their icebreaker had had propeller issues. We made ready to receive them aboard when from behind me came an authoritative and definitive "*Nyet*!"

"*Nyet* what?" I said. It was a *Nyet*, from our top KGB guy that no way in hell was he letting them get on board – that's what! It was unthinkable that foreign spies would be allowed free access to his domain. His job was not worth it. The salt mines were cold. The argument went back and forth. "But we *know* them!"

"*Nyet*!"

"But they are friends."

"*Nyet*!"

"But they are hungry."

"*Nyet*!" and on and on. In the end, I was permitted to allow the passengers, two at a time, to be escorted, under armed guard, to the bathrooms and back to their zodiac. We were allowed to give them nothing. In the meantime, I put the word out to the stewardesses that they had my full permission (and even encouragement) to entertain as many KGB as possible in whatever way they saw fit, to keep them distracted from what was going on. A zodiac at a time I told them to drift to the stern where we surreptitiously lowered fuel (of which we were already low due to the storm in Alaska), a soup cannister and cups and even radio batteries. It was never a good idea to have people below, or nearly below, any crane operation but the KGB gave us no choice. It was truly disgraceful on their part and I shall forever hold them in a bad light. Ablutions over with, the three zodiacs, with their much-relieved cargo, kept close alongside under their own power until the Yamal was in sight. It was by now long past midnight. Never did the Yamal captain thank Captain Lampe, nor for that matter, their expedition leader. Galen acquainted me later with the gist of the passenger debrief on board the Russian vessel where it was declared that, for the record, they had never been in any danger. It seems that the expedition leader's girlfriend had been reading the compass upside-down and they had travelled 180 degrees away from the ship, sliding further and further into distress.

Another special place for me in the Bering Sea are the Commander Islands, both entities being named after Commander Vitus Bering a Danish cartographer working for the Russians. He died on the islands from scurvy after being shipwrecked there. They lie 100 miles or so east of the Kamchatka Peninsula, slightly north of Petropavlovsk. We would begin the trip in Anchorage and sail the entire length of the Aleutian Chain as far as Attu, the westernmost point of the USA and some 1500 miles away (looking at it from a different perspective however Attu could also be considered the most eastern point of the USA as it is actually in the eastern hemisphere. A good pub quiz question). On the Russian side of the date line lie the futuristic (joking) Commander Islands still geologically part of the same chain. They are crammed with marine-based wildlife. There are perhaps 200,000 northern fur seals, 5000 of the impressive Steller's sea lions, sea otters and lots of cetaceans. There are more than a million sea birds that nest there and the curious Arctic foxes are common. Apart from the natural abundance, it is also marked by extinction. The Steller's sea cow is the most poignant. A direct relative of the dugong and manatees it was in the order *Sirenia* meaning mermaid. It was massive, possibly reaching over eight tons and possibly up to 30 feet long. It was scientifically described by Steller in 1741. Its range was only around the Commander Islands. Being a sluggish animal that lived in the shallows it was tragically hunted to extinction a mere 27 years later. A similar fate befell the large and flightless spectacled cormorant which was endemic to the Commander Islands. It lasted until around the 1850s when the sea otter pelt hunters were most active. Woe the hand of Man. It really pisses me off that even today there is nothing that we cannot leave alone. As staff, we would miss lunch or breakfast and rush ashore on a treasure hunt, having an hour to ourselves before we brought the guests ashore. I think without exception, we found bones of Steller's sea cows every landing, personally I found a whole rib and vertebra. Like gold to a biologist! A second treasure to be found were Japanese glass fishing floats. Between us, we could find up to 30 in a single outing. In the early part of last century, Japanese fishermen would leave port with a hold full of sand for ballast as they head out to sea to fish I am told. They would then hand blow molten sand into glass balls of varying sizes. After they had cooled an intricate rope mesh was tied around each ball and it was attached to a fishing net. Sand ballast was replaced by fish until the hold was full and home they went. Perhaps millions of these balls were lost at sea and due to the north Pacific gyre, the currents wash them up onto beaches from Alaska to Kamchatka. The Commanders are right in their path leaving nobody else to find them but us – treasure indeed!

# A Maggot in My Head
# Amazon Rainforest, Ecuador

With all the pros of travel come the cons and I have certainly had my share of illness which has included, dengue fever, hepatitis, amoebic dysentery (often), round worms, Africa tick bite fever, typhoid, double pneumonia (which seriously nearly killed me), bilharzia (twice), a mystery illness in India and another five weeks in South Africa of complete and total lethargy for a while diagnosed as CFS then later as early Covid-19. Externally, I've had things lay eggs under my toenails in the Amazon, gazillions of ticks, chiggers, hundreds of leeches and a bot fly. It is the story of the botfly maggot that I want to tell. I was working on a book about the Yasuni National Park in the Ecuadorian Amazon which is an area scientifically proven to be the most biodiverse area on the planet within certain groups. It is truly megadiverse. There are 600 bird species found in Yasuni for example, with only 965 found in the whole of the lower 48 United States. Scientists have documented 644 tree species in one hectare (100 x 100 metres) of Yasuni, whereas there are only 32 in the whole of the UK. Not only is Yasuni extremely diverse but the biomass is still very high. It is a great place to see Amazonian megafauna such as peccaries, tapir and monkeys. It is, naturally, under threat, this time from oil exploration and illegal logging, the same threats which the Huaorani people face (as Yasuni is also their home). Hence the need for a book.

I was based out of the Tiputini Biodiversity Station and wanted to photograph monkeys. It made sense to rotate through the various primatologists who were each working on different groups. They were all women and mostly worked alone. If they were not women, I would call them macho but I'm not sure if a female equivalent exists. They are as tough as nails but don't even know it. Leaving the station at dawn and returning perhaps after dark they spend the entire day, every day, in the forest following the monkeys wherever they take them.

Monkeys in the canopy do not follow trails on the ground and the primatologists are schlepped through the understory, over fallen logs, through deep creeks and beyond. Anything could happen to them at any time and they would be impossible to find. Spider monkeys, particularly, cover large distances often at some speed. I was always in awe of the researchers. Once, with Amy, who was 1/3 of my size, a bullet ant fell down my shirt and stung me on the stomach. It is an ant that is over an inch long and is widely recognised to deliver the world's most painful insect sting. The hurt was instantaneous and I quickly got the idea of why it was called a bullet ant. It doubled me over and I whimpered as loudly as I could without losing my perceived credibility as a crackerjack jungle boffin. Amy was eating a sandwich, and nonchalantly asked what was wrong. A bullet ant got me I hissed between clenched teeth. "Oh yeah, they hurt," she said, as she took another bite.

I needed some spider monkey images and Sara showed me a place where they sometimes came to the forest floor to eat clay and I decided to stake it out at a time when she was with another group. I spent the entire day scrunched up, under some camouflaged hessian with just my head and camera sticking out. It took a while but it was worth it and I got the images. Having become very used to mosquito bites, I ignored any that I had suffered during that day. Reneé and I were due back to Quito several days later and, with a good measure of nostalgia left the forest, unknowing that the forest had not left me. As you have already learned Reneé is a very capable nurse, so naturally I asked her to check out the back of my head as something was bothering me. "You are just imagining it," she said and walked out. Over the next few days, her response was the same so I guessed I must have been imagining it after all and stopped asking. It was now well over two weeks since leaving the spider monkeys, which, in retrospect was where I believe I was parasitised and I had had several sharp jolts of pain. Reneé had had a look by now but said that she could not see anything. "Probably just a tick that has fallen off." A couple more days and I insisted she look again. By this time, I was repeatedly suffering more and more sharp pains and weird sensations within my scalp. There was a lump too. She parted my hair at the affected area as I sat in a chair fidgeting. Suddenly, she screamed, pushed my head away and said, "You've got to go to the doctor!" Through the little hole in my head, she had seen the breathing siphon of the maggot sticking in the air and wriggling. It was confirmed, I had a bot fly. The 'MO' of a bot fly is that the adult, which resembles a small bumble bee, actually grabs a flying insect that drinks blood, such as a mosquito, it then lays its eggs on it and releases it. The maggots develop inside the egg case and when the mosquito bites a mammal, the maggots detect the temperature of the host, hatch quickly and disappear in through the skin. The pains I had felt were consistent with every time the maggot took a mouthful of my flesh, which not only kept it nourished but enlarged the chamber where its big, bulbous body now lived. OK so I was freaking out too, it wasn't a good feeling to know that I was being eaten alive. I found some forceps and asked Reneé to help. We both calmed down and she waited, hair parted, with forceps at the ready, above the hole. Eventually, the little monster needed a breath and gingerly protruded its snorkel once more. She grabbed it, the bot fly jabbed its rings of backward pointing spines into my flesh for grip, Reneé could not pull it out and it squelched back in with a sucking noise. Too much for Reneé, I went straight down to our wonderful doctor John Rosenberg. He knew exactly what to do and broke the handle off a plastic spoon, filled it with Vaseline and stuck it too my head with what looked like a little yarmulke, held in place by an elaborate chin bandage. We waited until morning, sure that by now it had suffocated in the petroleum grease. The time came for the spoon's removal, but it had slipped a bit in the night. Reneé watched in horror, as the brute gulped a deep breath and hid back inside my head. We had to try again. One solution is to tie fresh meat to the wound, the maggot happily eats its way through it to breathe and you remove the meat, maggot and all. Reneé was not keen but we did now take on removal of the unwelcome guest as a challenge. Reneé was disgusted that she had to share a bed with it and it had to go. She reapplied a pile of Vaseline, bandages, plasters and anything else she could think of. This time, she was ready in the morning with the forceps to grab it. Removing the patch there was the animal, it was lying half out of its hole with the siphon extended limply on my scalp. It was dead and must have suffered terribly – with any luck. Now, a better grip on the body Reneé tugged on it. The incarcerated corpse was however much too fat for the hole and wasn't designed to come out yet. With a heave, it jerked free making a sound like the tooth being removed at the end of the track 'Unfinished Sweet' on Alice Cooper's Billion Dollar Babies album, if you can remember it.

# Ice Is Nice
# Antarctica

I have only ever managed 15 trips to Antarctica which is far from being enough. I often rate it as my favourite place in the world but have not been back down for years. Some trips I was hired as a naturalist, lecturer and zodiac driver, others with the expedition leader (EL) hat on as well. It was the golden age of Antarctic tourism when there were just a handful of boats in operation. Our time was spent between the World Discoverer, the Caledonian Star or one of the Russian icebreakers. It was always different but never anything less than spectacular.

Many folks I talk to cannot believe that it could be my favourite destination and want to know why. Well, it is pristine, busting with wildlife, stunningly scenic, otherworldly, the quality of the light is amazing and just because ice is nice. When is the best time to visit, I am asked. It depends on what you want. Early in the season, the snow is pristine with the recently arrived penguins finding their mate and building a nest, as the season progresses rings of pink guano circle the nests belying their krill diet. Later still, after the chicks are born, there is guano everywhere and things get messy but the parent-chick feeding chases are fun to watch. In the New Year, the humpback whales arrive which can also be very entertaining and a highlight for many. I was in a Zodiac with Reneé on one outing, she was driving and I was the naturalist on board. We got into a pod of playful humpback whales. She turned the engine off and pulled the prop out of the water. Drifting on the glassy smooth water, the humpbacks came over. They were playing and a little boisterous, bumping each other but with no aggression. One of them then deliberately dove a little way and came up underneath us. All the guests fell into the well of the boat and while standing on the bow holding a rope, I screamed in delight with Reneé. It was magical. The whale gently lowered us into the water from his back and returned to playing with his friends!

Nobody it seemed liked the whales more than our old friend Captain Lampe. I was on the bridge with him, close to Paradise Bay, in utterly balmy conditions one day as we were discussing the itinerary. In the distance, we noticed a disturbance on the oily calm water. Putting up our binoculars, we could see that it was a lot of splashing. Closer still and it looked like a couple of humpback whales tail lobbing. Something was not quite right though and as we steamed even closer could see that the whale's flukes were not hitting the water parallel to it but violently slicing the surface at a 45-degree angle. Then we noticed the erect dorsal fin of a bull killer whale, which I prefer to call orca, in amongst them along with a group of females. The orcas were attacking the whales which were trying to defend themselves by karate chopping the orcas with their impressive flukes. As soon as the realisation hit of what was going on, the captain declared, "Nobody is going to hurt *my* whales!" And he steamed into the melee. The ship's rails were packed with guests and the setting was beyond spectacular. The orcas split off, drifted away and milled around in circles some three miles distant. We were unprepared for what happened next. For a full 45 minutes, I kid you not, the two humpbacks simultaneously breached, again and again at our bow. It was the most spectacular and convincing display of a 'Thank you' by any animal that I have ever witnessed.

Another fabulous encounter with orcas that I once had was in the Crozet Islands, deep in the Southern Indian Ocean. They are a French territory and one of the most remote places on earth. The nearest permanent population being Madagascar. Not really Antarctica, they are considered Subantarctic islands. Bleak and primordial they are beautiful in their desolation. Very few tourists have ever visited but there is a permanent scientific presence. But, if bragging rights are worth anything, far fewer people have ever visited the relatively nearby (about 1750 km) Heard Island, an incredible volcanic Antarctic Island administered by Australia. We certainly felt privileged to be there which was only possible with special permits from the Australian Antarctic Division and were told that only a few dozen non-scientists had ever gone before us.

On Crozet, we were all exploring in different areas and some of us found a pair of orcas close in to shore. They were fixated on a certain spot in the rocks underwater and we could not work out why. I climbed down to a small rocky ledge that jutted out over the water five metres above them to see if I could make out anything in the water. After several minutes more a weaner elephant seal ran out of breath. It had been hiding underwater in a rock crevice. As it came to breathe, one of the orcas rushed in and grabbed it, the momentum forcing it out of the water just below me. It was quite a shock but very cool to see the orca with what was effectively a big fat sausage hanging out of both sides of its maw.

Another incredibly special Subantarctic island is South Georgia. It is, as we say in the business, where God goes on holiday. The biomass of penguins alone is phenomenal and anyone who has been to Salisbury Plain will agree with me. Acres of adult king penguins coo into the air, with their brown and fluffy young, the 'oakum boys', looking dejected as if they have been tarred and feathered, scattered amongst them. Southern fur seals by the ton aggressively defend their territories, as do the humungous bull elephant seals while the females just take it all in. Wandering albatross are a highlight and so massive that a grown man could lie in the shade of each outstretched wing. A good friend of mine, Tony Martin, spearheaded and recently, against all odds, removed the invasive rats from the islands. It was a truly impressive feat which took many years. As if South Georgia was not good before, it is even better now. Owned by the British, claimed by the Argentinians, there is not much by the way of human inhabitants apart from a small military garrison and a post office (one of the ways to stake a legal claim to an area is to have a post office). Pat Lurcock with his wife Sarah ran the post office and did so for many years past the terms of the original contract. Pat and I were in the Falklands Fisheries department together and when the job of Postmaster on South Georgia came up, it was the two of us who applied. He did a fantastic job. They were based in Grytviken, near the British Army barracks. It had been a commercial whaling station in its day and the bay was full of degenerating artifacts, many of which Pat and Sarah were able to preserve in the museum that they helped set up. It is to Sarah that I owe a great debt of gratitude.

Grytviken is integral to the Sir Ernest Shackleton story. He was a British explorer a motivator, an icon and hero to all of us working down south. His incredible story of survival after his trans Antarctic expedition, where his crew became stranded on Elephant Island, is well known. I have visited the beach where the men were stranded. It is a high-energy, narrow, cobble beach and desolate in the extreme. To have survived that, let alone anything else was a near miracle. Leaving 22 men on Elephant Island, Shackleton and five others made the 800-mile journey across some of the roughest seas in the world in a tiny craft, the James Caird, a 22 ½ foot lifeboat, to the 'wrong' side of South Georgia, whose mountains and glaciers they crossed in a superhuman feat to arrive at

Stromness whaling Station. A full 127 days later, after several attempts, Shackleton returned to Elephant Island and rescued all of his crew! He never lost a man and is known simply as 'The Boss'. I recommend you read the book 'Endurance' which tells the tale. On another expedition, while anchored at Grytviken, he suffered a heart attack and died. His grave stands across the bay from the post office. Whenever we visited, we would always gather at the gravesite raise our glasses full of Irish whiskey, give a toast to 'The Boss', leaving enough to pour on his remains for good measure.

I was expedition leader, we were in Grytviken and the zodiac drivers had brought all passengers and naturalists on shore. The boats were lined up on the beach leaving one in the water on rotation for shuttle duty. Enjoying the beautiful day, Sarah approached me and said that she had noticed something did not look quite right with one of our zodiacs about one kilometre offshore. Looking through binoculars, it appeared that the propeller was sticking up into the air and the boat was upside-down. I called all staff on the radio, as I grabbed a boat and staff myself, and told them to respond urgently. We raced to the moribund zodiac not knowing what was going on. As we arrived, I saw it was Reneé. She was in the water, very close to death, with one arm draped between the upturned engine and the transom, holding her in place. She was a zombie and had been in the water a while. As she was returning to shore in an empty boat a strong williwaw, a katabatic wind, came barrelling down from the mountains, blew offshore and flipped the oncoming zodiac. With so much windage and the centre of gravity at the rear, it was an easy thing to do. Reneé became trapped under the boat with one of the ropes on the zodiac tube entangling her clothing. The float coat she was wearing was buoyant and she could only breathe in the trapped air. It was very hard for her to get free, especially with the total shock to body and mind of the near-freezing water. She was almost gone when we got to her and totally incoherent. We yanked her aboard and I raced her back to the ship, leaving other staff to right the zodiac. At the ship's ladder, grabbing her coat by the scruff of the neck and the small of her back, I force-marched her up the stairs and around and around the deck to get her circulation going before taking her to our cabin for a warm shower fully dressed. The galley staff brought down hot soup and slowly but surely, she came around. It was a very frightening experience. Reneé said that all she could see whilst in the water was Shackleton's grave across the bay which she considered a really bad omen.

We had a few near misses during our trips in Antarctica and after Reneé nearly meeting her maker, the one that scared me most was in the South Sandwich Islands. We had visited Zavodovski Island, an uninhabited volcano in the north of the archipelago, with its chinstrap penguin colony more than one million pairs strong, that offered a glimpse of what the natural world should look like and now headed further south towards Saunders Island. It was cloudy as we dropped anchor but we were surrounded by a perfect sea of pancake ice not too thick that the zodiacs couldn't pass between the slabs. Mike was the expedition leader on this trip and decided to arrange a zodiac tour. We dropped all the boats and one by one, the drivers filled up with passengers. We each went our own way, which was normal, to explore on our own. When, completely out of nowhere and taking us all by total surprise a very heavy fog moved in all around us. We had no more than about 50 feet of visibility. Onboard joviality dissipated instantly, the mood was sombre and we now had to make a plan. Our tour was already entering its second hour, so it was natural for folks to want to return to the ship. They asked if we could go 'home' now. We were totally disoriented in the fog and could reasonably have been pointing in any direction. A swell was picking up, fuel was low and I decided to use my radio sparingly to save the battery. The South Sandwich Islands are a long string of islands and the worst thing that could happen in my opinion was to get between them, pass them and come out the other side, getting into major seas, with no fuel and many scared guests. I had to find land. Secretly, I realised that we were imminently close to real danger. We heard an outboard and another zodiac came into visibility. It was Jonas, the impetuous, kid-that-got-away-with-everything-while-growing-up. He was racing around blindly. He was the son of important players in the industry but I really had seniority and said that we should stick closely together. He wanted to go and I wanted to take our time. There was immediate tension which was picked up by our passengers. We were in contact with the ship but had no way of letting them know where we were, all other boats, that had been closer had made it back after hearing the foghorn being blown repeatedly. We had not heard it. Nor could the captain distinguish our small zodiac on the radar from the thousands of large slabs of pancake ice that were everywhere. It was the days before GPS was mandatory in each zodiac. In fact, this was the event that changed that. The fog was a very thick layer but for a split second, I saw the peak of a snow-capped mountain. I took a compass bearing and had to convince Jonas to follow me. We made the island, felt much safer and clung to the cliff wall in a tiny bay. Nobody knew where we were. Mike was on the bridge with the geologist asking if we could see copper seams in the rock to give him a clue. No. No landmarks were visible either. Guests were relieved to be at an island but very angsty *not* to be there at the same time. Mike, with a handheld GPS, took a position of the ship and left with his rescue party and extra fuel. He hugged the coastline of two islands until he found us huddled up and cold. They had brought hot chocolate as a bonus. Mike plotted 'home' and we made it back safely with some stories to tell.

Antarctica has lured many types to marvel at her wonders and in almost every case, they have been enthralled. On one Christmas cruise, we left Ushuaia to cross the infamous Drake Passage *en-route* to the Antarctic Peninsula. After two full days at sea, the Filipino stewardesses approached Reneé to advise her that a single, elderly, woman, had not yet unpacked her suitcase. Reneé spoke to her; she was confused but said that there was no need to unpack as she was getting off in a couple of days. She lived at home with two full-time carers, 24/7, attending to her. She was incontinent and required nursing care. Her family had deliberately sent her packing to get her out of the way for Christmas, not a nice bunch. Reneé was forced to draw up a rotor for the staff, men and women, to attend to her needs. I could not believe that, of all places to pack up a fragile old lady, they chose Antarctica. To get there by ship, either from Chile or Argentina you are forced to cross the Drake Passage. It is literally a rite of passage to reach the southern continent. Large squalls, running west to east, are squeezed through the landmasses of South America's Southern Cone and the northward protruding Antarctic Peninsula. Rarely, the sea is so calm that we call it the Drake Lake and people feel cheated. It is approximately a 48-hour traverse and 25% of the crossings, on average, get hit, some pretty hard. You've got to come back so the odds raise to 50% chance of bad weather. Like I said, not fair on an incontinent old lady. Our worst crossing was in the World Discover, she was a good ship in rough water. Having many previous 'Drakes' under our belts this one was exceptional. At mid-crossing, we were hit by very heavy seas and strong wind. It was the only time on board that I ever saw blue water (not spray) hit the bridge as waves came over the bow. The Discoverer had an elevator, seawater poured into the vessel and down the elevator shaft to below decks. Passengers were confined to their cabins and staff crawled the corridors to bring them cold sandwiches and to check on them. One man was in the lecture theatre on the top deck when the storm hit and was flung off his chair. He broke a leg. The staff were making an inspection of all public areas and found him. We had to splint his leg and leave him strapped to immobile furniture lying on the floor until the storm had passed.

On the other side of the coin, we had a woman come aboard for a trip south in her wheelchair. I was gobsmacked that she thought it was even feasible on a boat. We were not set up for it and indeed, it wasn't really feasible. However, she was lovely and helpfully, of very slight build. When it came to landings, we would lift her on to the zodiac, I would drive her ashore first and carrying her around in my arms, would show her quickly the penguins, then the elephant seals or whatever there might be, ask where she wanted to sit and arrange a time a couple of hours later to carry her back. It really was so rewarding for all of us to see her getting so much out of the experience. It's all a question of attitude and as mentioned previously, a jaded view of the world, with very little interest and no passion are the hardest traits for a guide to deal with. One such traveller was a member of the Century Club whose community have each visited 100 or more countries and territories. He needed a tick for the Antarctic Continent. It was another fabulous cruise and everyone was making the most of every minute – except him. He did not leave the ship until we came to a particular landing site, some bare rock, without even any wildlife. The Antarctic Peninsula is actually a series of rocky islands joined by ice so that it appears to be one long, contiguous peninsula. At this particular spot, a small area of rock is exposed which is actually part of the continent itself. We all got out for the fun of it but the Century Club member, in all seriousness, waited for everyone to disembark, came out in a zodiac, slid all the way to the bow as the driver held the boat against the shore with the engine. He then swivelled around, placed both booted feet against the exposed rock, swivelled back to face inboard and asked to be taken back to the ship. He was done. He did not have respect enough for the continent, in my opinion, to even get off the boat and stand on Antarctica. It was his only time off the ship. I was very disappointed in him. A similar thing happened up north in the Aleutian Islands off Alaska. Hard-core birders can sometimes be all about ticking, rather like our Century Club friend. To attain high rankings in the world, they have to travel very aggressively and hire the right guides who are able to take them to the exact spot where their particular quarry can be. It sounds a lot more about a function of money buying bragging rights than love of natural history. We had the 7$^{th}$ ranked birder in the world on our trip. His goal was to see the spoon-billed sandpiper, a critically endangered, diminutive wader with an oddly flattened bill, found in only a few localities in the north (and Thailand) their total population numbering in the low hundreds. Finally, reaching the end of the long chain of the US Aleutians at Attu our ornithologists spotted the sandpiper. There was quite a commotion of genuine interest which was tempered by now having to radio the ship, to find number '7', get him into a zodiac and bring him to the bird. Duly ticked, it was, likewise, his only foray off the ship.

Another way of seeing Antarctica is by using a Russian icebreaker. The two styles of travel being extremely different. The main reason for an icebreaker trip is to get down to the emperor penguins. Standing four feet in height and weighing up to 100 pounds, they have become very popular in the public domain through various movies and the glut of photographs of them that abound in magazines. They are indeed enchanting, all the more so as the males incubate the single egg on their feet while huddled tightly, with other males, in the harshest of conditions through the Antarctic winter. A super dad! Emperors are much stockier, as well as being taller than their cousins the king penguins which are infinitely easier to see. Once down where the emperors live, there is not much else to see in the way of wildlife. They live 'inland' of the sea ice edge actually breeding on the frozen ocean that is attached to shore, the fast ice. It is truly a remote area and one that requires a certain mindset and wallet thickness to want to get to. The scenery of course is, once again, simply spectacular. Weather can vary from gorgeous sunshine and almost warm to thoroughly and totally foul. Conditions can change from one to the other within minutes and we always have to be prepared for the worst. Before the real adventure begins and we break ice to get close (but not too close) to the colony, we navigate the huge icebreaker south, in this case, having left from Hobart, Tasmania, towards the West Ice Shelf. We set up a round-the-clock watch system for the staff to see if we could spot any individuals before we arrived in a known colony. I had 02:00–04:00. It was beautiful from the bridge, as we cruised the ice edge. Even with 24 hours of daylight, the sun still rose and set and the early morning was gorgeous. I spotted an emperor, all alone standing on the very edge of the ice. We stopped the ship, turned it around and went in for a closer look. I called the cabins of those who had asked to be woken up. First on the bridge was the number one ranked bird watcher in the world. A woman who had seen more birds than anyone else dead or alive. Unlike number '7', she had a much more pleasant attitude, thorough knowledge of any bird she might see as well as a genuine passion for, not only birds but life in general. Having been diagnosed with cancer at 50 years old and not given long to live, she decided to go the way of all flesh doing what she most wanted to, which was watch birds. She was able to draw on ample means and travelled extensively in her pursuit of her feathered quarry. She did not, however, die as prophesised and was able to keep going and going. Her name was Phoebe Snetsinger and it was both an honour and a pleasure to show to her first emperor penguin, such an iconic bird to add to her list. Not all birders (by any means) are like number '7'. Phoebe was hard-core by the time I met her, you have to be to be top of the ranking, but she was a very interesting and pleasant woman. She had a lot of trials in her life, including being gang-raped in Port Moresby, Papua New Guinea but she seemed to believe that her constant exposure in nature was what kept her cancer in remission. Years later, we were leading a trip in Madagascar and a birding group was a few days in front of us on a similar route. Phoebe was amongst them. We were told that she was watching out of the bus window when it crashed. She was decapitated. It was a real loss to the birding community. She died instantly, while watching birds.

Once Mike, the expedition leader, was on the bridge we studied the scene with binoculars and it looked very much like there were tracks coming from 'inland' of many more than the one bird that was still alone at the edge. He decided to launch a staff scouting party for a recce. We dressed in many layers, with full protection of hats, gloves, goggles, a survival suit and two ski poles. Most had heavy duty Sorels, boots for the Canadian Arctic, but I didn't have any. I did have a pair of reindeer skin Sami boots from Finmark, more as a curiosity than anything else. They were calf high, had big curly toes and zero tread. I usually wore regular rubber boots but as the weather was deteriorating rapidly, I chose my Sami boots at the last minute. They were warm. We headed inland, in close contact with one another as conditions were really not good. There were many sets of tracks and we followed them. We found 35 chicks and three adults in our path but still more tracks inland to follow. If there were chicks, it was a colony! After arriving at the end of any sign of tracks or soiled ice, we had counted a total of 108 chicks and 11 adults. I have to say we were all pretty elated and very chuffed with ourselves. Our way back to the ship was now in severe weather. The wind came very hard and kept blowing me over because of my lack of grip. While the others thought it was funny, they didn't want to carry me either if I got hurt. We got into a complete whiteout which was an amazing experience. Buckled into the wind, marching hard with our ski poles, getting blown over, struggling to stand up with no reference to any horizon or any feature took its toll. Finally after at least half an hour, we arrived to be picked up. I was completely over-heated and suffered heat stroke! Nevertheless, we had discovered an unknown colony! Either that or it was the remnants of the Pingvin Island colony last heard of in the 1960s. John Splettstoesser, our team geologist, even wrote up a scientific paper about it citing our names as co-authors.

Obviously as we arrive further south, zodiacs cannot be used to ferry passengers, as the ship has to punch through fast ice until we arrive within reasonable helicopter range. Impressively, the Kapitan Khlebnikov, or KK as we called her, could manage one knot of speed through ice five feet thick. She is huge and looks rather like a ten-storey building sitting on a big black hull. The two basic criteria we follow are to keep the passengers safe and not disturb the wildlife. On the aft deck, there is a big helipad and a hangar for two Russian Mi-8 helicopters, each with a capacity for about 24 passengers. We used them just like zodiacs, but they are better. The first thing that had to be done when we 'arrived' is that the staff have to prepare the visit. It was the real highlight of the landing when we would all get to be alone out at the rookery. It was hard work and we all had our jobs to do. Basically, we had to set up a camp, fit for 100 people for three days. There was a large amount of heavy gear to take ashore and it was all loaded into the choppers along with us, sprawled out on top of it, as there was nowhere else to sit. Because we were always so heavy with cargo, the crew, for our staff flight in, would take off the floats on the choppers to help lighten the load. They would put them back on for passenger flights. Taking off was a nightmare. The choppers would just about get airborne and peel off the deck then fall violently towards the sea (where if we hit we would have sunk with no floats) before the pilot could get enough uumph to gain altitude. Once landed on the ice, a kilometre or more from the colony our work began. We had to erect large tents that we called TURDS which was supposed to be an acronym for something but I never knew what. Fully equipped with sleeping bags, a stove, dried foods and soups, a VHF radio the tents were actually pretty comfortable when finished. One fun thing to build was an open-air igloo, with the emphasis on loo. Using an ice saw, blocks of ice were cut to build three ice walls with the opening facing away from the main colony. We brought a toilet seat and raised on blocks of ice, a black plastic bag was opened beneath it. Anything collected in the bag, brown or yellow, would quickly freeze and was eventually taken back to the ship for disposal. It was the best loo in the world. When sitting on it, minding your own business, so to speak, there was always a string of curious visitors to keep you company. Emperor penguins would waddle up to within touching distance, stretch out their necks for a closer, more detailed inspection and whimper, whistle and coo in your face. My job was to lay a trail that could be followed, even in a whiteout. I took a small man-hauled sled to Antarctica with me which I loaded with red metal flags on stakes. The idea was to create a path between the colony and the TURDS avoiding any obstacles such as crevasses. For me, it was absolutely the best job. I was able to approach the whole colony, alone and in total solitude, both physically and mentally, to just suck it all in, to zoom out in my mind to where I was on the globe. What a privilege!

The whole thing was magical; it felt like a city from another world. The gigantic tabular icebergs, held fast by the frozen ocean, were the skyscrapers, the gaps between them the streets and the penguins, continuously coming and going in orderly lines, were the people. It was a true winter wonderland where we were the outsiders, the foreigners who knew nothing about incubating eggs or creching. Even though the penguins seemed quite happy to walk over long distances, they would readily toboggan if the going was good. One after the next, in single file, they would flop on to their bellies and paddle over the ice with their flippers. It was a much faster mode of transport and very entertaining – surreal!

At one colony, I think it was Atka Bay, this time in the Weddell Sea, it was a beautiful day and we had begun early. The passengers were always several hours behind us – the time it took us to set up camp. As a photographer, I was in my element, there were not too many emperor penguin shots out yet in the big wide world and I knew I was shooting some useful images. I hate sunglasses, even more when photographing or when they get steamed up and I wasn't using them. Both passengers and staff have a certain latitude to come and go in the choppers back for meals or a rest. I stayed, returning 22 hours later after looking through my camera lens most of that time. That evening, I was in excruciating pain. It felt like there was ground glass in my eyes. I could not open them; they were swollen and weeping. I was in the cabin, eyes shut, sunglasses on (finally), curtains closed but could still detect if anybody passed in front of the porthole, my eyes were so sensitive. It lasted the whole of the next day until I could begin to open my eyes. I had no idea until then that you did not feel the effects of snow-blindness coming on but I was properly snow blind.

One of our landings went a little bit awry. Everything was going well until conditions changed. The radio spluttered and the captain told us that we had a short weather window for the helicopters to shuttle people back to the KK. We rounded everyone up and sent them back in the choppers, by the time of the last flight, it was already a bit edgy but they returned safely. Everyone was back except the staff. No more flights were allowed and Lisa, the only staff member to have remained on board, now had the full complement of 100+ passengers to regale on her own. She was less than happy according to her radio transmissions. The rest of us, on the other hand, completely guilt free, having no control over the weather whatsoever enjoyed hot soup and time down on our own for the next ten hours.

An icebreaker trip includes scenic helicopter flights for everyone and it is a glorious perspective, flying over the icebergs looking down at the colony or even the KK herself. It made her look small. Mike figured that it would be pretty cool to land a chopper on top of one of the tabular icebergs. Flying with John Splettstoesser who was closely scrutinising a likely looking berg for fractures or weak points, he gave the OK and we landed. The view was to die for. Jumping out, we took out the Frisbee and had a game. It felt like the height of decadence to be on top of a pristine, beautiful iceberg, where nobody had ever been before, with great friends throwing around a Frisbee. In fact, we thought it was so cool that we should get the passengers involved. The chopper flew back to the ship and brought us out a case of champagne, glasses a table and tablecloth. We set the bottles in the light snow on the top of the berg to chill, arranged the table and brought out the guests for a drink of bubbly on ice.

# Guyana's Rupununi
# Guyana

Guyana is not in Africa as most people think but is nestled in the northeast corner of South America with Venezuela, Brazil and Suriname as neighbours. There are three Guyanas: Guyana (once British Guiana), Surinam (once Dutch Guiana) and French Guiana. I only know Guyana, whose name translates as 'Land of many waters' in one of the native languages. It is a small country with less than a million inhabitants, 90% of which live on a very thin coastal strip which includes Georgetown, the capital, which is actually below sea level. The entire coast is a low-lying area, the shore is muddy and there are still some very impressive stands of mangroves. Large flocks of scarlet ibis can often be seen in the mornings and evenings on their daily commute. Georgetown is barricaded from the Atlantic Ocean by a sea wall and an elaborate pump system removes excess water. An ex-British colony, the bulk of the population today is descended from indentured labourers from India, China and Africa. Immediately behind the coast lies a massive swathe of primary rainforest, behind that the expansive Rupununi savannahs. The forest and savannahs are the homes of many groups of Amerindians. Guyana is the only English-speaking country in South America.

I first travelled to the north Rupununi (which includes rainforest) of Guyana with Reneé, for six weeks, around the turn of the century and loved it. We had gone to visit Graham who was the friend with whom I had begun guiding in Galapagos. He was born in Guyana and had taken a job as Director General of the Iwokrama International Centre for Rain Forest Conservation and Development. Set in fabulous rainforest, Iwokrama was a parcel of one million acres that had been 'given to the people of the world' by the Guyanese government to show that truly sustainable logging was possible. I was told at the time that having drunk water directly from the creeks I would be back!

During my subsequent extended visits during 2009 and 2010, where Graham and I collaborated on our second book, my thoughts on the Rupununi matured. A relationship evolved. The area became intoxicating; I was drawn into its unexplainable and inextricable web, its infectious magnetism and allure. The spectacular wildlife, extraordinary biodiversity and scenery remain pristine (to a large extent); jaguars, tapir, giant river otters, macaws and black caiman are still readily seen.

What tugged at my emotions on these latter visits were the people. The area is dominated by Makushi Amerindians and today I feel privileged to count many among my friends. They are a people who are quick to welcome you into their culture; they have a sense of contentment, balance, connection and quality of life. The area may be a vast expanse physically, yet it remains small socially – the Rupununi is a network of friends, with a high comfort level between them and always with a space to tie a hammock – a term of respect to elders, even those unrelated by blood, being 'auntie' or 'uncle'.

The pace and approach to life in the Rupununi is very foreign to the 'developed' western world. It is very relaxed. There is a sense of patience and tolerance. The reality being that no matter how hard you plan there will always be something to deal with – a vehicle may wait a day at the river for the water to go down to be able to cross – "You can't fight life," they tell me. However, if such a wait is called for, there will very soon be hammocks slung, freshly caught fish roasting on an open fire and everyone involved in a good 'gaff' (conversation).

Water levels dominate the way of life, especially in the savannah, a land of unrelenting vistas, with a freedom to roam. 'Roads' criss-cross the plains. Most are dry season only. The wet season changes everything, houses are stranded on islands, roads turn to a sucking mud and the general economy inflates as transport costs soar. Where we might talk about the weather, a Rupununian will talk about water levels. 'River low' – i.e. good fishing and certain roads open, 'River more low' (going down) – fish coming back in, access improving, 'River high' – more kabouras (sand flies), boats are required for transport (which in turn opens new areas) and hunting is better as animals retreat to the islands, 'River more high' (coming up) – fish are 'marching' upriver to spawn – and be careful which road you chose!

The rivers are home to many perceived dangers from giant caiman, anaconda, piranha, sting rays, electric eels and the mythical 'water anteater' yet despite the threats they are socially important, places to 'lime around' (hang out), bathe, swim, play, wash clothes or cars, motorcycles and bicycles.

There is a real patriotism for the area. It is one thing to be Guyanese but so much more to be from the Rupununi. There is a sense of belonging. The people live hard, live rough, live tough and party hard too. Sir Walter Raleigh may not have found 'El Dorado' but El Dorado (the local brand of rum) has found the Rupununi.

'Coast landers' and 'white-men' are said to have soft skin. English in the Rupununi is spoken in a local Creolese. It is a unique treat within South America however to be able to communicate with everyone in my native tongue, even though it took a while to tune my ears. You do not shave out here; you 'shine your face'. You do not take something with you; you 'walk with it'. Enough means more than enough. An angry man is 'vexed'. A person, or guy, is a 'bannah'. 'Just now' means anything from right now to a long time hence. You do not leave, you 'beat out'. It is a place where fish stew is known as 'boiley boiley'. Where a blonde tourist is a girl with 'shiny hair'. Instead of 'his' and 'him' or 'her' and 'hers', he and she are used in their place. Where to go shopping is to 'pick up rations' and where a machete is still referred to as a 'cutlass' evoking days of old.

Monarch bicycles from Brazil were once the most common means of transport; today, as technology bludgeons the tranquillity of yesteryear, they are left in the dust of off-road motorbikes. Land Rovers and Bedford trucks were the veritable pioneers that opened up the savannah, when windscreens were a luxury. Today Land Rover skeletons pepper the landscape, dissolving back to nature, as brand-new Toyotas whistle past. With myriad roads and tracks, non-native travellers are quick to get lost. With the lack of signage to mark the way, distances are measured in hours and directions given by referencing trees, mountains, ponds or past events. Even by boat on the rivers, the number of bends in the river to reach it defines a place. There are no telegraph wires and poles; there are no roundabouts, traffic lights or road signs (except for a sprawling vanguard of a few bilingual signs as one enters the Rupununi capital, the border-town of Lethem). With new improved access in and out of Brazil, this affront on a harmonious lifestyle is surely a sign of things to come. Today the Bedford trucks survive, negotiating the main axis road through the Iwokrama forest that bursts out into the savannah joining the dots between Georgetown and Lethem. Plying their trade between the coast and the 'Interior,' the trucks access places that the huge majority of Guyanese has neither ventured nor dared to venture for fear of the unknown. No form of transport, however, no matter how big or small can ever be too overloaded. Motorbikes carry whole families with baggage up front. Trucks swell with goods while bicycles buckle under extraordinary weight. Even the ubiquitous oxcarts that make frequent journeys from farm to market strain the yokes of the bullocks that pull them. Nevertheless, a true outback spirit pervades no matter what you are driving, no one broken-down on the road is ever passed by a Rupununian without an offer of help.

The Makushi are a well-organised group and well informed, one might just as easily gaff with many individuals on the latest Wilbur Smith novel or world affairs as hear tales of ancient folklore. They love gatherings, where the best storyteller is king for the night. Dialogue is lubricated by *kari* – a fermented cassava beer – drunk freely; it helps loosen wicked jokes which are shared into nightfall. The sense of belonging is strong and a village council that, in turn, is led by a *Toshao* or headman, directs the communities – as powerful as he is however, important decisions are taken at the community level.

Cassava, or manioc, is the main staple and is produced in many forms, most popular being *farine*, a coarse flour which accompanies nearly all fish and meat dishes. It is a lot of work to produce cassava and households are upgrading, with appropriate technology and broken bicycles are now harnessed to spin a mechanical cassava grater.

People are at peace in the Rupununi, houses are small but they have a natural escape every day and still rely heavily on their environment as a resource, they do not seem to suffer the disease of avarice, which permeates the 'developed' world, it being seemingly tempered by the strongly held traditional values of their elders. There is a kind of gift economy in place whereby a visitor can always be fed and watered for no charge.

The Makushi are a savannah people, living close to primary rainforest, *ité* palm swamps, oxbow lakes and meandering rivers. Industry is absent, the air is pure and the skies are big. Cattle, locally important, still dot the grasslands in a land where the cowboys are Indians. The lifestyle is pure, expansive and energised, raw and full.

'Progress', from outside influence, is threatening to inundate the Rupununi like a colossal tsunami; rice, soy, commercial fishing, gold mining and oil all menace the equilibrium held so dear by so many. A brand-new oil industry in the country anticipates that Guyana may soon be the wealthiest country *per capita* in the world. A potential disaster – or not. The Rupununi of today and yesterday may not be perfect – but it does come close!

# Anaconda, Giant Otters and Animal Planet Guyana

Seldom in the news, little is therefore known about Guyana and few people have it on their bucket list despite all it has to offer. I have been privileged to have travelled all over Guyana, having been many times and published arguably the two most important coffee table books on the country. I still go, every year, leading groups of intrepid explorers. 'Rubbers' usually picks me up at the airport, so named apparently as he can always be relied on to provide condoms in an emergency. He drives fast but well, leaning back hard into his seat so that his arms are straight as he grips the wheel. The drive into Georgetown could take an hour from the airport. Very little has changed in all the years I have been visiting. It is still rough and untidy, carcasses of vehicles lay rusting on verges, horses pull heavily laden carts, pedestrians weave between traffic and my absolute pet hate, live iguanas, in the full sun, are hog-tied and suspended at the roadside like victims of the Cameroon security forces. Guyanese eat a lot of iguanas, especially in curry. I hate the cruelty that goes with it. We follow the right bank of the Demerara River and drive past the familiar smell of the rum factory with the same name. Once we pass the Demerara pontoon bridge, the city is almost upon us. My first point of arrival is at the Rainforest B&B, a Georgetown oasis, where I get caught up on all the news with an old friend Syeada, a warrior against animal cruelty. I tell her how many trussed iguanas I counted on the way in. Georgetown has a certain colonial charm but is very run down. The only things I can say I enjoy are the furthest recesses of Stabroek market, under the famous clock tower where each of the four faces tells a different time. Time to get repaired I guess. I always go to the fish stall and check out what has been caught. Nothing beats a golden catfish the locals tell me. Then it's to go and feed the manatees in what is known as the 'national park'. At about three metres long and over 500 kg, they are miniature versions of the Steller's sea cows that Bering, his crew and others, ate to extinction. They are seriously cool and while holding tightly on to a thick handful of grass you get to play tug of war with a manatee until its thick muscular top lips, which are split vertically, work up the bundle and your hand feels the array of very stiff, backwardly pointing bristles on its lips and tongue. You've got to hold on or you don't get the intimate encounter. Apparently, they have had a captive population there for a 100 years and I love to see the Guyanese picnicking alongside their large pool where there are no barriers. In the US or UK, it would be nothing of the kind, for fear of litigation and where I would personally worry more for the safety of the animals. Someone might just feed them a broken bottle for malicious fun, as a schoolkid did to an elephant in the zoo I remember when I was growing up. The elephant died. The reality is that the best thing about Georgetown is leaving. The place to be is either the forest or the savannah. In the old days, I used to drive a lot with Graham. There is a main road that bisects the country from the coast at the 'front' to the Brazilian border at the 'back'. It is the only road and I have to say is much better than it ever was. It is still not paved. In those days, there were truck-eating potholes the journey might take a full day, or several days and in a good rain it was not even passable. I have spent most time in the savannah, particularly hanging out with the late Diane McTurk (pronounced DeeAnne). Di's father, Tiny McTurk, was one of the original pioneers that opened up the Rupununi for cattle. He owned the Karanambu Ranch. In the South Rupununi, another ranch, Dadanawa, run by Duane DeFreitas, at one time, was the largest cattle ranch in the world. Today the herds are thin and hardly commercial. Dadanawa is another favourite place to hang out. Recently Erin, a Scottish geologist who married Justin DeFrietas (Big Duane's son) has given the place a serious makeover and things look good. Behind the scenes, the same old gang come to *lime* and drink rum. Their stories of everyday happenings is each an adventure to an outsider. Having been out riding on the ranch with the *vaqueros* (cowboys), who are mostly Wapishana Indians, on a round up, the hard day ends with looking for a place to sling a hammock, building a fire to cook and slugging more rum. At home on the range.

When I first tried to arrange to meet with Diane in Karanambu, the radio crackled a response, bad weather hampering reception. We adjusted frequencies and, as if by magic, her well-spoken brocade came to life. She complained lovingly about Peter who was in the kitchen waiting to be fed. We finalised the details of our visit and cleared the airwaves. I was elated at the prospect of meeting both Diane and Peter in person, for he was no ordinary teenager but a very tame South American giant river otter.

Diane, who had a spell in London working at the Savoy hotel, dressed in a pencil skirt, being nice to people, saw the light and ditched it all in to move back to the bush. She was a truly elegant lady, already somewhat steep in age, a striking woman, tall, elegant, slim and lightly tanned. A flowing headscarf lent panache to her otherwise casual clothes and if she needed, say, the carrots to be passed to her at dinner she would never ask directly, which would have been uncouth, but would ask, "Pete, do you need some carrots?"

Her lack was noted and I would have to reply, "No, thank you, Di, but may I pass them to you?" She is credited as the pioneer of Guyana's ecotourism industry, not ever meaning to be but simply by being a gracious hostess. As people occasionally passed through, the likes of David Attenborough, they would need a place to stay and slowly, aided by her famous rum punch, became *the* place to stay when in the area, meaning several hundred square miles. She was more famous as the 'otter lady' and rehabilitated dozens back to the wild. A large part of the reason for any of my visits was to get in the river and play hard with her tame giant river otters. In a pack situation, the otters can be considered dominant over all other forest animals, even large black caiman keep their distance while jaguar have been known to be run off a kill.

All that considered, I remember clearly on my first visit with 'Peter the Great' within thirty seconds of him coming out of his pen I was already tickling his stomach. Lying prone in a typical submissive posture, he shook his head and whinnied whilst emitting a strong musty odour from his anal musk glands. We walked the two hundred metres to the edge of the Rupununi River, Diane carrying Peter across the coarse gravel section of path. Although heavy for her to manage, it was encouraging to notice how Peter was in such lean, sleek and perfect condition. Unlike so many other fat wild-animal pets we had seen. Once at the river Peter received his first fish, freshly caught by one of the workforce. The attendant black caiman on the opposite shore slunk away as Peter immersed himself. We pushed off in a small skiff and rowed to a nearby sandbank. Peter swam. He was now in his element, even catching fish of his own. While we watched, he cruised up and down the river, disappearing occasionally into the woods, but making frequent visits back to Diane where they both enjoyed playing together in the water. At nearly six feet long with a very powerful bite, both of us would end up being bitten. Me with a loud 'Owh!' and Di with a mere 'mmn'.

These days, I don't drive to Karanambu but come with one of my groups in a chartered light aircraft, a Cessna caravan. Apart from, of course, being a so much more efficient use of our time it allows us to stop off at Kaieteur Falls, Guyana's tallest and the tallest single-drop waterfall in the world. Another one of my favourite places in the world (I don't know how many I have listed already). The falls have an airstrip nearby but at the falls themselves, there is zero infrastructure. No fence, nothing. Set in a huge expanse of primary rainforest, it really echoes Arthur Conan Doyle's Lost World which was inspired by Guyana. It is a powerful, primordial place and to lie on the ancient rock, some of the oldest rock in the world, shuffle until your head is over the edge and absorb the experience is giddyingly exhilarating. Continuing, what a pleasure to land directly at Karanambu's private strip. Flying from Georgetown, you get a true appreciation of the vastness of the rainforest, almost like no other place I have been. The abrupt transition to savannah is startling, but the height advantage as we approach the ranch shows off well the sinusoidal rivers, moriche palms and beautiful lakes covered with the super-sized giant water lilies, *Victoria amazonica*, many of the pads with a diameter of five feet (some say they reach up to nine feet). Certainly big enough to float a human baby on, as photographer, Loren McIntyre, famously proved for the cover of his book on South America.

Apart from giant otters, Karanambu is well known for its population of giant anteaters. One of the most bizarre mammals alive, they may be seven foot in total length but are super thin from one side to the other, like a cardboard cut-out. They have a really bushy tail, that I have seen them cover themselves with to go to sleep, shaggy fur, huge claws for digging up termites, a long snout with a tiny mouth at the tip through which protrudes a long sticky tongue to slurp up the insects and if that was not enough they have a dark 'go-faster' stripe along their shoulders. If wind direction is taken into account, they are easy to approach. Basically, watch their general direction of travel, go downwind and stay completely still. It will come to you and if you are lucky, it could be pretty close. The mothers carry their babies on their backs, the first time I saw this I didn't see the baby at first. It is a miniature adult and also has a go-faster stripe which blends into the female's. The first giant anteater I ever saw was before I went to Karanambu. Reneé and I were driving around in the savannah somewhere, talking about wildlife to locals as we explored when someone mentioned a pet giant anteater nearby. We went to have a look. Sure enough, we found it. Lying on its side, in the mud, in the pig pen, with the pigs, the distressed animal had all four feet tied tightly together. It had been captured to sell to a Dutch zoo collector roaming the area. I went ballistic. "How the hell can you expect to keep this animal alive?" I ranted. "It eats fifty million ants a day," I exaggerated. "Where are you going to get fifty million ants?" I challenged. "It is going to die, you have to let it go," I said with compassion. I told them how weak it already was and under duress, they agreed. I went in, untied the ropes and stood the poor animal up. I held it as I tried to encourage it towards the door. At the opening, it stood there for a minute and then broke our hearts as it turned around weakly and went back inside. "See what you have done," I admonished. I tried again, it walked with my support and we got to the open door. I let go and stepped back. The anteater raised its long snout in the air and sniffed deeply. Suddenly, it took off! Boy can they gallop when they want to. Nobody had a chance of getting near it and now I was in deep doodoo.

"You said it was weak," they shouted agitatedly, as we got in the car. "You said it was going to die," they said and we switched on the engine. They said a lot more too but their voices were already fading as we sped away with a very warm-and-fuzzy, do-gooder feeling inside.

Normally, we leave the lodge early morning, drive out to the savannah behind Karanambu, where, with luck, the cowboy in charge of the outstation has spotted an anteater working its way 'home' to some shade before the heat of the day. We all get a lovely look at one and go back for breakfast. On this one particular morning, we had had no luck. We gave up and Marvin, the *vaquero*, headed back home to the Mackiedon outstation. As we watched him go, we could see his wife standing, waving, in the distance. Marvin changed gear into a canter and I said, "Let's go," to our driver. A giant anteater had fallen into their well, a hole about 30 feet deep. It was swimming even though it had already clawed a 'foot hold' in the sidewall. It surely could not possibly last too much longer. Where was it going to get fifty million ants after all? It was a dilemma. They are surprisingly strong and have two very powerful front claws. Urban legend in Guyana tells of a jaguar and a giant anteater both deceased in a mutual embrace – a death hug. We used the bucket rope with a loop tied in the end and went fishing for an anteater. I'm sure it was half an hour before we finally got the rope over its head and one front limb. We hauled it up. As it hit the top of the well wall, the loop was slipping and it was instantly free when it hit solid ground.

Marvin jumped so fast out of the way, he almost landed down the well himself. We all laughed and, once again, I got to feel good about saving an anteater.

Not far from Karanambu is the Amerindian village of Yupukari where I have several close friends. It is a place I spent a lot of time while photographing for the book, 'Rupunuri, rediscovering a Lost World', that Graham and I produced. Fernando and Ashley are two of the closest and gave me tremendous support. One aspect I was keen to cover was the underwater life in the savannahs. I had already tried in the forest lakes to photograph *arapaima* but eerily only managing a caiman's tail in the gloom. Here the water was a little clearer but very foreboding. It felt more and more creepy as I went further and further out to the middle of the lake, into the ever thicker weed. I was horizontal and looking for fish. Anaconda would be great too, or a caiman as long as I got to see it before it saw me which was very doubtful. Piranhas would be perfect but I tried and it was hard to even get close to them! So much for their reputation. I crept up on several beautiful specimens including a lovely peacock bass guarding her fry and some nice demon fish. I pretty much jumped out of my skin though when a large tiger catfish came straight at me, fast and in no more than 2 ½ feet of water swam under me and between my legs. It's always good to have the chance to make other people laugh.

On one trip, Ashley was to take me deep in to the forest. We were with two Amerindians from the village, Brian the boat assistant and José the cook. We set off in Ashley's aluminium boat with heavy supplies, including a lot of camera gear, to reach Rewa village at the confluence of the Rewa and Rupununi rivers. It was our last night for a while in a bed. We stayed at the Rewa ecolodge. I'd been there several times before but once in particular was special.

*Arapaima* are one of the largest freshwater fish in the world, they were abundant in the oxbow lakes around the village. Gradually, the villagers noticed a decline in numbers through too much hunting pressure and self-imposed a moratorium on fishing *arapaima* for five years. It is a territorial fish species and also an obligate air-breather meaning that it regularly surfaces to gulp air. Through meticulous observation the locals can tell you how many there are in any one lake, how big they are and what sex. Once stocks had increased, they began limited, selective, sustainable hunting. It is a beautiful example of a successful conservation effort. Graham and I were with them on one of the hunts. Having identified a particular fish the hunter stands stoically, for as long as it takes, on the bow of the dugout canoe with a bow and arrow. As the behemoth surfaced, within range and at a good angle he let the arrow fly. Of course, he would never miss and the fish took off, with the arrow embedded in its flesh letting out line as it went. The canoe paddled to shore, the fish was played on the end of the line, there were screams of advice from everyone but the guy holding the line. Eventually it tired and they landed it onshore. It truly was a monster, about eight feet long. It was dinosaurial with large, piranha-proof, overlapping armoured scales and a long, flattened snout. We had set up camp in the main river on a sand island and the fish had to be carried overland to get there. A pole was passed through its mouth and out the gill slit. A man at each end then shouldered the weight as its tail dragged on the ground. It was an impressive fish and I wondered about its life. I'm a bit soft when it comes to fish. Once you get to know one, year after year, say a grouper, that is always in the same place it becomes an individual. By extraction they all are. I've certainly known fish that respond to me and not others. I like fish. Like little people really. I haven't eaten fish for years and admit to getting annoyed when everyone thinks it is so cool to go fishing. Usually I respond with. "OK, guys, have fun, I'm just going off to shoot a few songbirds." Is there a difference? In this case, I didn't mind at all, despite the magnificence. It was not a specimen yanked from somewhere 'out of sight out of mind', where 'what the eye doesn't see we don't care about'. This individual had been specifically targeted there was no bycatch, the population, the hunter knew, could sustain its loss. The fish was butchered, pieces strung up to dry and we settled in for a night of jokes and storytelling.

Ashley and the rest of us left up-river early the next morning. We had three weeks. Within a few hours, we had already left behind the last of the Rewa villagers on the river. It was magical. The banks of the Rewa were much closer than the Rupununi and in some places, the trees on either bank almost touched to form an archway. We were looking for anything really but particularly the big stuff, jaguar, tapir, anaconda, harpy eagle to name a few. Each night, a campsite was chosen on the riverbank. It was cleared a little with machete, a fire boiled water, food was cooked, hammocks were slung and we relaxed – completely. The Rewa is often fast, often shallow and often rocky. There are many large boulders offering beautiful scenery. On some of them are petroglyphs possibly carved thousands of years before, they represent animal motifs, similar to those still seen in the villages today. Also on the Rewa are waterfalls. At each waterfall, we had to portage everything perhaps a kilometre around the impasse. All the camping gear, food, engine and cameras was carried on the shoulder. The boat we dragged over rollers that we cut, through a path we cleared. Loaded back on the boat, we carried on upriver to the next one. Unsurprisingly in such a pristine area, we did get to see some very cool wildlife including tapirs, harpy and gigantic anaconda. Ashley has had experience catching anaconda for scientific research and knows how to gauge size. The one we were closest to was a twenty-foot animal, half in and half out of the water. I have hardly ever been as impressed as when the entire terrestrial half of this massively thick snake turned on a dime, in a millisecond and flung itself entirely into the river, not even a metre from me. Another highlight was arriving to a place where we began looking for another Guyana giant (after the lily, the otter, the anteater, the harpy eagle, the jaguar and the tapir) the Goliath bird-eating spider. And there it was, a seriously impressive spider. As we approached, it raised its four front legs, held out its ebony-like fangs and then with one of its other legs began flicking an airborne stream of fine urticating hairs. These barbed hairs can work their way into your skin, or worse your eyes, to cause a severe irritation. After a while of us being non-threatening it settled down, relaxed its body position and I could easily ascertain that it was greater in diameter than the spread of my hand. It was a big spider.

After seven major portages and a lot of river travelled, it was time to head back. We had seen more than I had hoped, dipped on jaguars, but made up elsewhere. Drifting quietly downstream at night was usually productive picking up such things as paca, boat-billed herons and ocelot. In the end, it became as important to me, not what we had seen but what we had not. For three weeks of constant travel, in the middle of mind-nurturing wilderness we had not seen a single other human being.

In 2016, Guyana celebrated 50 years of independence from the likes of me – the Brits so it was with some amusement that I accepted the irony of being asked to do another book on the country in time for the official celebrations. In conjunction with WWF, this was to be primarily shot from an aerial perspective.

With everything in place, I found myself being dropped off by Rubbers at the Rainforest B&B. The plan was to fly the length and breadth of the country in one of the military helicopters. There were certain obvious highlights to cover but the rest was up to my photographic eye to decide. There were some problems of course and it was a full eight days before I got anywhere near a chopper. I was interested in good light. My pilot, a captain of the Guyana Defence Force, on the other hand, wanted to wait for good conditions at our destination before taking off from Georgetown. We were pretty much always late starting and home early, shooting in the worst of the tropical light. The other possible contributing factor, I gleaned later, was that he had just gone and got himself a new girlfriend. We took the doors off and I set myself up with a 'monkey tail' to tie me off to a rigid stanchion allowing me to lean out and take the shots I needed. Of course, I loved it, I love helicopters, they are fantastic tools. We flew to the far north, overflying the coast, the mangroves and the incredible water bodies behind the beach. We flew over large flocks of scarlet ibis, acres and acres of flooded rice paddies and sugar plantations, over a sea of rainforest, to innumerable and inaccessible waterfalls. We flew to the deep south to the Wai Wai community, dropping in, to their great surprise, for lunch. We overnighted at Dadanawa Ranch and refuelled. I invited Justin to sit co-pilot as we flew south from the ranch to a stunning monolithic formation towering above the canopy. Called Bottle Mountain he had been there before, it had taken days and he had only seen it from the bottom up. He was like a child with unabashed excitement, hardly controlling his pleasure. We did a turn around the mountain and headed back to Dadanawa low on fuel. I didn't quite expect his reaction but he came to me immediately and told me, "Pete, that was so f…in' orgasmic!" I was glad to be of service.

One last icon of Guyana that I was not able to shoot from the chopper was Mount Roraima a large tepui, or flat-topped mountain, on top of which was the tripartite border of Guyana, Venezuela and Brazil. To get there, I had to use a light aircraft which we flew to the nearest village, took the doors off the plane and again I tied off my monkey tail so that I would not fall out if it got too bumpy. Part of the Pakaraima Mountain chain. Mt Roraima is the highest point of Guyana at 2,810 metres. Once again, the clichéd adjective of spectacular comes to mind. Never having actually set foot on the plateau, it's on my bucket list.

A negative aspect that I was quick to notice from the air, while flying over the country, was the extent of the illegal gold mining in the forest. In certain remote areas, it was very extensive. Whole river drainages were now settling pond after settling pond. Mercury, being used to amalgamate with the yellow metal, means the whole system is annihilated, sterile and remains toxic for a long, long time. We saw blackwater rivers being dredged for gold the process also polluting heavily as well as churning up the blackwater to turn it to silt-loaded whitewater. Blackwater ecosystems are now becoming rarer and many species live nowhere else. It is an issue that the government needs to address.

Relaxing in Yupukari with Mike, Fernando and Ashley, having just returned from one of the excursions, while working on the first book, I received an email that I had been recommended to apply for a host position on an Animal Planet TV series. Interesting I thought, loving the idea of the massive audience that could be reached for conservation messaging. I had to produce a promo video of myself to submit. Not so easy at the time in Yupukari. There was one video cassette camera in the village, Mike knew basically what to do and so with a mini production team from the Amerindian community behind me we got down to filming. I figured it should be hands on, so I joined the guys out at night and we caught big black caimen, as part of their ongoing research project. We weighed them, sexed them and I got to talk about their perfect adaptations on film. I paddled around the lake talking to the camera, mixed with the locals at the river and went over to Karanambu to play with Diane McTurk in the water with Peter the otter. After a lot of fun, I sent it off and won the selection process.

# They Wiped Me Down with a Fish
# Brazil

It was a California based production company which had made the pitch for a series to Animal Planet, who first had to see my demo tape and approve me as one of their hosts. With that out of the way, all that was left was to go and shoot the pilot. A producer, a sound guy, a cameraman, Reneé and I went down to Brazil straight into a hotel on Ipanema beachfront in Rio de Janeiro. I was given the first day off and Reneé and I crossed the road to check out the scene. It was classic Brazil. Beach culture is integral to Brazilian lifestyle; there are exercise frames, very serious beach volleyball games going on, business meetings being conducted, some thieving and guys selling coconuts, bikinis and flip-flops. Everyone busy doing something. It was the Okavango Delta of man watching and there was really nothing better that we could do. Sometimes rated as the sexiest beach in the world, it is probably because people think that Brazilian women in tangas are the sexiest women in the world. Something which I dispute though they are however probably the best at carrying themselves off as being sexy, no matter what their body shape. On Ipanema, there were all kinds. We went up to the Christ the Redeemer statue which was certainly a potent symbol of the Catholic faith. I enjoyed Sugarloaf Mountain more, having no idea beforehand that we would be sharing the experience with a group of habituated marmosets.

The whole idea of the series was to document present day cultures or tribes who held animals as sacred, often those that actually sacrificed them to their gods. There was a list of pretty cool ideas but they had chosen to start with my least favourite episode, the supposedly secretive religion of Candomblé. It is an African religion brought to South America by slaves. Whilst the Portuguese masters thought that they had converted their slaves to Christianity many were secretly praying to their own African gods. The outlawed Candomblé cult that developed used the Catholic effigies to represent their own African orishas. Eventually the two religions intertwined to where Candomblé is today. The holy city is Salvador de Bahia on the coast of Brazil but Rio is also another large centre. There are today approximately 2,000,000 followers, most of whom are in South America. It is not so unlike voodoo or black magic to the uninitiated, especially with regard to the ritualistic animal sacrifice.

The following morning, I went off with the crew to film while Reneé stayed on the beach being robbed. Apparently, according to the script, it would be an arduous journey for me, taking several days before I was able to find and introduce myself to the secretive priest of a clandestine cult. Such is the complete deception of most of these kinds of documentaries, which are fake, fraudulent and phony that we hired a boat on the outskirts of Rio, in an area that looked like rainforest. We drove around to get a few different angles, got off on a small beach, I walked around in circles for 20 minutes which was scripted as a two-day hike. We got to a road. I 'hitchhiked' and our own truck picked me up. We got the shot and drove the rest of the way. After arranging payment with the priest, I came around the corner to be filmed knocking on his door where he was told to answer as if suspicious of me. I spoke in Spanish, he answered in Portuguese and after explaining that I wanted to learn more about the Candomblé religion for the sake of the camera, he let me in. No further than the courtyard, however, until he had asked permission from the gods. I pretended to be at their mercy. We knew already what they would say as money can be quite persuasive, even to a deity it seems. I now sat with José Antonio, the priest, at a table in a small cloister. There was a beaded circle on the table between us into which he threw a handful of cowrie shells. He vocalised what the spirits told him in the message that they sent. Basically, yes, I was given permission to enter and also to great luck would be able to participate in an initiation ceremony. Well, well. First, however, I was to go to the market, buy some live animals and make an offering. Once having done that, José Antonio said I would have great prosperity in my life. I told him to thank the spirits for their benediction and if that was to be the case, I liked this religion and that things were looking very positive already. I was given a grocery list of the live animals that I needed.

The market truly was impressive, in a negative way. The front section was full of hundreds of religious icons, the *orishas* of the faith, then there were the beads, the cowries, knives and other accoutrements that one might need. The section in the rear was full of hundreds of cages with, ducks, chickens, pigeons, guineafowl, turkeys and pheasants; there was even a corral full of goats. All this could hardly have been a big secret within the society that all these animals were destined for sacrifice. I arrived back at the *terreiro*, the house of worship, with several boxes full of live birds. So, the priest went ahead and sacrificed a few chickens and pigeons as a warmup to alert the spirits that we were all getting ready. He cut their heads off, skewered them onto one of the many prongs of the mini tridents in the altar and then emptied the blood over the rest. I was, by now, dressed completely in white, as was everybody else, apart from the priest who was shirtless. The women, in particular, sported what I would describe as white turbans with voluminous white skirts; they looked pure and dashing. I was filmed in all my interactions with the people and even sitting with the women helping to cut up the vegetables to prepare the meal, where it occurred to me that never, in my wildest dreams, had I considered that I might one day end up as a TV chef. In the meantime, a makeshift 'bedroom' had been constructed, with straw bedding and a bit of a thatch which I was to share for the night, according to the script, with a gay Brazilian guy, lying next to me, who was also about to go through initiation. We lay there and were filmed in apparent deep sleep, then awakening sleepily at the dawn of a new and very special day. We were taken to a nearby river. I was told to wade into the water knee deep and take my shirt off. Several Candomblé disciples gathered around me and each began to wipe down my body with a fish. I had no idea why and could only think of Monty Python's Fish-slapping Dance.

Witnessing the sacrifice of an animal, to bless the spirits, was certainly different from watching one being killed for food. It was the evening of the second day and the *terreiro* was filled with 50 or more Candomblé participants. There was a palpable excitement and tension, the portent of things to come. Drums were continuous and rhythmic, egging on the dancing and I watched women genuinely go into trances to receive their *orisha*. Talking to one lady post-trance she said when the spirit entered her it felt very heavy and her crying was a release for her rather than a sadness. It was night-time and things were definitely hotting up. The drums were louder and there were more of them. The worshippers danced. I believed in their belief. I was dancing with them. The cameraman put a green filter over the lens to create an even more outlandish scenario. The priest took me by the hand, presented me with a live chicken and lead me to the altar. He 'made' me hold the body of the chicken while he cut off its head. It kicked and spasmed in my hands. I regret it to this day. It was something that I would never normally do but because I was being filmed felt that it was justified. It is unnerving how the thought, or power, of fame will deflect a moral compass. By making an offering to my specific *orisha*, he told me that I would be visited and become possessed by the spirit of a dead relative. In Candomblé, wildlife or animals are seen as energy, as a force. A sacrifice is not about giving a dead animal as an offering but about giving the life of that animal to the god. I never was possessed, or at least I didn't think so, I am not even religious so did not expect to be. I was witness, however, to the power of absolute faith.

# A Pig Valve for a BFF
# Delhi, India

Tom, from my guiding days in La Selva, is still one of my best friends. He married Mariela. The union is certainly my most successful matchmake from the many times I have tried to play Cupid. Tom is from the deep south in the US of A, Gulfport, Mississippi. His family and friends in the States are rednecks. Mariela is gorgeous, vivacious and a strong woman. She has a huge Afro hairstyle, when she lets it lose and is proudly black. They didn't go back together to Mississippi for many years after they were married. On the northwest coast of Ecuador, there is a population of black Africans descended from a slave boat that shipwrecked on the shore around what is the city of Esmeraldas today. That is where Mariela is from. Together they have a beautiful lifestyle, having built a chique, but rustic, ecolodge in the Ecuadorian cloud forest, called 'El Monte', close to Mindo, a birder's paradise. It is forty hectares of primary cloud forest, with no other building in site and surrounded by hills. Wildlife on the property is excellent and includes ocelot, jaguarundi and puma amongst the cats. Access over the raging Mindo River is by man-hauled cable car. It is like a moat defending an ancient castle and offers a deep sense of peace, security and solitude once having been welcomed on the other side.

Neither Tom nor Mariela is particularly well travelled and as we regale them with our travel stories, they seem to enjoy our tales as friends, because travel makes us happy, but there is no sense of them needing to see any of the places we have been to for themselves. They are supremely content. It is often a very enviable state. At the time of this story, in general terms, they had been to Mississipi, Quito, Esmeraldas, Mindo and Chicago. It was their world map.

Tom came to our apartment in Quito with a story that he had gone to his doctor for a routine checkup. As a fit jogger, he was not expecting anything but a clean bill of health. All good said the doctor, except for your heart. Tom's fitness was masking the symptoms, but a second opinion from a heart specialist had confirmed that he had a very leaky valve which needed fixing urgently. He contacted doctors in the States and was told that the operation would run between US$250,000–$300,000. That was not even a consideration. In Ecuador, the heart doctor, in a less than confidence-inspiring pitch, told him that they could cobble a team together of a surgeon, anaesthesiologist and nurses; it would be open-heart surgery, 10% chance of dying, six months recovery and no less than $25,000. The price was better but it all sounded a bit dodgy. Reneé was listening in and said immediately, "Why don't you go to India?" She reminded him that when she had very nearly died of cholera in India the hospital gave excellent service. Reneé and I secretly hoped that heart surgery would be a better experience than her cholera.

On the visit in question, whilst at Bandhavgarh Tiger Reserve, Reneé was suffering a bad bout of diarrhoea. We put it down to a classic case of Gandhi's Revenge she stayed in bed and one of the guests gave her a course of 'cure anything Cipro'. There was no improvement, by day three Reneé was losing fluids in every way possible. She had lost thirteen pounds in the process and was barely coherent. Now it was looking scary and we were a long way from any medical support. The lodge became involved and summoned the nearest doctor. He arrived, leather case of instruments, white lab coat, spectacles and around his neck a stethoscope. He looked the part. Next to him stood a tall man with bare feet, an orange robe draped across one shoulder, a beaded necklace, a long grey beard and bold yellow and red face paint. His long hair was tied at his neck. He held a trident. Reneé opened her eyes, took one look and in her delirium thought she had died. In rural India, western doctors work hand-in-hand with traditional healers. They both stated the obvious that she was very sick and needed a hospital. Our ground agent, Pradeep, was travelling with us. For the first time ever I left one of our groups, Pradeep took over, knowing the itinerary better than anyone. Reneé and I took an ambassador car and drove to Khajuraho Airport. I had to roll her frequently out of the vehicle to void some more. She was in a really bad way; we flew to Delhi where she stayed glued to the toilet on the plane. A little Suzuki jeep picked her up. It was an ambulance and she lay beside the driver with no passenger seat, just a bed. No room for me, I followed. We became stuck in traffic the blaring siren made no difference at all. In the 1950s style hospital, she was well treated. The very first question the doctor asked was had she taken Immodium. No. He was visibly relieved and set her up on an IV drip of Tetracycline, the only thing he said that would touch cholera. She recovered fully and was very happy to have gone through the 'best weight-loss program in the world'. The doctor said she would have been dead in two days.

For Tom, to go to India was an interesting idea but way out of his comfort zone. India of all places could hardly be more foreign. Desperate times call for desperate measures and the next day, he phoned and told us he had decided to go! We started him off with a medical recommendation from a good Indian friend of ours in Delhi. In the end, Tom ended up talking to the hospital directly. Medical history and ECG's were sent and Tom was very pleased with the efficient and knowledgeable response. Reneé helped them with international air tickets, I arranged emergency medical visas. Four days later, they were set to go. Reneé and I both knew that we could not leave them in the deep end and on the spur of the moment bought tickets too.

There were four of us, each with two bags of luggage allowance on the flights. Mariela, particularly, is a very no-nonsense minimalist and regularly gives anything away that has not been used within a certain time limit. Between them, they only needed one bag. After deciding that we should accompany them, we realised that we would have an unprecedented seven bags to bring back! For a crazy basket collector like Reneé, this was something to get very excited about. Surely, we could squeeze them all in somewhere when we got home.

It was Mariela's 50th birthday. She was a nervous wreck with stress. On our second flight, out of Tokyo's Narita airport, I struck up a conversation in the galley with an air stewardess and told her Tom and Mariela's story. She invited the four of us back and popped open a bottle of champagne over the Gobi Desert. We'd effectively had breakfast in Quito, a sushi lunch in Tokyo, pre-dinner drinks in China and went on to eat a curry supper in India. For such non-travellers, they both got into it quickly and thought it was pretty cool.

The hospital in Delhi is a heart and cancer hospital only. It was very imposing and stuffed to the gills with brand new, expensive equipment of cutting-edge technology. We were duly impressed.

Tom was prepared by the medical team which included dietary restrictions, a briefing of what to expect and a full body shave with a cutthroat razor. Full body, even the crinkly bits. Reneé took Mariela, both fabulous cooks, to the spice market. We assured her that our baskets would not be too heavy and could find room for all her extra kilos of luggage in one of our bags. Three days after arrival, he had the operation. It was an expert team, that work together as a unit. It was matter of fact to the medics, as if heart operation patients were on a slick conveyor belt. There were four surgeons during the surgery and at least one full surgeon, not nurse, on 24/7 in postop ICU. Once inside, they realised that Tom's valve was too badly damaged to repair and fitted him with a 'brand new', pre-loved, pig valve. No matter how good it smells, Tom will never eat bacon again. In initial recovery, he looked terrible with tubes coming out of him all over the place. Reneé went in with Mariela and cushioned the visual shock. Pretty soon, they were holed up in the heart-operation-friendly hotel next door for a three-week lockdown with a remote control in Tom's hand and cable TV.

# Living Bridges
# Meghalaya

Now that we had three weeks downtime, while Tom was recuperating with Mariela in Delhi, we took the gap and headed to the far northeast. Known as the Seven Sisters, the seven states of northeast India are perhaps the least travelled of the Subcontinent. Apart from the thin corridor that skirts Bangladesh, connecting them to the India, and Indians, that we are more familiar with they are not really India at all. In fact, a young Indian Administrative officer, while based, many years ago, in Manipur, one of the sister states, famously stated that "On a clear day, you can see India." As mentioned earlier, the people themselves are more Asian, closer to Burmese, Nepalese, Chinese and Tibetan with whom they share borders, narrow eyes in all the indigenous tribes betray their more Asiatic roots.

    We had previously arranged our trip with a local Assamese tour operator who sorted out the plethora of necessary government permissions needed, even simply to enter some of the states. He arranged vehicles and drivers, along with accommodation, which was always pretty rustic. Our goal was to visit and photograph, three major points of interest, the Living Bridges of Meghalaya, the Naga tribes of Nagaland and the Apatani tribe of Arunachal Pradesh, and buy as many baskets as able to fit in seven large, soft-sided duffels. It was to be a people trip, because, apart from Assam the rest of the sister states, following in their Asian ways, have basically eaten everything, songbirds, rats, squirrels, dogs and insects to name but a few, of the delicacies on the menu. We saw no wildlife, only people with guns, bows, fish traps, rattraps and bird traps. Enough said. I do however love traditional cultures around the world and spend a lot of time immersed in them. I have photographed many but, it seems to me, that I spend my life going from one to the next documenting their cultural extinction. Maybe my images may have a purpose one day from an historical perspective. While

I'm looking for imagery on our travels, Reneé collects the baskets from the cultures. I have to say that they are fabulous. The skill involved in weaving them is far beyond my capabilities. That each shape and style has a particular use is fascinating. That local materials vary widely but manage a similar result is proof of necessity being the mother of invention. A large percentage of Reneé's collection can no longer be found in the societies that we collected them from. Plastic has virtually, totally replaced, or is in the process of replacing hand-woven, wicker, bamboo or palm baskets around the world. As the elderly keepers of the craft die off, their knowhow dies with them and these seductive cultures, living encyclopaedias of cultural knowledge, take another step towards insipid homogenisation and loss of identity. The youth race headlong into a world that doesn't really want them and they end up not knowing who they are or where they belong.

After landing in Guwahati from Delhi, we were immediately happy to be back in perhaps our favourite Indian state – Assam. With our car, guide and driver we set off south, via Shillong, to the small town of Cherrapunji. Passing markets *en route* women held up live frogs, thread on a split vine string, for sale as food, others silkworm caterpillars, strange fruit or fish. All of the vendors smiled however through red and blackened teeth, the result of incessant chewing of the ubiquitous betel nut. On the way, we spotted two women each with what reminded me of a lacrosse stick but with a longer shaft and the basket made from woven bamboo. It looked interesting so we parked the car and followed them down the dirt track. The basket end was tied on a long string to a post, the basket filled with hairy caterpillars and with the woman at the other end rhythmically jigging the whole thing backwards and forwards, they removed the nasty hairs from the caterpillars so that they could be eaten. Never having been photographed in this everyday activity before, I am sure that it was completed with more smiles and vigour than normal. Our accommodation for the night was a modest hotel set on a hill. Dusk fell early, at 17:00, but before we were fully engulfed by mist and darkness we could see, far, far below, the hint of a small village – Nongriat, populated by the Khasi tribe, our destination in the morning.

A porter was there at dawn to help us carry all our gear down to the village that we were separated from by 2800 steps. Steps made for Asians – tiny! Not even halfway down to the village, between Reneé and I all four legs were like jelly, and muscles ached in places she didn't even know I had!

Arriving, stiff and wobbly at our much more basic 'lodge' called 'Byron's Serene Homestay'. Our joy at arriving was tempered by our outside 'Indian style' toilet, cold water from a hosepipe for showering and my bed which was too short. We literally had to have the footboard sawn off enabling me to lie down while allowing my legs and feet to dangle over the end!

The village was famous for its living bridges, a series of bridges formed by training, over generations, the roots of two or more fig trees, *Ficus elastica*, to span a river and anastomise together, eventually bridging the river to become transitable by humans. Over time and with careful training, the bridges become beautiful works of natural living art. Often stones are laid in the roots which become incorporated by the trees in the bridge and form a more comfortable footpath over the river for the villagers. Little or no maintenance required, the bridges actually become stronger over time rather than weaker like those of our society!

Reneé, with hawk-like eyes, had already spied several appealing baskets and I was sent to close a deal. Although in certain situations haggling is one of my favourite sports, when it comes to utilitarian items in traditional cultures my first question about something of interest that I might want to buy is to enquire how much it would cost to replace. I always give the seller at least that amount. And so, it was that we have some baskets from Meghalaya.

We dropped our bags, grabbed a cool drink from the only fridge in the entire village (which had been carried on the back of the village 'mad-man' down the same steps that had just tortured us) and left to explore. Within two minutes from Byron's we were at the famous double-decker living bridge. An impressive structure of two stunning fig trees reaching out two gigantic 'arms' across the river to each other in a show of perpetual strength, support and solidarity while the Khasi people, who have given the trees their grace, use them to cross from one bank to the other as the wet-season river rages below and as they have done for generations.

The Khasi people were outwardly relatively uninteresting as a culture. Their clothes were now westernised, made of cheap, Chinese synthetic material and decorated with Mickey Mouse and other western icons. Inherent to the culture however was bamboo which was omnipresent. Apart from the basic utilitarian objects such as baskets, everything seemed to me made, expertly, from this incredibly versatile, tough and convenient material. Tongs for the fire, knife holders, chicken coops and even raincoats were woven from bamboo. The raincoat being not so much a coat but a grossly extended hat, leaving arms and hands free to work but giving the wearer the appearance of a giant cockroach.

Over the days, we spent in the village we visited many Living Bridges, each beautiful and each totally unique. We were left transfixed, both by the bridges themselves as well as the ingenuity of the tribe that had made them.

# The Last of the Head-Hunters
# Nagaland, India

On our next leg of the journey driving long and hard from Meghalaya state, over several days, we were aiming for the heart of the last remaining head-hunter territory of India. Our journey, from the living bridges of Nongriat and the Khasi tribe, had taken us north and then east, halfway through the state of Assam. We stopped at each working elephant that we passed on the road and jumped out of our vehicle for a gratuitous pachyderm hug in exchange for a wide-eyed treat of ripe bananas (always on hand for this very reason!) We had seen wild greater one-horned Indian rhinos from the roadside (how cool is that!) as we drove through the very impressive Kaziranga National Park. Nothing could later stop me from jumping out and wading through waist high bushes of Assam tea. Risking a shoe-full of terrestrial, blood-sucking leeches with each step, the reward of photographing the exquisite tea-picking women was worth it. Sporting large, brimmed hats and heavy baskets, these dark-skinned women, from, mostly Orissa and Bhopal, were staggered that a white man with a camera could ever find them worthy of a second glance, let alone a photograph. It humbled me and I tried to do them justice as I took their image.

Arriving to the border of Nagaland, we handed in photocopies of passports and visas as well as our prearranged government permits to travel within the state. We would build up to the headhunters, the Konyak Nagas, by first visiting the Ao Naga tribe and then the Chang Nagas to adjust to the cadence of the Naga way of life. Still very Asian in appearance, the Nagas were immediately different from the Assamese, told by their dress and their knives. Traditional shawls were decorated with tigers and *mithun* and knives were carried on the back in open wooden sheaths. Buffalo were used to haul logs from the forest and hot water was boiled for tea in green bamboo, stood next to an open fire. It was Diwali, one of 'mainland' India's largest festivals but it passed unnoticed here in

Nagaland. Our first visit was to an Ao Naga village where the centrepiece was a massive, log drum. Hauled as a solid trunk by hundreds of Nagas in a unified effort it was brought to a high point, carved and decorated to a hollow drum where a score of Naga warriors would beat out a pulse. People were very friendly and welcoming and the older women would even let me get in close to their legs with my camera to document their fading leg tattoos. A young man approached us and asked if we would like him to put on his traditional dress for a photo. He did so, for no money, and no other apparent reason than to help us get the most out of our visit. We ate in the Naga houses, cooking Chinese noodles over an open fire in the centre of the house. The smoke and warmth rose to cure meat, dry herbs and keep weevils out of the baskets on the suspended tray which hung over the hearth, covered in stalactites of soot. Even soot was not enough to put Reneé off and we added to our collection. Perhaps our favourite baskets of the sojourn were from the Ao Nagas. They are large, carried with a tumpline, leaving a sizable opening at shoulder height behind the head. The baskets taper dramatically, being well over a metre in length. They are rice-collecting baskets. As the women work on the terraces, the narrow 'foot' of the basket rests on the step of the terrace behind and carries the weight. We have two of them.

Pushing further into Nagaland, we drove the incredible precipitous dirt roads that snaked their way along mountainsides leaving an overgrown edge to free-fall into oblivion. We even stopped once to join a crowd that were peering over the edge trying to spot the car that had just gone over. The hillsides were forested with thick stands of bamboo, giant tree ferns and wild bananas, the scenery was stunning but no birds or animals, at all, shared our journey. It had all long since been eaten.

From the town of Tuensang, we ranged into nearby Chang Naga villages. Houses were decorated with sometimes scores of buffalo skulls, demonstrating the social status of those both rich and generous enough to be able to slaughter a buffalo to share with fellow villagers. It was a sign of generosity, not wealth, which, something like the culture on Fatu Hiva, translated back to wealth. Women ran from me, a white man, in apparent terror yet peered through slits in bamboo walls once safely behind cover. It was clear that the area had not many foreign visitors. Darkness fell at 16:45 and we headed home to our rundown guesthouse.

Our flat tyre, on a Sunday, caused problems. Having been ruled over for a hundred years by Baptists, the Sabbath meant that no one would supply compressed air to keep us on the move. Our spare was also flat! We trans-shipped and left the driver with the car and our baskets. The next morning, after a bucket shower over the Indian toilet, we headed towards the town of Mon in Konyak Naga territory. We came across a man with a strap to his traditional helmet made entirely from tiger claws, that had been hunted locally and who was proud to be photographed as a warrior. While most people were dressed throughout the state in cheap, synthetic Chinese-made clothes once again, there was still a strong sense of cultural pride below the surface. We arrived to Mongnyaksu village where we arranged to stay three days in the village chairman's house. It was befitting of his position that foreign 'dignitaries' should do so and advantageous to us as it gave us a presumed elevated status. I slept fully clothed on a table covered with a plastic sheet and only thawed out the next morning by almost sitting on top of the central log fire. Reneé was given a bed after the son was moved out. Ranging into nearby villages, our arrival needed always to be announced first at the Chief's (Ang's) house where a traditional token payment for our visit was offered. We were looking for *bona fide* headhunters. Warriors who had brought home one or more heads severed from enemy clans during battle. Not cannibals, the heads were revered and ceremoniously carried home, in special baskets, where the skulls were then displayed as trophies. In recognition of his prowess as a headhunter, the warrior was entitled to his badge of honour – a set of elaborate tattoos decorating his face and chest! He also wears a mixture of a set of five brass heads around his neck, beaded necklaces, sometimes including the teeth of wild boar, bracelets worn above the elbow and sometimes an antelope horn passed through each pierced earlobe or a waistband of rattan loops.

The reward of facial tattooing gave ultimate social status to the warriors in their prime. Today the few tattooed men that remain are now old and their status is gone. Some look incredibly melancholic, others still sport a wry, mischievous smile. Once again, the documentation of cultural extinction. I am proud to have their images for posterity and if I look hard at some of their portraits, their character and individuality begins to show.

At one of the Ang's houses that we visited, half the house was in Myanmar and the other in India, the border bisecting the dwelling. We were invited in and sat with the Ang and his two friends. All three men were heavily decorated with facial tattoos and I looked deeply at them for a hint of their murderous forays of days gone by. I could only find bright glimmers of roguishness and playful childlike grins. My head grew heavy as I sucked in the dense smoke billowing from the brass crucible bubbling in the fire. Opium was being rendered down in readiness to top up the three men in their state of relative oblivion. We walked visa-less through the Burmese side of the village and found more men wearing their tattoos, all were friendly and not one of them was even slightly aggressive nor gave me the feeling that he might want to cut off my head. The last time that happened was sometime back in the 1970s – at least that is the official story!

# Pig-Nosed Women
# Arunachal Pradesh, India

Heading north, down from the hills, we arrived back in the flat expanse of the giant floodplain and stood on the banks of the mighty Brahmaputra River, sister of the sacred Ganges. Holy cows grazed on food scraps and sodden cardboard while hordes of brightly coloured boats, each with a pot plant on the prow lay listing at rest in the shallows. It took a while before I realised that one of these boats was the ferry that we were waiting for. Once it was our turn, a rather unriverworthy, rustic, wooden vessel was punted into position. Two planks were laid at tyre-width apart, connecting the edge of the deck to the sandy riverbank, expecting our heavily over-laden SUV to climb aboard! Baskets by now blocked the entire rear visibility, except for a single wing mirror. Who needed to look behind, I thought. It was a one-shot deal. Forward and up or nothing. We had prudently disembarked the vehicle and watched in fascinated horror as the tyres screeched for purchase. It was done and, in true Indian fashion two more vehicles filled the deck space while impossible crowds inserted themselves into all other areas, many staying on the roof, joining the crush of top-heavy motorbikes already there. An hour and forty minutes was spent on the river. It was beautiful and majestic. Several times *en-route* we watched rare, Gangetic River dolphins cavort in play close by. We passed Majuli Island, where, on a previous visit, we had stayed amongst the beautiful Mishing tribe, visited the monks in the Hindu Monastery of the 'clean sect of Vishnu' and watched a traditional mask maker act out the depicted characters bringing his *Raas* festival masks to life. Disembarking our vehicle on the Brahmaputra's north shore was the reverse procedure of boarding but not before the multitudes on board had caused a dangerous list as they crowded onto the portside in readiness to get off.

Northbound to Along, we handed in our paperwork including more government-issued restricted-access permits for travel into Arunachal Pradesh.

The roads in these highly mountainous 'foothills' of the Himalayas were now even more sinuous, precipitous, eroded and dangerous than those in Nagaland where we had come from. We were both actually very nervous and got out to walk several narrow spots. It was bizarre how the modern dress worn by everyone did not match the overwhelming traditionalism of the village houses and agriculture. Baptists were the catalysts of these cultural changes and we realised once again that these tribes had long since been missionarised. We passed houses of Adi Galong people where men greeted us, some of them sporting a beautifully woven and distinctive 'Bolop' hat. Most of them were smoking from an ornate and flamboyant metal pipe. Mithum, a local domestic breed of cattle, close to the wild cattle of the area in looks, were a huge source of stature and could be seen commonly, left grazing close to the road by their owners.

We traversed the homelands of the Tagin tribe where most men still wore a backpack woven from split cane. The Suban Siri River glistened in the valley below as we mirrored its path until another nightfall forced a break in our journey. From our small hostel in Legu village, we continued into a thick mountain mist, passing through new tribal areas of the Nishi and Hill Miri tribes. We visited an extraordinary Hill Miri longhouse, built on stilts and constructed of bamboo, where we shared our breakfast. Truly it was long, possibly thirty metres, totally open it was divvied into five equal portions each dominated by a firepit. One for each son, with their wives and children claiming the floor close to their fire as bedroom, kitchen, dining room and social area.

Our target town of Ziro still felt like an eternity away as the snaking road forced a hazardous journey at least five times longer than the distance a crow would fly. The following day, we arrived and went to what we were told was the 'good' hotel in town for a late lunch. It was false hope and far from good, the toilets were disgusting, the kitchen was grimy and thankfully closed, as militant students had taken over the establishment in protest.

After a light lunch elsewhere, I wanted to see the produce market, as I do pretty much everywhere I go. Although in India politically, we were definitely amongst Asians. Scattered between the stalls of more usual produce a lot of the food on display was less appetising. Rats were common, mostly they were skewered on a stick and pre-smoked over a fire, ready for eating. Some were fresh. Sections of hornets' nests, a valuable delicacy, were on sale at high prices. The hornet grubs, or recently pupated adults, would be picked out and eaten as a treat in a traditional family home. Perhaps instead of hornets shield bugs could be the fare of the day. Flying insects are caught in large nets suspended from bridges over rivers at night. Maybe I could get excited by a plate of homegrown silkworms. At least their bright green colour added perhaps a somewhat more appetising appeal. If it was colour I wanted however, then I could simply pick out one of the many piles of tiny songbirds. Set in scruffy heaps their bright iridescent feathers of blues and green gave a hint of the bird's former glory in life. They are caught by first tying a live bird to a branch and then applying a very sticky glue to branches next to it where other birds land to investigate. To my mind, it would not have been worth the effort to pick off the tiniest morsels of meat from their minute bodies. We were with a guide and I asked her about this. A pile of songbirds, which weighed much less than a chicken, was several times more expensive. How could she explain the discrepancy of why more chickens were not eaten? People like the taste of 'wild' was her best answer, perhaps summing up the reason for the huge number of Asian exotic, wild-caught, animal markets.

We were now in Apatani territory, home of the people we had made so much effort to come and know. I had noticed some of the women already in the marketplace, crouching cross-legged next to their pile of wares. It was always a doubletake. They were certainly bizarre to look at. I had seen no others like them before in my travels. Of course, the most striking feature were the two impressive, wooden nose-plugs, perhaps an inch in diameter, inserted into the fleshy flanges above the nostrils. I was told that nearly every woman over the age of forty was disfigured in this way. They also were dressed in a median-line, tattooed from forehead to the tip of the nose with perhaps five parallel, vertical lines on the chin. It was a deliberate effort to look ugly. The practice stemming from the days, up until the mid-'70s, when neighbouring tribes would raid villages and steal the Apatani women who were considered the most beautiful in the area. It was decided, by the men apparently, that large nose plugs and facial tattoos, would render the so-called 'pig-nosed women' so ugly that the raiding parties would no longer want to steal them. The practice of 'self-mutilation' has since been outlawed by the Indian government and women under forty years old do not have the plugs, nor the accompanying facial tattoos. I had long known about these women having seen photographs in one of the many ethnicity books in my collection. It was the power of those photographs that were the driving force for our visit now. Reneé, meanwhile, had extensively researched the kind of baskets to expect on our trip and was happy to find the oddly shaped, almost conical, basket, typical of the tribe, still in use. We were able to buy one but were now running out of space in the car. Another, which was unexpected, was gifted to her by an old woman. It was in disuse but intact in the rafters, blackened from soot. Her mother had made it for her to commemorate the birth of her first child. A real treasure for Reneé, I believe more than the woman could ever have imagined, considering that in her eyes, it was way past its useful life.

The first sighting of the nose-plugs, although expected, was still shocking. It surprised me however how quickly I became totally used to seeing them and looked past the wooden disks to the woman wearing them. Indeed the host of our homestay had nose plugs and we sat with her every morning around the fire for breakfast. Possibly 70 years old, but still with a very human sparkle in her eye, made her far from ugly. Very soon, I failed to notice that she even had them.

The culture of the Apatani people was still very much deeply engrained in their everyday beliefs. Shamanism was widely practiced and at every house, there was a sacrificial altar where chickens or eggs are sacrificed to bring luck and to cure ills. There were also, larger communal sacrificial sites on the edges of the villages where desires of bigger things were asked of the spirits. The villages were crowded and houses densely packed side by side. The central fire was omnipresent and we often sat around one drinking a welcome cup of tea offered by our Apatani hosts. Every household had its cats and chickens while the dogs, which were more 'outdoorsy' decorated the steps and sidewalk. If a dog gave birth to a big litter, the solution was easy. Grow up one or two as pets and eat the rest when plump enough.

Everywhere we went, kids would shout 'Foreigner' to us, not in a nasty way at all, but simply as an excited exclamation. It was true that in the land of the Apatani we were the strange ones. It is always top in our minds when we visit faraway cultures to recognise that *we* are the foreigners not them. It is important for us to let the local people satiate their curiosity of us, unguardedly, as we wish to do of them. Indeed in a full three weeks of travel, we had only seen a total of four other foreigners ourselves!

Time had run out and Tom must have been well on his way to recovery by now we reasoned. After packing the baskets as best we could and paying significant excess baggage, we returned on a flight from Guwahati and made it back to Delhi. Tom and Mariela were happy to see us, as we were them. We swapped stories to learn that things had gone well and routinely on their side. It was almost time to leave back to Ecuador but, as he was obviously in fine fettle we decided to accompany them down to Bharatpur, a gorgeous little park several hours south of Delhi, which is stuffed with Indian birds and wildlife. The beauty being that the whole system is accessed on tarred roads via man-peddled rickshaws. It was the most relaxing way we could think to give a little natural history fix to our friend and fellow guide. It went so well that we continued on to the Taj Mahal after a few days. I got hold of a wheelchair and we took it in turns, between the three of us, to give him the full guided tour. It was a deep relief to see him doing so well and we headed home the 'other' way around, back to South America, making a full circuit of the world to consummate the experience for our globetrotting friends. After all that, the flights, five-star surgery, by a five-star specialist team, a pig valve, the hotel, food and a bit of shopping, their total bill was under US$14,000. I'd recommend it to anyone.

# Horse's Sweat, Hairy Pasta and a Bottle of Wine
# Mongolia

As a child, the threat I endured, by way of chastisement, was being sent to Outer Mongolia. Perhaps that is why it has always stuck in my mind as a place to explore. Far from being the punishment it might have been, we were sucked in and it quickly became another country that we grew to like very much. It is huge and can be roughly divided into five regions, the eastern steppes, the Gobi Desert, the northern lakes and Taiga Forest, the Altai Mountains and the capital Ulaanbaatar. Removing 'UB', as the capital is called, Mongolia is the central Eurasian convergence zone of the four, abovementioned, major ecosystems. Biodiversity is high as a result while cultures too vary from region to region. Mongolia is landlocked, bordered by Russia to the north and China to the south. It has been influenced heavily by both. The average elevation is more than 1500 metres and the name means 'The Land of Blue Sky'. Most fabulous factoid of all is that it is the least densely populated country in the world when taken as a whole. Consider that UB is home to roughly half of the approximately 3,000,000 souls, then average density in the countryside halves. Mongolia is about wide-open spaces. Japanese tourists now go there simply for that reason.

We were approached by a wealthy Mongolian, whose home and business was in New Jersey. It seemed that Genghis Khan's tomb had been found. It was going to be big news globally and he, personally, was going to be arranging to bring an exhibition to the North American museums. He wanted a book on Mongolia and he wanted us to do it. Naturally, 'no expense would be spared', there would be a 'massive' print run and we would ultimately be 'cloaked in riches'. What could we say, it is once in a blue moon that you get a contract *that* good? We loved the idea, didn't quite get taken in hook, line and sinker but we did get hooked.

Genghis Khan was obviously a phenomenal man. He conquered the largest contiguous land empire of all time. How he managed it is a worthy read, in a different book, by a different author. One interesting tactic that I did hear though was that marmots, carrying bubonic plague, were flung over fortified walls of yet-to-be-conquered towns. A pre-cursor to the WMDs of today. What we do need to know however is that Mongolians are tough.

We were to come back over different seasons to get a full overview of the country and be based out of UB (pronounced YouBee by the way). We were set up in a flat in town, which I have to say left a lot to be desired and was a bit rough with graphic graffiti wrapped around the centralised, indoor, vertical chute into which you would empty your rubbish that would then cascade from each floor to a messy collection point at street level. We thought it was bad actually until we learned that one of the most revered Mongols, in all the land, lived in the same building. He was the nation's top wrestler. I had to look up his title but it is this; *'Dayar dursagdah, dalai dayan, tumniig bayasuulagch, darkhan avarga Bat-Erdene'* which translates as 'Renowned by all, oceanic, makes people happy, strong titan Bat-Erdene'. I actually thought that it included, Champion and Elephant in there somewhere but who am I to know. What more could we say? Luxury, we thought. UB is not an attractive city. Sure there are some beautiful elements and it is becoming nicer lately. Originally, it was basically Stalinistic in its architecture – a little severe. Building was heavily influenced by communist Russians. There are large asbestos covered pipes, for example, that deliver government-controlled centrally heated water to individual houses throughout town. The locals in town, we find, are completely different to those of the vast countryside. Shopkeepers tend to give you a look like 'What the hell are you doing in my shop?' While we were there for the book project, in the bitter, bitter winter, gangs of children were living and cooking in the storm drains of the city, surfacing, *en masse* to 'forage' from passers-by. They were dangerous. In essence, Mongolia is best experienced outside of the city. Having just said that let me make an exception. Well worth being in town for are the Naadams, winter and summer. Essentially, they are massive public holidays dominated by the three, so-called, 'manly' sports, wrestling, horse-racing and archery. The wrestlers are pretty large guys, dressed in calf length, leather boots, 'Speedo' lookalikes and two sleeves, attached from behind and with a rope around the belly keeping it all in place, leaving a bare chest. Apparently, the bare-chested design is relatively new since a woman once won while hiding her gender (her breasts) behind the full tunic. There may be 1000+ wrestlers who compete for advancement towards the title described. A true spectacle. Archery is a much-adored sport and any culture that can conquer such a big empire, with horses, bows and arrows, you know they are good at it. The horseracing fascinated me most of all. It was the jockeys really. They range between about five and 12 years old. Experience and lightweight being the essential ingredients. Hard to get much experience by five, so I guess they really must be light. Basically, all Mongolians can ride from a very early age and it is pretty much taken for granted. They wear bright colours, a big number and stand proudly on the weigh scales before the ride. Races vary in length. The one that impressed me most was the 30 km race for the six- to seven-year-old horses. I had a special vantage point as a government-approved photographer and watched as the police forced the bruising crowds behind the chain-link fence. The horses took off in a group at a lazy canter, far up a distant slope behind a standard-bearer. Turning around the starting post, they galloped hard to the finish. The jockeys themselves are not really seen as doing much and even a riderless horse over the line still counts. It is the trainers and the horse itself who get the glory. I'm guessing there were 50 horses in the race I was watching and they came barrelling down the long home run in a cloud of dust. Horses fell, jockeys came off. The final approach was something to behold as horses began funnelling into the narrow finish line. The lead horse crossed and I was totally unprepared for the next chaotic scene of complete bedlam. All the spectators poured over the fence in hordes, the track swarmed with people, horses were still coming hard at full gallop between them, it looked like the Pamplona bull run. I saw a horse collapse, dead, not 20 metres from the finish line, the young jockey sat on the track by its side sobbing, horses galloped past. The crowd was chasing the winning steed. It was a complete scrum. They were each trying to wipe some sweat, with a cloth, from the brow of the horse. It would be put on their altar at home and bring good luck to the family. The horse meanwhile was overwhelmed and desperate to escape the attention. The winner made good its escape, the crowds dispersed, stragglers kept coming, some with jockeys some without and a bulldozer went down the track to scoop up the bodies of the horses that didn't make it. It was a tough race for a tough race.

We never saw the winter Naadam in UB but were told some stories. Girls, they say, after being jockeys so young, in such cold, have birthing problems later in life and it has been known that the eyeballs of the young jockeys have frozen solid in the cold.

*Après* shooting, riding or fighting the order of the day was to swan from one exotic, uniquely Mongolian, marquee to the next where it would have been extremely rude not to have indulged in some snuff swapping and a nip of *airag* – the national drink of fermented mare's milk, served from a large bowl with an intricately carved wooden horse-head ladle. Horses are obviously revered in Mongolia and while music is prominent throughout the various celebrations even the principal instrument is a horsehead fiddle. An unusual addition to any rendition is the accompaniment of a throat singer. I have been inches from a singer's throat while performing, being invited to 'inspect' him up close. It is the most bizarre sound I think I have ever heard to emanate from a human and has to be witnessed to be believed.

Outside of town things are quieter, more relaxed, although everywhere is changing. We have spent a lot of time in the Gobi Desert. Agriculture is nigh impossible and the people who live there are mostly herders of camels or goats and like most country folk (even some city dwellers), they live in gers (yurts to a Russian) cylindrical felt tents with a conical roof, covered in cloth over a wooden latticework frame. It has a central stove and the whole dwelling can be dismantled or reassembled in less than an hour. It has a wooden door. Gers are unbelievably cosy and once broken down can be strapped to a couple of large Bactrian (two-humped) camels as the herders move seasonally between pastures. Camels serve as transport, beasts of burden, milk on the hoof and donators of hair for camel hair coats. Goats are for meat, milk and cashmere. Both are for status. Motorbikes have become more and more prevalent over the years and have largely replaced camels as transport. The problem is that they need fuel and repairs, which costs money and throws the locals further into the harder reality of a cash economy than the days when a camel was good enough. One way to earn money was to sell the camel's feet to the Chinese, a delicacy no doubt. A vicious circle which I believe is being addressed. Unlike motorbikes, of course camels are pretty much self-sufficient and even reproduce themselves. In general, to our palate, Gobi food is pretty bad. It is simply boiled meat, with no seasoning except for the infused taste of wild garlic eaten by the boiled animal. I once photographed a goat slaughter. A harsh word to describe the reality. A goat was caught and against the outside wall of the ger, the herdsman, who knows all his goats, laid it on its back in his lap as he sat stroking and caressing it as one would a dog. The goat was totally relaxed and obviously enjoying the affection. The herdsman took a very sharp blade and made an incision adjacent to the heart. The goat did not flinch and continued receiving affection. He gently put his forefinger and thumb through the slit and pinched the aorta. Again, the goat apparently felt nothing as it gradually drifted through oblivion to death. It was all very touching. Come milking time the goat herd is tied up, the women corral them and then rope their horns, one goat to the next, so that they are in two rows with their heads facing inwards. This leaves the udders on the outside and from the milking stool, the women can easily pass down the lines to harvest the milk. In the springtime, the goats are combed, with a special comb with curved tines, for the luxuriously fine cashmere hairs that are shed after winter. This has become an increasingly important economy, especially as the western world has come to realise that hand-combed cashmere is a humane and sustainable product.

An area of the Gobi that we like to visit is the Flaming Cliffs. The evening sun sets them 'alight', hence their name. Made famous by the American palaeontologist, Roy Chapman Andrews, who discovered the first ever fossilised dinosaur eggs at the site in the 1920s. We run regular trips today to Mongolia for small groups and always include the Flaming Cliffs, either arriving by camel or jeep. Camels are fun for a while, especially being in the company of the herders, summer camels however are a bit too bony for a long ride.

Charmaine, our large traveller whom I have already mentioned in 'Muslim Uprising', was with us when we decided to arrive by camel. She had already declined to get on a horse earlier in the trip rightly stating that she refused to sit on anything that weighed less than she did. To mount a camel, it squats and, with help if necessary, your right leg is passed between the humps as you wriggle on. We were all mounted. Charmaine had tried but the camel, realising what it was in for if she succeeded, fully rotated its head to face her and in no uncertain terms let out a blaring, mouth-wide-open-gob-spitting scream. It did not want her onboard and we were obliged to let her bring up the rear in the back of a camel cart.

Once at the cliffs we separate and look for fossils. It is pretty much guaranteed to find some small fragments of dinosaur bones with always the possibility of something big. *Velociraptor* claws are relatively 'common'. We were once with a local palaeontologist who was in the process of uncovering the entire hand and claws of a *Protoceratops*, enough to boggle the mind of any young fans of the 'Ice Age' movies. Or, in the case of my generation, fans of the 'Flintstones'.

While travelling around Mongolia, it is normal to stop at family gers along the way. Even though they are complete strangers, the families are unreservedly welcoming. The first protocol to remember is that it is considered very rude to knock on the wooden 'front' door. The only thing that is acceptable to say by way of announcing your presence is 'Hold your dogs'. This should of course be said in Mongolian or is useless. I let the guide speak for me. The appeal is as much an act of self-preservation as politeness to avoid being savaged by the hugely territorial Tibetan mastifs. Once entering the ger, custom dictates that males sit to the right of the man of the house, who himself is to the right of the family altar i.e. enter to your left, ladies to your right. Take a small gift of some kind, greet the members of the household, keep your sleeves rolled down, don't point your feet at anyone and accept the copious amounts of food the lady of the house will offer you. Common curtesy really. It is culturally 'obligatory' to offer a guest tea, usually made from buttermilk, sweets, then biscuits, to hard cheese and cream. If the guest wants to stay, then a full meal should be offered and then if he or she wants to stay longer, a bed for the night. Sometimes while scouting for the book project we would go to bed in a ger with six people and wake up with a dozen. It is a system that has grown from necessity. Winters would be fatally cold if a traveller were not to find hospice for the night, hence a permanent open-house policy. What goes around comes around and so it perpetuates. Unfortunately, it is a system that is open to abuse and there is many a western backpacking blogger who has boasted that he 'did Mongolia' on a few dollars a day.

It was our 10th wedding anniversary and after much time and many dusty miles in the desert, we had the promise of a return to a cheap hotel, with running water and a bed, in Kharakhorum, near the famous Erdene Zuu Buddhist Monastery. We had lugged a bottle of wine with us the whole way through the country and tonight was going to be the night. Relaxed, washed, shaved and unhurried, it sounded like a good plan – of mice and men. Our jeep broke down long before we were even close to the small town. Reneé and I walked towards a ger, with smoke coming from the chimney that we could see a couple of kilometres away. The driver stayed to try and fix the car and our guide left in the opposite direction heading for help at the last ger we had passed. "Hold your dogs!" I called, still not having learned the phrase in Mongolian. There was nobody to hold them nor were they anywhere to be seen. After a minute or two, we were assailed by curious children and their mother. I explained in sign language what had happened and we were immediately put to work. I was led by one of the kids, back to where he had come from to help bring in the horses while Reneé was sent to draw water from the well. Dropping our bags in the ger, we completed our chores and reconvened. The mother had five hungry progeny to feed. In preparation for the evening meal, she rolled out strips of what I can only describe as pencil-thick cords of homemade pasta. Not on a kitchen board as you might expect but on the yak hair blanket covering the bed. Each skinny cylindrical piece was cut into sections and used in the boiled meat dish. I couldn't help but notice that each section had also picked up several yak hairs with each roll. Nobody seemed to care, why should we? When in Rome, or some distance from Karakhorum… She had made enough food for all of us but there were only five bowls. Kids came first and as the first one finished the mother took the bowl and licked it completely clean, in front of us, before serving another portion which she handed to me. Reneé shot me a worried glance. I made gestures of great appreciation and dared her with my eyes to eat. We both finished our bowls, I had seconds and then it was time for tea. With no milk in the house, a child was sent out to get some fresh milk and squeezed enough from the udder of the tethered camel that we could all enjoy a good cuppa. A little light in the gift department all we had was our wine. Summarily opened and all in good spirits, there was barely enough in the bottle for the guide, driver and new friend who rocked up in the newly repaired vehicle. We made it late to town and crashed for the night. There was no hot water and the wine was finished anyway.

Our book sponsor also lays claim to being the principal co-founder responsible for setting up the now famous Kazakh Golden Eagle Festival in the province of Bayan-Ölgii. I'm sure there were some others involved but such is his boastful character. Having done a little falconry in my past, I was definitely excited to get close access to some of the last practitioners of another ancient culture.

Despite being forewarned, I was overawed by the spectacle when it finally happened. Fifty proud Kazakh men on horseback, in full traditional regalia, rode slowly past in stately splendour. For a moment, I came close to ignoring them all.

On each heavily gloved right arm, resting on a wooden, 'Y' shaped ornate support, the riders carried a magnificent golden eagle – the epitome of power.

My eyes were transfixed on the birds. With every passing unhooded eagle, an involuntary, primeval shudder flashed down my spine as the piercing gaze of the predators seemed to stare into my soul, from only a few inches away.

It was October and we were in Western Mongolia, participating in the opening ceremony of the second-ever annual eagle festival. The stakes were high. A trophy, glory and personal esteem were sufficient to lure the hunters, with their trained eagles, from as far away as four days ride.

Isolated from the rest of Mongolia by the daunting Altai Mountains, ancient Kazakh traditions remain virtually pristine. For hundreds, perhaps thousands of years Kazakhs have used eagles to hunt wild animals for their pelage. Dressed, sometimes from head to foot in fur the hunters look magnificent. Winter is the time for hunting when fur is at its thickest and a prime hunting eagle (larger females are used which are claimed to reach weights up to eight kgs when fat) will regularly take foxes, hares and occasionally even adult wolves! To take a wolf, the eagle swoops in from behind the fleeing animal and grabs it by the head, the powerful talons piercing the skull in a vice-like grip until the rider catches up for the final dispatch. A desperate way to die but an impressive feat for an eagle.

Removed from the nest as fledglings (eyasses), the birds are revered and doted on by their owners. Apart from personal satisfaction, a proficient eagle trainer also greatly elevates his social status, the practice being highly venerated by the community. Without such respect for the eagle, through the continuance of the tradition and in the face of the insipid encroachment of the western world, (particularly where modern synthetics are replacing fur), it was feared that the custom would fade, leaving the eagle to be considered a threat to livestock and shot.

The event itself was a kaleidoscope of colour, suffused with a rich blend of tradition and warm hospitality. With my special VIP photographer permit, I had *carte blanche*, free to wander at will interacting with the excited throng and visiting with the hunters in the few gers erected for the tournament. They really were cool guys, most of them however had no idea. Hooded eagles, some with false ruby eyes sewn onto their hoods were tethered haphazardly all over the place attracting inquisitive comments from younger members of the community. Some eagles arrived wrapped in a *papoose* and strapped to a motorbike. Stories were swapped and techniques exchanged. The strongholds of the eagle trainer populations are now fragmented. Today they eagerly exchanged ideas, finding solutions to their problems and learning from other's mistakes. The atmosphere was vibrant as the aims of the event, to maintain and foment the culture, were unconsciously being realised.

Experts in handling their charges Mongolian eagle hunters have been deemed by western falconers as masters of the craft. Each hood is so well fitting that no straps are necessary, no bells are used (as in the west) to follow errant birds. Instead, Mongolian eagles are taught to call in response to their owners. Care and devotion go into making the jesses (leg straps) and even 'gloves' which are used in cold weather. Eagle-owl feathers too are often tied to the wing coverts to give power to the eagle (it is believed that an eagle-owl can kill a golden eagle). In addition, in the way of true conservationists, ten-year-old birds are successfully 'hacked' back to the wild to breed (on release the owner ties a marker to a wing to be able to later identify the bird).

An overall winner had to be found during the three-day event and Kazakh judges deliberated hard over the presentation of the contestants. Not only were they judged on the intricacies of their hunting equipment but the clothing itself and how closely it followed tradition. Kazakh women, famous for their exceptional skills in embroidery and appliqué had however seen to it that their husbands were well turned out. Horsemanship too was a major consideration, including rough games, of two riders tugging for possession of a wolf skin as they spilled jubilantly into the buoyant crowd. Mostly, however, the competition was about the eagle. Flown onto dragged lures from the dominant hilltop, eagles swooped in a ferocious display of predatory power to hit hard, in a tumble of dust, the fake fox. Directness of flight, hardness of the hit and the speed of the strike from the time of release were critical. Repeatedly, the eagles upheld the honour of their trainers and only an expert eye was able to judge one strike better than another. Apart from the comical incident where we watched a young bird landing instead on a red crash helmet (while the owner was wearing it!), the trials were exemplary. Eventually, a winner was singled out – a man we had previously befriended. Accepting his award and cash prize his pride was radiant. With true humility, the remaining competitors quietly dispersed, dissolving to all points of the compass. The winner, as was expected, would take several days to reach home as he visited one ger after another *en route* on his horse-borne 'lap of honour'.

Over the years, we have remained friends with many of the hunters and on our tours often stay with them in their summer pasture, involving ourselves in helping to milk the yaks or rounding up some fresh horses, before riding with them for four days to compete in the festival. The eagles are constantly with us as we ride and we become very intimate with them, holding them, feeling their weight, the grip of their talons and the softness of their feathers. Dalahan is our 'main man' with a rock star personality. He is a true showman and delights a crowd. It makes all the difference in the world to be at the festival, which is today very busy with foreign tourists, to actually have competing friends to cheer on. There was a documentary, released in 2016, called The Eagle Huntress which became very popular and tells the story of Aisholpan a 13-year-old Kazakh girl, trained by Dalahan, who competed in the festival to win the overall title. A remarkable achievement. It was a man's world and she won. She became instantly famous. We know Aisholpan; she is a smart but very unassuming young woman. On our last visit, she joined our group too and shared a tent with our lady guests.

The Kazakh people are Muslims and some of the warmest and most generous of spirit that you could ever meet. Apart from the eagles, I always get a kick out of shattering any negative Muslim stereotype to our American guests. Familiarisation and understanding, true values of travel.

Mongolia is rich in wildlife and was where I saw my first pet wolf. It was tied by a rope and stood outside of the ger entrance as a young boy squatted next to it stroking its fur. It is not uncommon to raise wolves in parts of Mongolia. Folklore tells that if a wild wolf sees you first, you must kill it or it will take your spirit. UB in winter is a sorry place for wolves. Scores of their pelts can be seen hanging, in the cold dry air, from balconies. Sometimes orphaned puppies are left after a killing and adopted by folk in the country. Mongolia is a good place to see wolves, and apart from one in India, is the only place I *have* seen them. Our first sighting was in winter, the easiest time to spot them and from our vehicle we saw a small pack of six adults that we watched until they disappeared over a rise. In the same region, we came across a single wolf running through crisp snow, ravens were mobbing it. We were virtually alongside keeping up with it in our vehicle as it ran hard. Powder snow was billowing while four or five ravens at a time mobbed the wolf. It was a superb image, an unquestionable award winner. My camera was ready, settings were perfect, just stick the lens out of the window. I couldn't open it. The window was frozen shut! Impossible to open, we watched the wolf run until finally the ravens gave up and it became a memory.

Perhaps my most cherished encounter was after having walked a long way up some ancient steps to photograph a shrine. I was on my own and one third of the way back down when a lone wolf came up the steps towards me to no more than eight metres away. It has happened to me before with a jaguar in Peru and an Iberian lynx in Spain. In each case, the animal, a predator and I were calm and made deliberate, curious appraisals of each other. I was ecstatic that a wolf and I trusted each other. He, persecuted to the ends of the earth and I with innate genetic fear. Why? It would be easy to say body language, or it smelled no fear, or a host of other excuses for not admitting that we both 'saw' each other on a subconscious level, two sentient beings, conscious of mutual awareness.

Winter in Mongolia is fabulous, pristine, white, dry and cold. Indeed, it is cold enough, to use an old naval term, to freeze the balls off a brass monkey. Camels are rotund and very much hairier than their summer selves. Their humps are upright and gorged with fat. They can be seen carrying huge bundles of hay for livestock fodder and look gorgeous. The strangest thing for me was to see them in the snow. Even the Gobi has snow. The whole country is clad in snow, the sheep wade through snow up to their bellies, yaks stand steadfast and resolute in defiance of the wind and cold. Goats huddle, sometimes the kids are brought into the gers for extra warmth and care. Horses are ridden hard, their excessively long manes and tails flowing freely as they gallop jubilantly like Haflingers from another world. Horses to be ridden are shoed for winter leaving protruding nails to add grip on ice and purchase when pulling sleds.

Far from being a time to cosy up in a nice warm ger, winter is ripe for socialising, especially in the more northern areas of lakes and forest. Homemade ice skates are strapped on and a ger that was a long summer walk away is now a few minutes in a straight line over a frozen lake. Lake Hovsgol, the largest lake in Mongolia, is up in the northwest, close to the Russian border. It freezes so profoundly in winter that Russian goods trucks enter Mongolia and cross the frozen lake to ply their wares. Winter is a time of access and plenty in the Taiga. Tyres are changed for winter tyres, they are also studded, like the horse's hooves, and now the frozen rivers become roads. It's amazing to be driving up a frozen river through a frozen forest. Pathogens die. My cat allergy also disappeared and I could tolerate one on my pillow at night. Allergens freeze, I guess.

For the book project, we needed to cover various regions and from Lake Hovsgol travelled to the Darkhad Depression. We were in a ubiquitous UAZ 452, Russian minibus; they are so capable as 4x4 vehicles that one of our clients once had one shipped to him when he got home. Known affectionately as 'The Loaf' after looking like a loaf of bread, they are the best thing to be in if you are off the beaten track in Mongolia. There is always someone with a spare part or the skill to fix it. Mornings were so cold that a fire was lit directly under the sump of the loaf to warm the gelled diesel back to liquid before it would start. We were working in 40 degrees Celsius – below zero!

We first stayed with a family in a small cluster of wooden houses near a lake. The evening meal was mutton from one of their fat-tailed sheep. An extraordinary animal, it actually has a huge fatty lump for a tail, equivalent to a camel's hump, which can easily weigh in excess of four kg of pure fat, a very valuable commodity in such a cold environment. The following day, we accompanied a father and son on an ice-fishing trip. Once again, I had to admire the ingenuity of the Chinese. A hole was first drilled in the ice, which had to be no more than six or eight inches thick, with no snow on top. The hole was large enough for a little submarine 'tractor' to pass through. This tractor was made in China, positively buoyant and had two large metal wheels which were each lined on their edges with backward pointing heavy serrations. The tractor had a thin, strong cord attached to its rear end as it clawed its way along the underneath surface of the ice. On the upward facing side of the little clockwork machine was a bright red flashing light. The light enabled the fishermen to track its progress. Once sufficient cord had been played out another hole was dug in the ice, a little bigger and the device, with the cord it had towed behind it were pulled on to the surface. Now with both guys holding one end of the string each, a net, with floats at the top and weights at the bottom was passed through the hole until it was left suspended under the ice to actively fish. Returning several hours later, we pulled the net, some good-sized salmonids and all, through the larger hole and went home proudly with the catch to drink vodka.

The toilet was interesting. It was an outhouse at the end of a well-used and very icy path. Opening the rickety door, there were two wooden planks spanned, across a deep pit, on which to place your feet. They were icy too and were best negotiated with extreme caution in the reverse position. While squatting, I was slightly fearful of relaxing into a deep, more comfortable, squat due to the disturbing proximity of the tip of a stalagmite of frozen shit. As the 'defecant' hits, it is quickly frozen and the 'shitcicle', as I called it, builds in stature. This particular one was long due to be toppled, which is routinely done with an axe I was told.

We continued on our way in the trusty UAZ stopping for tea, to shelter from the bitter cold, at a ger whose occupants would be able to put us in touch with a local shaman. For tea, we needed water and a young boy was sent out to the sled parked 100 metres away to bring in some ice that had been collected. The door was opened for him and he struggled inside cradling a block of ice that he could hardly lift. Our bodies recalibrated, we wente to find the shaman. He was to be paid for his services both in banknotes and a bottle of vodka. That was his price. Dressed in blue with long flowing sky-blue scarves tied to his garment, a big leather drum and a hat that covered most of his face he performed an *ovoo* ceremony. I let him whip me with some birch twigs, not really aware of any spiritual intimacy, I was more conscious of his eagerness to get the ceremony over with and get stuck into his vodka.

Finally, we arrived at our furthest destination, the tepees of the Tsaatan people. The Tsaatan are a nomadic tribe living far in the north of Mongolia. They are reindeer herders and migrate between summer and winter pastures. There are few of them left that continue a traditional lifestyle. To them, a reindeer is everything, meat, leather, warm skins for clothing and blankets, a mount from which to hunt and a pack animal. I had no idea until our visit how much they actually used the reindeer for riding. It seemed obvious once we were there. They would often make hunting forays looking for deer or smaller prey which they would let their pack of dogs flush and then shoot from reindeer back. For the night, the headman gave Reneé and I the use of his tepee. I had only ever before been inside the tepees of the Sami reindeer herders of Finmark, in northern Norway, for comparison. These were smaller and less substantial. We cooked the food we had brought and shared liberally between the Tsaatan, our driver, his assistant, our guide and us. Although the night was young, we decided to turn in; it had been a long day. Our bed was a reindeer pelt, lying directly on the permafrost, on which we unrolled our two double sleeping bags, one inside the other. Our toiletries came in the bag with us for good measure. It was a night of fitful sleep punctuated by the flap of the tepee being brushed aside ushering in the owner to stoke a little fire that we had going inside. It was a kind gesture but we froze anyway. Come morning, even the toothpaste was frozen solid. It could wait, first there were reindeer to round up. Not really fully domesticated, I wondered what it might entail. I left the tepee while Reneé was doing what she could to prepare to face the cold. I noticed a Tsaatan man peeing on the ground and extraordinarily, a group of reindeer flocked to him and began eating the yellow snow, something I had always been told not to do. He grabbed a couple by the antlers and led them away. So that's how it was done – easy! I had not told Reneé, she emerged and set off a discreet distance to pee herself. I heard a scream, guessed what had happened and ran to her aid. With her pants down and bare bum to the air, she peed, not realising that a wily reindeer was creeping up on her. Suddenly, she felt a cold wet muzzle nuzzle her between her legs as the reindeer, desperate for minerals, went directly for the flow of amber nectar.

A flight out of Murun, near Lake Hovsgol, takes about 90 minutes to arrive back to UB. Although the situation is a little more controlled these days, generally Mongolians want to travel with as much cargo, hand luggage and kids-on-laps-that-don't-count as possible. I remember when, after managing my cameras past the first security station, and eventually seated on the plane, the whole entity would be towed to a weighing scale. Only then could the critical, final weight be ascertained for the ageing turboprop and any extra kilos would be jettisoned. A pretty smart idea.

Something worth mentioning, close to UB, is the Hustain Nuruu National Park where, in the early 1990s, the Przewalski's horse, extinct in the wild, was reintroduced. Considered possibly the only truly wild horse still living in the world. The population was resurrected from breeding populations in zoos. The effort has been successful and it feels special when watching the stallions protecting a harem at home, back in their natural habitat.

Our time photographing for the book was very rewarding. Back in Ecuador, a top designer laid the whole thing out, a writer completed every chapter and in my opinion, it was our best book to date. There *was* no Genghis Khan grave ever found, no international museum tour and no book was ever printed. The sponsor pulled out leaving Reneé and I financially in the lurch. I had learned that Outer Mongolia was not a place of dread, rather one of welcome and we had cemented many friendships in the country, characters with whom we had shared untold adventures. It turned out that these were the riches in which we were cloaked.

# Camel Blood Wine
# China

To fly to UB from Ecuador, we connected through Beijing. Coming or going, we always made the most of our location and spent time exploring in China.

Friends had duly warned us that China was changing fast and the 'real' China, the one which was most interesting to us, was becoming harder and harder to find. Undaunted, we landed in the capital and decided on a hotel close to Tiananmen Square. Indeed, there was no question that China was well into the twenty-first century. Everything we passed was brand new, roads, cars, buildings – even the hordes of bicycles crowding their purpose-built bicycle lanes looked new. There was order and a certain sense of calmness. Even the traffic was relatively light as people preferred pedal power over expensive gasoline. Equipped with bicycle umbrellas and an all-in-one shoulder wrap and gloves, the Chinese ladies however were determined to keep their skin as white as possible while cycling in the searing heat. Our first mission was the Great Wall of China, but in the meantime, we soaked up some local sights. We decided to take in an early evening show of spectacular acrobatics and dancing, which included the phenomenal *bian lian* or face-changing dance where masks are imperceptibly changed throughout the routine. The lights were dimmed and snacks were served, a mixture of dishes from crunchy dried fish and sliced carrots to diced squid. The show over, drained by the spectacle the lights came on and we were ready to leave. The remains of our snacks were still there. The crunchy fish had been grasshoppers and the squid pieces were chunks of a cockerel's comb.

Unfortunately, the classic tourist circuit is very much a treadmill and lately caters for thousands of tourists daily, they are pumped through Tiananmen Square, The Summer Palace, Peking Duck Restaurants and any number of obligatory government factory stores. For meals, we opted to go it alone, preferring to mix with the Chinese where English was neither written nor spoken.

I would literally take the shy waitress by the hand and walk around the restaurant with her until we found someone else's food that looked appealing. I pointed to it, indicated one each and within minutes an exact copy was laid at our table. If we enjoyed it, I would then ask the waitress to write the name in Chinese characters in my notebook. I would add my own description alongside and next time we were good to go just by pointing in my book. While in Beijing, we did find one restaurant that we liked, it was called South Beauty and very near to the railway station. Mostly, I went for an unadventurous *Kung Pao* chicken. It was however interesting to note the many varied plates being served to the tables around us which included a plate of goose tongues, chicken feet or crispy pig's ears.

In any new town in the world we visit, our priority is always to unearth the local meat and fish markets. In China (even Asia in general), these are a whole world unto themselves. In Beijing, we wandered, without another western face to be seen, freely taking pictures of the weird and exotic foods for sale. Most of the produce was still alive and included fish tanks of catch-your-own-fish, baskets of frogs, trussed crabs, squirming buckets of eels, live scorpions, baskets full of skinned songbirds, a tray of duck heads, soft-shelled terrapins whose shells are sliced off in front of you aided by the vendors foot on the animal to keep it still. There are sometimes large stalls selling nothing but animal penises. There were lots of snakes. I've seen many disturbing things in 'wet' markets around China. They are actually horrific. I go because I need to understand from personal experience to be able to best relate my thoughts and feelings to others. We were standing at a stall specialising in snakes. There were perhaps hundreds, all wild caught. I love snakes and for many years have been one of the directors of Ecuador's public vivarium where we teach communities the value of these amazing reptiles. A jogger came through the market and paused, while jogging on the spot to converse with the snake vendor. The jogger pointed to a live snake and the vendor reached into the cage and pulled it out. It was three feet long, black and yellow. Holding it firmly a few inches behind the head and with a large pair of scissors, he decapitated it. It shuddered. The jogger took the snake, with a hand at the neck and one at the tail. He then inverted the whole thing, holding it upright in the air and aimed, allowing all the snakes fluids to drain into his mouth. He returned the empty carcass with payment and jogged happily on. Eating dogs in China is apparently outlawed in many areas. It can still readily be uncovered. It is a practice that we, in the west, are uncomfortable with. What I have witnessed disturbed me. Not the eating of dogs or cats *per se* but the cruelty that goes with it. There were dogs of all models, from what source I do not know, suffice to say that they are not a standardised 'eating-dog' breed. I suspect they were rounded up as strays. Kept together in ridiculously cramped wire cages, they were killed, in the company of those next in line by the blow of a spiked hammer to the head. The bodies were thrown into a 45-gallon drum of water that had a fire underneath it to bring it to boil. The meat is cooked and the hair falls out. Then, one by one, they were taken outside, laid on their backs in a special rack where a woman spent her day browning them, to make the skin crispy, with a blow torch. The seller comes by, loads them into the wide-mouthed basket on her back and disappears off to do business. There is zero compassion. Why should there be it is an animal. Medicinal markets are a whole other phenomenon again. They are truly frightening. I don't mean that when I go in I tremble with fear, I mean that it is scary the sheer volume of animals present. Animals from all over the world, raped by locals from the wild to satiate the Chinese demand. The fact is that every little town has one, or more. China is huge, the collective hunger is ravenous. Of the many Chinese medicine stores that I have been into they are all variations on a theme. Everything is always neatly ordered, for example 50 large centipedes, dried fully extended, are strapped with great artistry to a split bamboo support, there will be sacks of small, dried snakes yet each one is perfectly coiled in a tight spiral. Tokay geckos, are 'butterflied' and skewered on sticks. There are sacks of dried pillbugs, sacks of dried ants, starfish, sea cucumbers and sea horses. There are pipefish, antelope horns and sacks of tortoise plastrons. At one particular shop, I went in pleading, in sign language again, a bad case of impotency. I needed a tiger penis to cure my ails. A little suspicious both of me and my camera I was persuasive enough that the shop-owner produced one. Due to its high cost, I reasoned that I needed to take some pictures to ask my knowledgeable Chinese friend to vouch for its authenticity. I would be back tomorrow. He allowed me to photograph and I left a sad conservationist but a happy photojournalist. In Beijing, there is actually a restaurant that serves nothing but penises. I presume an endangered tiger would be one of the most expensive.

I have to say that it shames me as a human being that, within my lifetime, an infinitesimally insignificant blip in the grand scheme of things, we have caused so much change and destruction to our planet.

To add further insult to injury, every restaurant, many shops and various public places have a large glass bottle that is stuffed with geckoes, snakes and other reptiles, pickling away in alcohol. The more you squeeze into the bottle, the more energy you suck out of the animals when you drink the liquor.

To beat the tourist rush and the hordes of street vendors and even the Chinese who dress to look like Mongolian warriors – for a photo fee, we left Beijing at 4 am out to the Great Wall. Not only were we the first but the only visitors on the wall for the first forty-five minutes after sunrise. Walking the ramparts and looking ahead as the monumental structure snaked its way over the distant ridge tops, we could only wonder at the mentality of the Chinese emperors who commanded its construction between the seventh and seventeenth centuries. The wall we see today dates basically from the Ming Dynasty (1368–1644), the centuries-long efforts of which culminated in an incredible 50,000 kilometres of defensive walls! I stood over-impressed, much more so than the first time I had seen the Taj Mahal, Stone Henge or even Machu Picchu, the Great Wall of China was indeed a wonder of Man's achievement. By the time the heat of the day had settled-in making climbing difficult, we were leaving the parapet as the main wave of tourists and hawkers were scaling the same ramparts – now generously dotted with brightly coloured parasols giving shade to the cold drinks for sale. As we reached ground level, I noticed a camel, kitted out ready to be ridden by any gullible tourist. The camel's keeper was squatting in the animal's shade with a fly swat in her hand. Every biting horse fly that landed on the camel, after drinking a little blood, was summarily swatted. The moribund insect (they are hard to kill) was picked up and dropped into a bottle. "Why?" I asked our guide.

"Wine," she said. It was a stupid question, who needs grapes when you can make horse-fly-camel-blood wine?

We have spent most time of all in the Yunnan province in the far west of China. Still one of the richest areas for wildlife it is also home to more than two dozen ethnic minorities, a good combination. Before we get there, however, two other cool things come to mind.

Chengdu, in the Sichuan Province is the home of Giant Pandas. As wildlife photographers and biologists, the panda was one of the greatest attractions that China had on offer. We decided to use almost a week, investigating all the panda hotspots. To see one in the wild, however, we regrettably decided, was close to impossible. Requiring up to a month camping in the thick, high forests in remote areas – just for a glimpse. We concentrated our efforts at the well-known Giant

Panda Breeding Centre, just outside of town. Our first impression of these incredible animals was how totally improbable they seemed. We found we couldn't take them seriously and they reminded us exactly of animated cuddly toys. Coupled with their very endearing, anthropomorphic gestures we at once fell in love with them. Using their chests as breakfast tables, as they munched bamboo, they spent many hours in a semi-reclined position eating during the day. Hotter in Chengdu than their native habitat, however, the pandas are offered large blocks of ice in each of their cages which they spend long, midday siestas hugging in their sleep. Ninety percent of all panda images that have been published come from the breeding centre. Pandas are commercial, photographically speaking, even today when there is virtually no editorial market left. We took a deep breath and paid our dues and were handed a receipt for US300 'Panda Handling Charges'. We were allowed 20 minutes with a mother panda and her baby in a cage with a bamboo backdrop. That included the first five minutes or so when she was given several carrots to keep her occupied without getting up. I waited out the carrot eating and then shot like crazy. It was very cute and the images still sell today. They are labelled as captive as we believe in truth in image captioning. The following day, after making friends with the head handler, I had much better fun. For a paltry fifty bucks, I got to take an adolescent panda out into the woods, for an hour with the keeper. Forgetting to photograph, I was playing and wrestling with it for at least 20 minutes. They are strong, with pretty big teeth too! I had an absolute blast, the keeper just looked on as the panda and I rolled around in the middle of the woods on our own.

Southeast of Chengdu is the magnificently scenic area of Guilin, studded with dramatic, self-standing limestone pinnacles around which the Li River weaves slowly to eventually mingle its waters with the South China Sea. Here in the river live a dying breed of fishermen which still use trained cormorants to hunt fish. With a string tied around the neck of the free-swimming bird, it is prevented from swallowing the fish which it captures and is trained to return it to its master who rewards the bird with a cube of chopped fish small enough to swallow. The birds live their lives tied to rafts alongside the fisherman's floating home. Come nightfall, the team sets out on to the river where a bright paraffin lamp attracts fish to the surface aiding the cormorants. At dawn, the hunters can be seen gently poling their way back to their houseboats in which a wife and hungry children wait for the night's catch. Tourists have set upon the area *en masse*, attracted primarily by the scenic beauty, reminiscent of the classic Chinese paintings so widely available. Many of the fishers have now turned their unique lifestyle into a fifteen-minute side-show at the dockside, profitable enough to buy more than the fish they could have caught on a night's foray. We had a pretty in-depth experience with the fishermen, getting to know the cormorants a little as well as spending time with the families in their rundown floating homes. The ancient lifestyle, of an unlikely relationship between man and bird, is probably in its last generation.

In the very south of Yunnan province is Xishuangbanna. It lies close to the Laos and Myanmar borders. We were drawn to the area on the reports of wild Asian elephants roaming in the protected area of the national park. Apart from the possibility of elephants, I was also keen to photograph as much other wildlife as possible, especially some of the exotic birds. There is a lot that is misunderstood or lost in translation in China but our guide really was below average, although I have to say, she was keen to help. Most registered tour guides, licensed to take foreigners, are given an official western name to guide with to make things easier. Ours was Mary.

It was a shock to her that we were planning to leave our cabin at dawn and had asked that she arrange for a park ranger to accompany us. I wanted to start photographing in the early morning light if possible. I asked her to explain to him that we would be looking for little birds, the more colourful the better. Dawn came quickly and everyone was on time. The park ranger looked pleased with himself. He approached me with a gorgeous green-tailed sunbird held high, dangling between the tips of his thumb and forefinger. "Here's one!" he said in the local Tai Lue language. He had shot it.

We had booked one night to sleep in the elephant observation tree house next to the river and perched on enormously tall stilts. It was rustic and mosquitos were bad but that was all outweighed by the chance of wild elephants. Unfortunately, we saw none that we could claim were wild as the three that did pass we could have sworn had chains for ankle bracelets.

Close by was something we were told was an 'Eco' park. We decided to take a look. From the outside, we were immediately dubious but paid our dues and went through the gate. It was obvious from the outset that Chinese 'eco' simply means animal and has nothing to do with 'responsible'. It was a show. Tigers, wolves, bears and more were permanently kept in such confining cages that they could barely turn around, about a foot longer than the animal excluding its tail, while loud Chinese music blared from speakers just above them. As there is no concept of being able to be cruel to an animal, because it is just an animal, nothing was wrong with this to a Chinese person or the multitude of Asian tourists. Tigers were harnessed to carts, which they pulled around within a large cage, while a woman sat on the cart clapping, while a wolf was made to jump backwards and forwards over a wall. Macaques were tightrope walking and playing basketball. Two tigers were made to climb a ladder and slide down the other side, the tiger in the rear being hit constantly. A tiger was riding around the cage on the back of a cantering horse. Bears were made to ride bicycles. A small bear, in a dress, did a little tightrope walking and then a few handstands. The show ended with a bear 'marriage' ceremony where one bear was in a litter, carried by two others and all the other animals including tigers, horse, goat, pig, wolf, dog and macaques followed in a procession behind.

Then it was time for tourists to pose with the animals. A tiger lay on a table, with a chain around its neck that passed through a hole in the table to restrain it. The keeper stood close by clutching a steel bar to assure good behaviour. We saw it being used to hit the tiger in the face. Mostly tourists sat on the animal and portrayed dominance over it for their photographic mementos. A more creative tourist might pose face to face with the tiger and snarl at it. An Asiatic black bear, restrained with a rope through its nostril that exits through a hole made in the bones of the snout, was also a favourite for tourist photos. Once again, a stout metal bar is close at hand. Some like to punch it, others enjoy dominating it while the keeper forces it to open its mouth and look more aggressive, I just talked to it nicely and paid nothing. Having been noticed taking pictures with a decent camera, I was approached surreptitiously by the staff and asked if I wanted them to arrange a private fight between a lion and a tiger, for a fee. It was a disgusting idea which I naturally refused. Images of this show have done well for me in competitions and books denouncing the cruelty, as we in the 'west' see it. For many years, I have done my best to raise public awareness and denounce these kind of practices. I'm sure the Chinese haven't seen them though.

We have managed to travel widely in Yunnan and visited many of the ethnic minorities, a few things have stuck in my mind. In a small Bai minority village, we were in the local market and there was a dentist touting his trade. His pitch, to rustle up business, was to sit at a small table on which was a gruesome photo of him working on a patient (aka victim), a pair of rusty pliers, a hammer, a roll of wire and an open tin containing several sets of false teeth and a large collection of the teeth he had hammered out. The empty chair next to him was there to tempt any would-be masochist.

The Grand Terraces in Yuanyang are absolutely mind-boggling. Tiered rice paddies they stretch for thousands of hectares. The reflected light, when they are full of water, makes for a photographer's dream. They are thousands of years old and are a truly exceptional example of ancient engineering, as well as efficient water usage, something modern society could perhaps learn from. China really is an amazing place in so many ways except for their relationship with nature.

In the north of Yunnan, we ended up spending four days at the Tibetan horse racing festival, known as the 'Heavenly Steed Festival', in Zhongdian, which changed its name in 2001 to Shangri-La. On our way north, we stopped at Lijiang and visited the Jade Dragon Snow Mountain, it was a visit specifically to find the famed red panda hats. Like a Davy Crockett racoon hat, but on steroids, we found lots of them dwarfing the heads of the Yi women that wore them. Red pandas are listed as endangered animals and now I knew why.

Our guide in the Tibetan Autonomous Prefecture region was a young woman called Numjie; it was her real name. She was probably the only guide that we ever had in China with whom we had a real and mutual understanding. She was Tibetan and our driver was Han Chinese. The festival was a lot of fun and we saw only a handful of other western tourists the entire time. I loved the social interaction that we enjoyed with everyone, despite the language barrier. I loved their outfits, full traditional dress and obviously only the finest for such an important annual event (which culminates on the 5th and 6th days of the fifth lunar month) and I loved the huge, black, fiercely loyal, Tibetan mastifs, each regaled in a fabulously flamboyant bright, red-coloured collar of bushy fur. Perhaps the most dramatic event was the scarf grabbing competition where twenty or so scarves were lined up, parallel to each other about two metres apart in a row some 40 metres long. A horse rider, on his Heavenly Steed, at full gallop had to lean all the way out of his saddle and grab the scarves off the ground. The most scarves wins. Riders came a cropper, with many hurt as the horse trod on them during the fall, it was all taken in good stead and the crowds just couldn't get enough.

Driving back from the festival to our hotel in town, I saw a crowd gathered by a narrow, shallow, rocky river, running next to the road in the open terrain. I asked the driver to stop. A crowd usually has something of interest to offer. We got out of the car. There was in the order of 25 people milling around amiably and chatting together a little way back from the river. There were two men each holding a long trident close to the river downstream of a party of three at the water's edge. One of the three was standing, the other, a priest as it turned out, was kneeling over the third who was an elderly woman lying down. She was naked and dead. Her clothes had already been tossed in the river by the time we had stopped and now we watched as the priest raised the woman's right leg and chopped it off at the knee with an axe. He threw the severed limb in the river. The remainder of the leg was then chopped off at the hip and thrown in the river. This was repeated for the left leg. The job of the men with the tridents was to push the chunks of amputated limbs as far downstream as possible as they were getting held up on the rocks in the shallows. Meanwhile, the crowd of 25 relatives, close family and friends continued talking amiably amongst themselves. The right arm was chopped off at the elbow, thrown in the river, then at the shoulder and thrown in the river. It was again repeated for the left arm. The limbless torso was now eviscerated and the intestines thrown in the river. The torso was cut in half on the spine and thrown in the river. The head was decapitated with the axe and the chest and ribcage was thrown in the river. The larger pieces causing the trident guys some issues. Now holding the head in his hand the priest took a sharp knife and scalped the woman, throwing her hair in the river. He peeled off her face and threw it in the river, then, like a coconut he cleaved the skull into two halves with the axe again and threw each in the river. Our Han driver was freaking out. He lost it and hid away in the car, as we refused to leave, screaming of barbarism. We were fascinated. I commented to Numjie that in our society, if a daughter, husband or son had watched their mother being brutally butchered and thrown, dismembered, into a river, it would have severe traumatic repercussions on that person and scar them for life. "Not at all," she said. "This is a sacred river; the fish are given the meat as a gift. A fitting end for the human body to be returned to nature. No fishing is allowed here. For us," she said, "once a person dies, the spirit leaves the body and all that is left is meat." She continued, "When I was a child I had to walk a long way to school, following the course of a sacred river. There were always pieces of human bodies, hands or legs in the river. For us, it is normal." I believed her.

# Fossa, a Frenchman and Farting Frogs
## Madagascar

As mentioned previously, Madagascar remains one of our favourite destinations. We have probably made 30 trips there, both with clients and on dedicated photo shoots. Madagascar is the fourth largest island in the world, after Greenland, New Guinea and Borneo. It lies off the southeast coast of Africa and is approximately 1000 miles long by 350 wide. Madagascar was once joined to the mainland but drifted apart from the African/South American plate 135 million years ago and then the India plate about 88 million years ago. It has been isolated ever since. Drifting on its own, it carried the early ancestors that evolved into the species we see today. 88 million years is a long time for the vagaries of evolution to experiment with what might work best. When you are pretty much starting from scratch, the end result is a lot of bizarre animals that are found nowhere else on earth. One hundred percent of the nearly 300 species of native frogs are found nowhere else, ninety-five percent of the reptiles, more than eighty percent of the plants and ninety-two percent of the native mammal species. It is quite literally like nowhere else on the planet. As the island drifted away, it carried the precursors to this wealth of species, including little 'pre-monkeys' called *prosimians*. There are no monkeys on the island but there are lemurs. Not quite as well-endowed in the intelligence department as modern primates on mainland Africa, they are still good at what they have to do. There are about 60 different types or taxa which are continually being revised by evolutionary biologists. They range from the smallest primate in the world, the ridiculously small mouse lemurs that can sit comfortably in the palm of your hand to the indri, a large, black-and-white, 9kg teddy bear. Indris, like many lemur species are critically endangered. They are prodigious leapers and quite rightly famous for their blood chilling call which pierces the forest air like a humpback's call cuts through the ocean. Today indris are the largest lemurs. That was not always so. There were

17 known species larger than the indri, all now extinct. The largest the size of a gorilla. The lucky Dutch, when they first arrived to the island, even got to see some of them, describing lemurs the size of baby cows.

The sifakas are second only to the indri in size. They belong to the *Propithecus* genus and there are nine species. Their name comes from the alarm call they make. It is an onomatopoeia. They are predominantly leaf-eaters which imparts a rather sedentary lifestyle. When alarmed however, they are very capable of a swift escape response covering huge distances through the forest in a series of massive leaps. Propelling themselves by their long, powerful hind limbs, they spring from one vertical tree limb to the next, maybe six metres or more away. We were the first photographers to photograph all nine species in the wild, which, because of their geographical ranges being circumjacent around the island, meant travelling pretty much the whole country. Some were relatively easy, such as the Verreaux's sifaka for example in the south of Madagascar. Not only does it frequently come down to the ground but, if you predict its direction of travel and sit quietly, it will famously 'dance' right past you. Others were harder and when the roads got too extreme for a 4x4 we were forced into ox-drawn carts which was definitely worse, on the hugely pot-holed tracks, than any other transport I can think of.

Our hardest species to photograph was the silky sifaka. There were no photographs that we knew of already taken. It required expeditionary planning and logistics before we were to complete our goal.

It was our twelfth day in the forest. Twice already, we had sent our Malagasy porter the long way back, down the steep rain forest path, to re-provision with rice and beans. Despondency was heavy in the air. By now, I was beginning to believe that perhaps wedding photography may have been a better option when, completely without warning, I heard a familiar dull thud close behind. Then another and then another. Cautiously, I turned to meet, eye to eye, the curious gaze of what seemed like an apparition – a spirit of the forest – the all-white silky sifaka. They had come to me!

Madagascar is a poor country, with very little industry to create employment, which, in turn, dictates that the vast majority of the young, burgeoning population is forced to live off the land. Many and varied problems face the diverse lemur populations, most general amongst them however is the demand on the remaining forests for wood collection (for charcoal) and swidden agriculture. Local *fadys* (taboos) have largely protected lemurs from hunting in the past but these are now breaking down due to local immigrations to new areas by Malagasy seeking fresh opportunities. The newcomers to an area may have *fadys* of their own, which prevents them hunting their own local species, but these do not pertain to the resident species of the new locale thereby rendering them fair game for the pot.

One of the joys of Madagascar is travelling by road. There is always so much to see, especially as most people are out in the fields working. Apart from baskets, Reneé and I have an odd assortment of various themes from around the world. Of all the people we know, we have the largest collection of skulls, books, baskets, wire bicycles and ammonites. None of it of any intrinsic value, but all of it with enormous personal attachment. Visitors usually liken our home to a museum.

We also have a large collection of utilitarian items that we find in the various cultures we visit, one of them is a rice-paddy spade from Madagascar. It is a beautiful object. The wooden shaft being highly polished from regular use and hard work. The distal end has a homemade round metal cap. The blade is long, nearly eighteen inches in length, but narrow, only a few inches wide. It is curved along its length and sharp at the working end. It is hand crafted by a local blacksmith and they are omnipresent in the countryside. I had always liked the idea of owning one when finally, I stopped our bus, full of a group we were leading and walked out to the middle of the paddy field. I immediately scouted the best-looking spade and approached its owner. Everyone downed tools and gathered around. The clients had caught up with me and we were quite a throng, all focused on the spade. I asked how much it would cost to replace. We struck a deal, paying more than it was worth in monetary terms and I walked away with my spade. The other farmers were totally floored. I believe it was probably the first time in the history of tourism that a tour bus had stopped to buy a five-foot spade! Running tours back-to-back, we were driving along the same road nearly three weeks later. I slowed the bus to a stop to tell the story to the new guests. As we stopped, thirty farmers came running out of the fields, waving their spades high in the air and converged on the bus trying to sell their tools. I guess word must have got out that I gave him a good price!

A very rewarding activity that we offer on a trip is the night walk. Often along a forested road edge, we each have a torch, the guide goes first, me second and single file behind. Mostly we look for chameleons, snakes and frogs. The guide that we work with is phenomenal and we generally have a very high reward-to-effort ratio. It was early in the trip and we were in Perinet. If we call stop at the front, everyone continues forward to have a look at what we have found. "Stop!" I hissed loudly. "Frog! You can hear it calling. Listen!" Sure enough, a frog was calling, regularly, about every second, a rather muted croak. It was getting closer. We all had our full attention now precisely focused on the sound. It *was* getting closer. Then, I nearly died of embarrassment. Thankfully, it was dark. I realised that the straggler of the group was letting out a little wind with each footfall, as she walked up to join us and see the frog. She arrived and the noise stopped. Little did she know that *she* was the frog.

If we are lucky on a trip, we may see one or two species of tenrec. They are gorgeous little animals ranging from the size of a mouse to a hedgehog. They are shrew-like in their high-energy activity, covered in spines like a hedgehog and can also roll into a protective ball. I had no idea, until Reneé and I were walking along a beach and I found a common tenrec skull, that they had such massive canines. "I'd hate to get bitten by one of those," was my comment, as we continued our stroll. A few weeks later, on our own, we were photographing golden-crowned sifakas near Daraina when a local boy came wandering down the track with a live tailless tenrec suspended by one leg from his basket. He had caught it and was going home to cook it. I considered it was equivalent to three cans of sardines from the local shops and asked how much they were per can. I gave him enough to buy four cans and I became the proud owner of a tenrec. Reneé, our driver and I walked far away from the road until it looked like a good spot to release the animal. Undoing the string which was biting into the flesh was not easy and on the last snip the tenrec managed to bite me getting a full lock on the fleshy section between the thumb and forefinger of my left hand. It hurt like hell and bled profusely. The little demon had a tenacious grip and vigorously shook his head like a terrier. It was too spiny to grab, I needed help to get it off but by now both my comrades, which included my wife, were out of control in hysterics. They couldn't help me if their life depended on it and there was no way that they were going to risk getting savaged either. I had to resort to a desperate plea. Full minutes later, they came to my rescue and we extracted the beast. It ran, happy that it had wreaked revenge on Man.

I know that I have a long list of favourite animals but, even before I saw one, fossa was high on my list. It is very cool and the type of mammal I enjoy, predatory, quick witted, smart and aloof. Something like a small puma to look at, with shorter legs, a very long tail a bulbous nose and large, rounded ears. Very cat-like, they are not felines but belong to a small subfamily of Madagascan mammals. It is a monotypic genus with 'loose' ankles allowing it to rotate its feet somewhat to climb down a tree headfirst. Incredibly agile, they eat lemurs and are a sifaka's worst nightmare. Through the canopy or along the ground fossas give chase at an astonishing rate. It is Madagascar's largest carnivore and there is nothing quite like a fossa. The best area to see one was recommended as the Kirindy forest. They are very shy and the locals are afraid of them claiming they will eat their children. It had not been photographed professionally in the wild before and I really wanted the scoop. So, long ago, we arrived at the reserve, our driver left and we spent time getting to know the park guards and scientists. Yes, there were fossa in the area; they often collected their scat to see what species they had been eating. They all agreed that it was unlikely I could ever photograph one. I asked questions and scouted the area. It was the hot dry season and water was limited. We were camping and there was no water in the well either. We had a crate of bottled water and that was it. I have mentioned how my father taught me patience and the way to watch animals and I knew that this stake-out would take a lot of resolve. I think differently to a lot of my wildlife photographer colleagues when it comes to photographing predators. I am good at waiting. My tactic is to sit it out in full view. I don't believe you can ever really hide from a predator and if it suspects you are there it may make it even shier. Know the enemy I think they think. I found a spot in a dry riverbed close to the last remaining surface water for a kilometre. Fossas have to drink I reasoned. The only caveat in my plan was that it could simply wait for me to leave and come after dark – which I am sure that it did. Every day, dawn till dusk I sat fully exposed in 40-degree heat, in a riverbed waiting for a fossa to come and drink. It was certainly hot and uncomfortable; my forearms were blackened with flies but I had a head net to keep them off my face. I pride myself in understanding animal behaviour, I had a 500mm lens mounted on a tripod, and I had it aimed and pre-focused at the point where I believed any self-respecting fossa would make an appearance. Things were starting to get a little desperate, we were running out of water and I was not getting any images. Day eleven, I heard an alarm call and a minute later, a fossa walked directly into my frame and stopped. It was one of my greatest ever 'think-like-an-animal-told-you-sos'. I literally did not move my camera one millimetre and started shooting. It was a huge release of tension and I was shaking with nerves not knowing if the dimly lit images were blurred or not. I had been accepted and it had decided it would allow itself to be seen. All I had to do was stay in my spot. And so it was, it drank, rested on a log, walked around a little and left. I was delighted. We managed to contact a driver by radio who came out from town to resupply us. The stakeout would continue. Once the ice had been broken, the visits were more regular and she became more curious. A mere few days later, she had come right up to me and stuffed her whole head into my partially unzipped camera backpack looking for anything of interest. Another two days and there were two fossas. They actually had a fight at my back while I was sitting on the ground and banged into me! By now, I could walk with her and follow. She led me to a den. I watched her disappear inside, in the heat of the day. She found another small pool of water in some rocks and lay half-submerged to cool off. I was not more than a metre away. I fell in love with her. Later, back in the real world, I had got my scoop. The readers will not know what it is, said the magazine editors! That was the whole point, I told them. Eventually, months later, the images made cover and feature article in Africa Geographic magazine, thanks to the foresight of Eve Gracie, the editor and only then other publications followed suit. I claimed they were the first professional images ever taken of fossa. One US magazine, before publishing told me that it was a false claim as a colleague had already shown them some images. I challenged the assertion, as I knew the story, it was a captive fossa set up in a forest enclosure. Eventually, it was admitted and my images regained their one-upmanship rights. Then there was flak from a well-known fossa biologist who publicly petitioned that I had drugged the animal. It was the only way I could have got the images he said. He is a scientist not a natural historian and likewise ended up eating his words. Several times, I have been back. Fossas are easy to see now, as there are a few that have become very habituated to people. Yes, I love them dearly but it is not the same anymore.

When working previously for a US company, before starting Pete Oxford Expeditions, we used to lead trips into Madagascar but had no control over who joined the trip, take Molly and Bob for example. So when I tell you that there was an American, a Frenchman and a Mexican, it is not the opening line of a joke. They were all single men but none had paid a single supplement so were obliged to share. Reneé, in her wisdom decided that they should rotate sharing at each stop always giving one of them the chance to be single by default. The trip was just beginning and we were at our hotel in the capital of Madagascar, Antananarivo, or simply Tana for short. We were, as usual, staying in the colonial style Hotel Colbert on top of the hill. The staff know us very well and even today, it is always like a homecoming each time we return from the bush. Outside of the entrance is a melee of humanity, fossil sellers, booksellers, working girls, embroidered linen sellers, beggars, sweet sellers, parking attendants and fruit sellers. Everything you could need. It was our second night; we sat for dinner, still getting to know each other as we placed our orders. For me it was always the zebu and French fries. There were things like oysters on the menu but Tana seemed too far inland to risk them. The Frenchman didn't seem to mind and I noticed him order a big plateful of the raw shellfish. Conversation was surprisingly animated which bode well for the trip ahead. We retired contented. Up early the next morning, Reneé and I were assailed viciously by the American. He had been sharing a room with the Frenchman who had brought in a prostitute. The Frenchman then went through a suite of elaborate sexual adventures with the woman, completely oblivious to and in full view of, the American. Not only that but he videoed the entire episode. We were stunned but felt we could not be blamed, as was the American's insinuation. He wanted his money back, he wanted to sue and he wanted to be taken to the American embassy to formally complain about the habits of the French. It took a while but Reneé managed to calm him down with the promise of a single for the rest of the trip. On discretely interrogating the Frenchman, he said he didn't understand what the problem was – he would have shared! The Mexican was now moved in with the Frenchman on a permanent basis and, suspiciously, never had anything to complain about. The Frenchman continued to video his entire trip. On our last night, at the farewell dinner, back in the Colbert, he ordered oysters again and then went on to offer to sell copies of his video to the group. Another passenger commented that they wanted the unedited version, which we thought was odd as we had believed that the whole issue was under wraps. It was time to order dessert, there was mousse, fruit, chocolate cake or apple tart. The waiter came to the Frenchman who was undecided what to have, when someone else piped up, "If you start with oysters you are bound to end up with a tart!" to which the whole table broke down in convulsions of laughter and we realised the cat had long since been out of the bag.

# Ocean's Ambassadors
# Mexico

"Don't end up as a kebab!" my friend Pete Atkinson Skyped me after I'd told him about my upcoming adventure.

It was March, in Mexico, off the Yucatan Peninsula on Isla Mujeres, and it was six o'clock in the morning. I was on the dock, ready to board one of the fleet of a dozen high-tech, game-fishing boats, each bristling with fishing poles, outriggers and antennas. Clients and crews were cocky with anticipation. Fishing was good – the annual migration of sailfish was in full swing.

Sailfish are one of the most highly prized gamefish in the world. The sport fishing industry sells them as 'providing thrilling leaps and a powerful and acrobatic fight'. Personally, I have to admit that I just don't get it. I fail to understand how the terror of a magnificent, hooked fish, in its desperate attempts to evade death can be entertaining, whether it leaps out of the water or not. Nor do I understand how we view the fish as 'providing' such a show as if it were doing it obligingly to please a human audience.

Nevertheless, my three *compañeros* and I were no exception, we were also there to get amongst the sailfish. Our intentions however were different. We wanted to peel back the barrier and witness one of the world's most incredible fish in its natural environment – from underwater.

Sailfish are members of the billfishes, *Istiophoridae*, family (which includes all the marlin, the spearfish and sailfish). They are a designated Highly Migratory Species (HMS) and will swim an average of 200,000 miles, through international waters, in their 16-year lifetime. They can grow quickly in their first year reaching up to five foot in length but from then on, their growth slows considerably. They are one of the most inshore ranging of the billfish feeding on flying fish, halfbeaks, sardines, small tuna, squid and octopi.

The problem of course is how do you find a few sailfish in a vast expanse of open water. Despite their size of up to nine feet in length and in excess of 120 pounds, they remain elusive. Except that is when they gather to feed.

We slipped away from the dock, scanning the surface out to the horizon in earnest, as we motored into blue water. We were not in fact looking for the sailfish themselves – but frigatebirds. With a six- to seven-foot wingspan and only a two-to three-pound body weight, these aerial masters dotted the sky, lazily cruising on outstretched wings. They were hungry and they too, indirectly, were looking for sailfish.

Then, a mere hour into our day, on the horizon we spotted what we were looking for – more frigates. This time, the birds were flying in a concentrated funnel, swooping down to the surface to snatch sardines from the water. We were already kitted up in wetsuits, weight belts, long fins, masks and cameras and excitement levels were high. By the time the skipper had reached the melee and turned our stern into the action, we were lined up on the back rail, filled with anticipation ready to jump. "*Délé*, go, go!" shouted the skipper and we launched ourselves into the water. The difference between what we had seen in air, watching the frenzy of the frigatebirds, coupled with the occasional, tantalising glimpse of action below, to what we witnessed as we passed through the invisibly thin surface, was, quite literally a world apart.

A large, living, silver ball of polarised sardines was being kept pressed against the surface by as many as 50 swift, dark shapes criss-crossing below and to the side. Sailfish! We kicked frantically, cameras at arms-length, aiming at the action and firing away with super wide lenses. We were lucky so far but this could well be our only encounter of these elusive fish. The sardines were trapped and the frigates were maximising on the bonanza held within their reach below the surface by the hunting sailfish. As we sped forward, the closer our approach, the more awesome the spectacle became. The whole group was working like a pack of wolves; they were cooperating in the hunt in the typical manner of other apex predators. Lions cooperate, wolves do and so do wild dogs and hyenas, yet for some reason, we don't normally associate fish with any character or individuality but merely within the limitations of 'tasty', 'tonnage' or 'something to hook' – let me tell you, now is the time to take a deeper look into what makes a fish.

Indeed, humans largely view fish as a resource. We continue to pull them out of the ocean as if the old adage were really true 'That there are plenty more of them in the sea'. That may have been true a century ago when fishing pressure was lower and the playing field was more level, when we did not totally outcompete the fish with advanced technological capabilities to find and catch them by the hundreds of thousands of tons. It was also, in a time when there were only two billion not seven billion people on the planet. Today, however, all the billfish populations are at an all-time low, several species may already be close to a non-viable population number and may not recover sufficiently, once the present long-lived adult population begins to die off, if the current kill rate is maintained.

As we moved in, yet closer, to the hunting pack we began to make sense of the apparent chaos. The prey were being herded into a tight bait-ball. Sailfish would swim close and flick up the huge sail-like dorsal fin like a fence to consolidate the sardines, another would work the opposite side while others stayed below. Colour patterns instantaneously flashed on the bodies of the hunters from a purple-with-blue-spots to a dramatic silver-and-blue-striping, to a stunning coppery-bronze colour; the revelation was that they were actually communicating. Reminiscent of squid or cuttlefish (mere molluscs), they appeared to be using a kind of chromatic semaphore. The meaning was lost on us except that as they turned in, one at a time, to the bait ball to feed, they most often lit up with a metallic bronze as if signalling, "It's my turn, I'm going in!" Their sails would erect explosively with the whooshing sound of a zip fastener and they would swim until their bill was inside the bait ball. I had been told that they would slash dramatically at the sardines with their rough-edged bill and stun a few fish to pick up later. The truth was so much more elegant as, with an almost imperceptible sidewise motion, (virtually only a vibration) it was enough to knock a sardine senseless which was scooped up there and then on the fly. The satisfied sailfish pulled out, the sardines baled up tighter and then another hungry hunter would flash bronze and move in effortlessly to the bait ball to grab itself a bite to eat. Through close observation, one could see that the whole process was in fact ordered, refined – gentlemanly almost.

In all my travels and close encounters with nature, to be in the intimate company of 50 Atlantic sailfish, in blue, oceanic water was already, after 45 minutes, a major wildlife highlight in my life. Part of the beauty of the experience was the fact that these top predators, who knew exactly that we were there, accepted us completely and let us simply observe.

Yet, these ambassadors of the high seas are threatened, like so much else in the oceans of the world. Even before humans have learned enough about their basic biology, from the moment we have been able we have rapidly and very effectively, been systematically ridding the planet of sailfish. Nor do we understand the consequences. We do know that apex predators in general are the keystone species of ecosystems and without sailfish being present in their pivotal role anything could happen. Maybe no billfish would mean that baitfish numbers exploded, just as no lions results in too many grazers and bush turning to desert so, an explosion of baitfish might eat all the plankton. But, guess what, 50% of the planet's oxygen comes from oceanic plankton. Who knows what will happen? I can tell you that seabirds would suffer. As in the case of the frigatebirds, if predatory fish do not trap the smaller bait fish at the surface, then they simply swim deeper and stay out of reach of the avian threat. Whatever happens, if the trend continues, it will not be good.

Why are they threatened? Throughout their range, sailfish regularly encounter 30- to 40-mile-long lengths of monofilament nylon, laced with tens of thousands of baited hooks. Easy prey, the sailfish take the bait and drown on the line. The cruel irony is that these highly non-selective fishing methods are actually targeting tuna and swordfish, yet alongside the dead sailfish may hang a drowned turtle or albatross. Sailfish have a rather tough, undesirable meat and are not even allowed to be landed commercially in the USA. When the fisherman comes to haul in the longline he berates the catch of 'trash' fish, turtles and birds as a waste of hook space and they get tossed overboard to pile up on the sea floor. Unbelievably, these incredible fish are caught for no other reason than to be thrown away as 'by-catch' – a politically correct euphemism meaning carnage and waste.

I could no more imagine killing one of these animals as I could a lion. Of course, there are people who would like to do both and I would say to those people, "What's the point? Haven't we done enough damage to the planet, our home, already? Why not just trash your bedroom, your living room or your back yard – surely, it's the same?"

As the bait ball was being eaten smaller and smaller, the desperate sardines became individually more and more vulnerable. Occasionally, one would break out from the ball and try to take sanctuary in our wetsuits or use us as a shield. An alert sailfish would soon swerve in perilously close to catch the errant sardine and, as thin as a knife would flex its body and shy away at the last instant in a supreme show of athleticism, the long, pointed bill missing my face by a foot or less. It was then I remembered Pete Atkinson's comments and knew that if a sailfish had the will it could pierce my body with its sword, like a hot knife through butter. Malice was absent however and I felt guilty on behalf of those of my species whose only thought was to wrangle a hooked one.

'Tag and release' is the cry from all the would-be conservationists amongst the anglers. Yes, of course, it is better than bringing ashore a dead sailfish just to have it weighed and I applaud the goodwill and common sense of the initiative. We even spotted a tagged animal swimming happily with the crowd and joining in the hunt. I also witnessed however, underwater, from a few feet, the effort, stress and damage (as the taut monofilament continually raked the animals flank) of a sailfish with a hook in its mouth at the end of a line while the oblivious topside crew waited for it to provide the 'thrilling leap'. It was not an easy thing to watch.

The fastest fish in the sea, not to mention one of the most beautiful, sailfish are a supreme blend of wolf, cheetah and chameleon. The time has come that they deserve our respect and understanding. Time too that we ban all indiscriminate long-line fishing and gill netting giving the sailfish, indeed all billfish, a chance to recover. I know it is a rant but I had to get it off my chest. I wish we could get over the 'Out of sight, out of mind' syndrome and accord them, and others the respect they deserve. For sailfish, I give them 'honorary mammal' status.

# Himba – The Ochre People
# Namibia

Namibia is a country where wilderness is totally dominant. Covering an area of more than 800,000 square kilometres, more than three times the size of the United Kingdom, it is home to a meagre human population of just 1.7 million people. It is a land where one is immediately struck by a sense of space. The people are hardy and live close to the land. Fifty percent or more are Ovambo people, but many ethnic groups make up the Namibian melting pot. Others include the Caprivians, the Damara people, the Herero, Kavango, Nama and the Bushmen. Their recent history has been a turbulent one.

Finally, as recently as March 1990, Namibia celebrated independence from South Africa after a long-drawn-out guerrilla war. The new country however inherited a well-developed infrastructure, the mood was peaceful and a new constitution was quickly written, (which was subsequently hailed, as one of the world's most democratic). Although perhaps one of the most rugged countries in the world, Namibia has to be considered one of the most beautiful. Even the roads seem to reflect the soul of the land. We have driven for days covering thousands of kilometres on dirt roads and seen less than a handful of other vehicles.

In the north-west corner, nestling quietly, far out of the way of what little metropolitan life there is in the country, lies Kaokoland – a spectacularly tortured landscape, dry, desolate and inhospitable. To the north, beyond the Kunene River lies the war-torn country of Angola, to the west the bleak and daunting shores of the Atlantic Ocean This dangerous, fog-bound desert shoreline, with strong marine currents, has claimed many the life of an unwitting seaman. Even making it successfully to terra firma after going aground, the hapless souls have succumbed quickly to the vagaries of the extreme desert climate. If the cold didn't kill them, the heat invariably did, if that failed then thirst was a swift release. The bleached bones of sailors and ribs of broken ships eventually gave the stretch of coast its morbid name – the Skeleton Coast. It is beautiful, yet austere.

With abundant fish stocks, the frigid coastal waters are home to African penguins and thousands of Cape fur seals. From the landward side come black-backed jackals, brown hyena, springbok, desert lion and black rhino. Apart from a gravel road, entry to Kaokoland is severely limited. The only overland access, from the south and east, usually being by fully kitted-out four-wheel drive vehicles, which, for safety reasons, should only travel in convoy with another. Surprisingly, this area is home to a few remaining desert elephant that manage to eke out a living from the unusual plants. Perhaps more surprising still, it is home to a dwindling tribe of proud people – the Himba.

Reneé and I had optimistically hired a little Volkswagon Golf in Johannesburg, filled it with provisions, bought an extra fuel tank and a big plastic water container and drove west, spending several nights in the Kalahari Gemsbok National Park, in South Africa. What a pleasure. We saw many raptor species for which the park is famed as well as a leopard for which it is not. Continuing north, we spent a few days at Okonjima. At the time, it was a cheetah rehabilitation centre and with work going on to rehabilitate livestock-killing leopards. We had a great several days and I played hard with the cheetahs who would run behind me and try to trip me with a determined swipe of my ankle with their dewclaw. The aim being to unbalance me as they would an antelope. I went in the compound with the manager to feed Dracula the brown hyena who managed to get hold of my leather shoe in his mouth. Luckily, he did not crush hard which may have broken bones. The most unusual encounter was with Elvis, a full-grown male chacma baboon. They are impressive animals and in fact, we work with them a lot today. Reneé being affectionately known locally as the 'baboon lady'. Elvis had been rescued as a baby. Somehow, the death of his mother was related to a kudu, a large antelope with spiral horns. I do not know how. When we met Elvis, he was chained to Wayne's belt. Wayne and his then wife Lisa, were part owners of Okonjima and managed the business. Elvis was a total chauvinist and misogynist, he felt dominant over Lisa and when she would serve food at the table he disdainfully looked the other way as she offered him his plate. He would smack his lips at me (a male) and ask to be groomed which I would oblige then, in turn, offer my head to him as he went, methodically through my scalp looking for lodgers. When driving, he would sit in the passenger seat, the window rolled down and his elbow leaning on the sill. Lisa sat in the back. Elvis was not a particularly nice character and on a subsequent visit a few years later, we laughed quietly to ourselves. There was Elvis but he had just had his tremendous canines removed after having bitten a guest. All he could do was look sorry for himself covering his mouth with his left hand and pointing to it with his right, looking for pity. There wasn't much of that going around. It turns out that while Elvis was being driven in the truck sometime later when a kudu ran out into the road, it might have even jumped over the car, I'm not sure, Elvis had a heart attack and died.

Continuing much further north, past Outjo and the turn off for the fabulous Etosha National Park, past its western border, we reached Opuwo, the Himba 'capital', a short hop from the Angolan border. The meagre stretch of tarred road in the middle of the settlement did however bequeath immediate status to the town, the next nearest tarred road being more than 100km away. Outwardly, the town has little more to offer than the long overdue chance to replenish fuel.

It is scruffy, scant, dusty, dry and hot. A town full of obvious characters it seems to be as far into the 'daylight' of civilisation that many dare to come to re-provision before skulking back into the depths of the desert. Himba huts are immediately obvious, small domes of bent sticks covered with cow dung on the edge of town, patched with plastic bags, cardboard and other artifacts. Himba women wander semi-naked through the town, into the sparsely stocked supermarket.

Many men have turned to alcoholism and some of the women even to prostitution. No gestures of friendship are offered and a mute, stone-faced appraisal of each other is the best we can muster. Opuwvo is the interface between traditional Himba and the West – the two have collided with the worst of both cultures seemingly manifesting themselves. Nevertheless, despite the harsh description Opuwvo is – at a Himba level – a fascinating place worthy of a visit. Eventually, after having stocked up on corn meal and flour to offer as gifts we left, heading into the hinterland in search of something more traditional. Directions were vague, as the Himba are not tied to any particular place but move according to the best pasture.

On first entering a traditional Himba settlement, one is struck with a sense of hardship, a feeling that for these people Nature is a worthy adversary. The balance between survival or not must indeed be a very fine line. With almost no vegetation of an edible nature to be found, the Himba are almost totally dependent on meat and animal products for sustenance. Semi-nomadic pastoralists they now number no more than seven thousand. (Less than 0.5% of the Namibian population.) They are today one of the last remaining, truly 'primitive', tribes in Africa many still lingering in the Stone Age, refreshingly a culture with almost no dependency on plastic.

We were immediately impressed. Not only were both the men and women extremely handsome, but they were also some of the most welcoming, gentle and proud people we had ever met on any of the world's continents. Apart from one or two of the community speaking *Afrikaans,* we communicated patiently through elaborate sign language. We were soon ushered to the centre of the cluster of huts and told we could pitch our tent. Bright yellow, amid the dull earthy tones of everything else around us, our tent looked conspicuous and out of place. Carefully pitched on a soft bed of dry goat droppings however we slept soundly, at ease with the world, safe under the wing of hospitality offered by the ochre people.

The Himba society is strongly dictated by a wealth of rules, governing social status, hierarchy and tradition. The most poignant feature of their physical appearance is their love of self-adornment and beautification. A tall people, with well-defined facial bone structures their appearance is enhanced by an elaborate display of jewellery, fashioned from mostly, metal, leather and shell. The women in particular are the more extravagantly decorated. It is ritualistic for a woman in the morning to put on her jewellery (that which is not permanently attached) after which she anoints her whole body with a red ochre made from a mixture of powdered red rock (hematite), butterfat and the fragrant sap of a local tree. The mixture, known as 'otjize' is patiently rubbed over the entire body and hair, where, naked from above the waist, the women glow a rich, red colour in the morning and evening light. Apart from the stunning appearance, which the ochre imparts to the skin, we were left with an indelible memory of both the exquisite texture, of that of fine, unglazed porcelain coupled with a delicate and rich fragrance of the perfume. Central to the women's decoration is a large 'cone' shell, collected from the Skeleton Coast and passed down from mother to daughter; it is a highly prized fertility symbol. Trade routes with the coast however have been lost as a result of war and subsequent migrations of people into safer areas such that the cone shells today have become even more valuable.

Each piece of jewellery, such as the heavy steel ankle beads or a copper bracelet is adopted by an individual according to strict tradition. It is permitted to be worn only after an initiation ritual and therefore is 'earned' and so becomes a graphic display of status. Hairstyle plays an important part in signalling the status of a woman in society. Until the age of about ten years old, at around puberty, two thick braids are worn in front of the face. After puberty, these are replaced with a multitude of much thinner strands, packed with ochre, which hang in all directions from the head. As the girl moves into adolescence and becomes of a marriageable age these strands are lengthened and tied back, away from her face. Below shoulder length hair being a Himba sign of beauty. A woman finally changes her hairstyle for the last time upon marriage. Her married status being denoted by a headpiece called an *'erembe'* which is a ruffled piece of tanned goat's leather tied to the top of her head. The hairstyle of a man is also indicative of marital status. Until married, a man's hair is worn in a single braid sweeping backwards from the centre of the crown of the head, called an *'ondatu'*. Upon marriage, his hair is tied up in a kind of turban, *(ondumbu),* where the hair is mixed with wood shavings to give it volume and thus the strange and characteristic profile. Nor is he ever allowed to remove this headpiece unless mourning the death of a close relative. The wire which you often see protruding from under the *'ondumbu'* is used as a tool to scratch the scalp and relieve the itching caused by the wood shavings under the turban.

Such did our relationship develop over the days, that the women thought it amusing to sit me down and plait my hair in the Himba style, my hair was a lot longer then. The smallest things were found amusing and for hours, we would sit around a fire and find things to laugh about.

Key to the Himba culture is cattle, a sleek, wide-horned breed adapted to dry and barren conditions. A family's wealth and subsequent status is measured in head of cattle. Goats and sheep are also important, all species providing milk, meat and skins. In the early 1980s, in the worst drought in living memory, 80–90% of the cattle in Kaokoland died of thirst and malnutrition. From being some of the wealthiest pastoralists in Africa, the tribesmen quickly became some of the poorest. The three desperate years are referred to by the Himba as 'the time when the people had to eat their leather garments'. By the end of the drought, a fair number of Himba had migrated to Opuwvo seeking government and Red Cross aid. It is since that time that many of them stayed. Some joining the army and earning a wage others went the way described earlier. Those that left the town after the drought walked hundreds of kilometres back into the desert and single-mindedly built stocks back up to what they are today.

Apart from the day-to-day duties of tending livestock, men occupy themselves in long discussions and decision-making. The women meanwhile care for the babies, prepare food and indulge in self-beautification. We found it such a 'homely' and idyllic feeling to sit on the ground with goats, a few lean dogs and Himba children milling around. Meanwhile, an adolescent girl might be scraping a goat skin of its hair as her mother lies on her side having her hair re-braided by another member of the community while her youngest child, in turn, suckles contentedly from her breast. One almost tends to forget the true nature of the surroundings until, a few steps from the shelter, the heat of the sun once again bakes down upon you.

Without pomp or ceremony, the men butchered a cow, after killing it by suffocation, and excitement quickly stirred amongst the tribe. After the headmen gathered to read the future in the entrails, carefully examining the way they had spilled, men and women came to inspect the carcass as it was being butchered. The select pieces are distributed according to special customs and tradition. The peritoneum was removed and draped over the head of a young girl as part of an initiation ceremony, being now eligible for a change of hairstyle, having passed through puberty. The blood dripped down her breast. She wore the peritoneum for the entire day before her hairstyle was changed, by which time it had dried to biscuit hard and taken on the shape of the two raised lumps of her thick braids signifying prepubescence.

Surprisingly, almost no flies gathered – as if the land is too harsh even for them. The remains of the butchered carcass and various joints of meat were wrapped in the cow's skin and covered in brushwood to refute access to the hungry dogs and chickens. A night of celebration began. Women in their finest goatskins and jewellery gathered from the various huts to dance, while men made rudimentary music with traditional instruments. The men were dressed in not much more than a belt, sandals, *'ondumbu'* and thick necklace. The belt supports a flap of cloth at their rear while another smaller cloth dangles in front. Young boys lacked even the cloth at the rear as they ran around barefoot over the hard ground playing in the light of the fire. The women support two or three layers of goat skin from their waist which covers their buttocks and serves admirably as a cushioned seat, finding a low rock on which to sit close to the hearth, between dancing.

By first light next morning, things were back to normal. Families awoke in their huts, their faces reflecting the orange glow of the fire's embers, still burning in the doorway. Soon the girls were going about their duties of collecting milk from the goats. A hind leg held under their arms as a restraining measure as they pulled roughly on the teats. The youngest children played while the boys rounded up the goats ready to take them to areas away from the village to find food for them. Ever watchful, the goat herders must always be on guard against desert lions and leopard which find the domesticated animals an easy target. The chickens have been let out of their cages of sticks and stones where they have spent the night free from the threat of jackals. The men are stoking the fires, using wood collected by the women the day before. They are chewing on meat, and smoking pipes. Gradually, the women emerge after a private session of self-adornment in their huts. After feeding their babies, the women began the morning's ritual of collecting water. Walking in convoy over the rough rocks, the nearest source of water may be several miles from the settlement. Eventually, they returned, some, with the added weight of babies strapped to their backs, carrying a heavy load of water on their heads. Still only mid-morning, the sun was already scorching the earth while the men were busily building corrals for their livestock. A day in the life of traditional Himba.

Each new day brings with it the inevitable encroachment of the western world. Despite their remoteness, these, beautiful people are coming more and more into contact with outsiders. A nomadic people cannot afford to have any more possessions than it can carry. Yet with civilisation comes a change of values, the young Himba are being channelled towards school, an institution where western ideas are instilled in them. The children are drifting away from their parents, a sense of materialism is creeping into their culture, cars, watches and radios are becoming more and more attractive to them, objects of their dreams, replacing the vision of a large herd of cattle. "Cattle are no longer in my grandson's heart," complains an elder to me, smoking his pipe in front of the fire. Now with the chance of waged labour these dreams are not so far over the horizon. As with most primitive cultures, which stand precariously on the edge of the abyss of civilisation, their problem is a lack of understanding of what is in store for them and the negative aspects of the western culture. Should they decide to take the plunge? More often than not, the two collide head-on with disastrous results. We can only hope that these proud and independent people of the desert can make the move, gradually at their own pace and of their own accord such that they retain their dignified demeanour, within the encroaching, polyglot, African society as well as within their own.

Our return journey was long. We headed for the coast, remembering the cardinal rule in Namibia to fill up your fuel tank and water containers every single time there is an opportunity, no matter when you last did it. Arriving at the coast at Torra Bay, it was not much more than the road turning right or left. We wanted to reach Terrace Bay in the north to sleep in a bed at the small guesthouse. Along the way, Reneé wanted to pee. We stopped the car and she walked away clutching a roll of toilet paper. She called to me to keep a look out. I reminded her that we had not even seen a handful of vehicles the whole day and went to look for scorpions. Suddenly, two light aircraft came barrelling in, very low from the south. They saw Reneé in full squat and the lead pilot thought it hilarious to buzz her so low that the toilet paper unravelled and blew like the streamers of a kite into the air. The second aeroplane followed in behind. Reneé, who easily suffers acute embarrassment started screaming at me, "I told you to keep a look out!" I turned my palms skyward and shrugged my shoulders. We arrived at the guesthouse in time for dinner, the only other occupants being the passengers on the two aircraft. Reneé was mortified, it could only have been her peeing out there in the desert. To make things 100 times worse, (I'm sure you don't believe me) but one of the couples knew who we were having travelled with us previously on a trip!

South along the Skeleton Coast, we saw no one before arriving to Cape Cross where there is a huge Cape fur seal colony. There were tens of thousands of them lounging on the windswept and blustery shore, a rare vista into a healthy system. Or was it? Even today, these Cape fur seals are harvested in vast numbers for their pelts, their genitals and their blubber which is rendered down to oil, rich in omega 3s. We even visited a drying station where pieces of fur seal bones, meat and fur were drying to be used in cattle feed. *Can we not leave anything alone,* I thought?

Continuing east through the Namib-Naukluft National Park, we took the scenic route all the way back to Cape Town to drop off our little Golf.

We were keen to revisit the Himba and, a few years later, we had the opportunity. We were lucky enough to do a Schoeman family safari. True pioneers of the area, they had been taking a small number of guests to the remotest parts of northwest Namibia to stay at their camps for decades. We were fortunate to be in that number. Bertus, the eldest son was our guide, pilot, host and driver. Beginning our trip in Windhoek, he flew us in a little Cessna 210 across the desert where we turned north along the amazing coastline, this time seeing it from the air. There was a lot that we did along the way. After some exciting flying, lower than the cormorants, we landed on a rough strip where Bertus had an old Land Rover waiting. We transferred to the 4x4 and hand-cranked it enough that it finally started whereupon we took off over the massive dunes coming to a sharp edge and then letting the car slide down over the other side. We were on the roof and it was a lot of fun. At another impromptu stop, on a gravel strip, was a second Land Rover, also in the middle of nowhere. After firing it up, we drove off to look for amethysts in the desert and found many.

Continuing on, we landed at one of the Schoeman ventures at a camp near a Himba village where we were to stay. I was delighted to be back amongst them. They were a different group of people than we had visited before but equally friendly and they obviously loved Bertus which gave us a big head start in socialising. We spent a few days at the camp, looking for desert elephant, brown hyena and other wildlife as well as finding lion tracks, animals that had recently moved into the area after many years of absence. I spent all the time I could in the company of Himba. On our previous visit, I had learned what was of value to them. During the three-year interval, I had travelled widely and always kept a look out for the specific cone shells that the Himba women wear. I found them in a London shell shop, in Madagascar, and other locations that I have since forgotten. I had five of them with me. As a parting gift to the five adult women (by sheer coincidence), I gave them one each. It was as if I had given them a gold ingot. They were delighted. I was thrilled because our mutual interest and curiosity had been genuine; they had not expected anything. Bertus was very taken aback at such an intuitive gift and I felt proud to have surprised him that way.

# Stolen Binoculars and a Black Panther
## Amazon, Ecuador

For Reneé and I, our time living in the Ecuadorian Amazon were good days. For me, it was a dream, for Reneé more of a surprise, but our relationship was young and we were keen to make the most of everything. While we were at Sacha Lodge, it became known as an ideal place to receive animals for rehabilitation, be they ex pets or confiscated by the military from the pet trade.

We had many charges including several sloths which are very endearing characters. Mostly, they were easy animals to relocate; we would usually keep them one or two nights in the cabin to make sure that they seemed fine before release. Spending a significant amount of time hanging upside-down the shaggy hair is layered from the belly towards the back to help shed rainwater. They are superb athletes with incredible strength in the grip of their ferocious claws. I was holding one once and it gripped a roll of flesh in my midriff which was excruciating and took Reneé to help extricate. A sloth can grip a branch in one hand and stretch its other arm in a long reach horizontally, followed by its body before it grabs a nearby branch. I doubt there is a human that can do that. We knew their favourite food trees and would look for a good area to include at least one or two of them. With my wooden paddle over my shoulder, the sloths were easy to manage, as they simply clung on to the paddle as we walked through the forest. It was always gratifying to watch their climb to freedom.

An animal with a boisterous character that we were once responsible for was a South American coati. Similar to a racoon, it is an omnivore with a long prehensile nose with which it makes it its business to root around in anything. The coati slept with us in our cabin, usually in the hammock, we were the only two people who were able to handle it without being bitten by its impressive teeth. Usually highly social, the animal would follow us everywhere, even on our walks with guests. The problem was that if I was to point out a frog, for example, it would muscle in and scoff it before all the guests had seen it. If we pushed off in a canoe, it would jump aboard too. Sitting in single file, the coati would visit us in turn, walking along the sides of the canoe to the person behind, where it had the disturbing habit of sniffing everyone's crotch by rummaging around with its wiggly nose. You had to let it happen or it would nip you. I always knew how far down the canoe he had gone by the cries of 'Ow!' as people tried to push it away. It all became too much in the end and it was obviously very capable of looking after itself. After demolishing all the butter and sugar bowls on the tables set for lunch, I decided it had to go before the chefs killed it. I took a sack, threw in a boiled sweet, the coati followed and I walked with it, in the sack, several kilometres before crossing a stream to let it go. It was sad but I felt confident that it would be fine. I returned to the lodge. As I arrived at the main building, there was the coati to meet me. How he had followed along a trail he had never walked and crossed a stream I am still not sure.

Our favourite animal of all was a grison. A gorgeous little mustelid, related to badgers, weasels and wolverines. Only reaching about 2–2 ½ kg in weight they look just like a petite African honey badger, a grizzled grey coat with a white line through the forehead and a black mask and chest. They are equally badass. I have never seen one in the wild, many of the natives did not even know what it was when it was brought to us. This particular individual had been kept as a pet since it was a kit. It lived in a house, ate bacon and was trained to shit on the tiles in the shower. My kind of mammal, it was absolutely adorable, despite its foibles. We were asked to rehabilitate it back to the wild. Of course, we agreed knowing that it would not be easy. It lived with us, as the coati had done, in our cabin. There was a spare mattress leaning against the wall and it decided that it would make a good place for a den. If ever we misplaced our smelly socks or used underwear we knew where to look as it had a penchant for collecting and 'nest making' with all things odorous, in fact, being also related to skunks they can produce a little whiff themselves. Grisons are diurnal and it took on the same circadian rhythm as us. At night-time, Reneé and I would go to bed under a sheet and no more. Within a minute or two of lights out, there would be a tug on the sheet at our feet. He would have grabbed the hem in his mouth and pulled himself up until able to duck his head under the sheet and crawl up between us. Once his head was sticking out the other side, level with ours, he fell asleep. In the morning, we actually had to shake him to wake him, he yawned and sauntered to the shower to ablute. He walked with us, sometimes for hours at a time, in the forest, hardly ever leaving our side. When we were close to home, he would scamper ahead, run to our bathroom, straight to the tiles and relieve himself. We eventually broke that habit by creating a latrine on the forest floor using some of his own urine and scat as the inoculum. Next was to get him to hunt. We asked the staff to supply us with any rats that they killed. With these, we baited the grison, getting him into a frenzy, holding the rat and attacking him with it until out of frustration he bit it. We let him taste and did it again until we got him to actually eat one. Next stage was to dig a large pit in which, every few days, we would put the grison with a live rat. Little by little, it successfully killed and ate them, until we figured it was ready for release. Somehow, it knew something was up and it grabbed one of my flip-flops as comfort and ran into its den. We released it a kilometre or so from the lodge and never saw it again although one of the guides, approximately three months after release, spotted a grison running across the trail with an agouchy in its mouth. We can only suppose it was 'ours' that had made the transition.

The Rio Napo is the main fluvial access route into Sacha Lodge. It is a major tributary of the Amazon and up to a mile wide in places. It is in a constant state of flux, with water levels, submerged sand banks and floating obstacles continuously changing. The hundreds of times I have travelled the river, I can still not read it like a native. We would often leave the lodge pre-dawn, or sometimes in dense fog and even then the drivers made it. Not always. I remember being grounded very hard onto a sandbank. There was no other thing for it but to get out of the canoe and lighten the load. There was a hierarchy to follow where each 'group', having disembarked, would try and push us off the sand before the next had to get out. First the native guides, then the crewman, then the naturalist guide – me, in my underpants and shirt, then the male passengers, dressed down the same, then the women. In the jungle, they say it how it is. If you have a big nose, you are called 'Condorito' (little condor), if you are fat, 'Gordo' (fat), skinny, 'Flaco' (skinny). We had one extremely large woman in the boat with us who could have saved at least the first five of us from having to get wet. The locals saw it and were gesturing to me that removing her would be the solution. I had to stay professional and run through the protocol. She was in group 5 for disembarkation. We were badly stuck and it came to her turn, the big river canoes are extremely heavy. She tried to swing over the side but lost her balance and fell, upside-down, back into the canoe, stuck fast between the bench seats. We now had to push like crazy on the canoe to float it as there was no way we could now unload her. Another fast canoe passed us, its wake gave us a little help and we pushed off. Now there must have been four of us trying to haul the woman back to vertical. As with Molly, her clothing was in disarray, everything was a little embarrassing but finally, all ship shape again, we pointed back upstream, the driver making very sure that we hit no more sandbars.

There used to be much more wildlife on the Napo than there is today, for example, I haven't seen spoonbills, horned screamers, tucuxi dolphins or boutu dolphins now for many years on the main river. I had heard, from a friend who was interested in developing community tourism, that there were some locals on a small tributary, a long way downstream, who were hand feeding wild boutus – Amazon pink river dolphins. It was an opportunity I was not going to miss and was able to arrange a canoe and driver for the long trip down river.

About halfway into our journey, we both saw something odd in the main river, it was twitching. As we came closer, we could see it was a human body, still with his clothes on. The fish were nibbling at him from below. There was just the boat driver and me. The only thing we could think of was to take a rope around the chest and under the arms and tow the body to shore. We saw a hut on the bank and alerted the occupants that we had tied off the corpse at the edge of the water such that when the next passenger canoe came upriver on its way to Coca that they should arrange to take the body with them and continued to the dolphins.

I had my underwater camera with me and slipped into the tannic water, the colour of tea. I was attached to shore by rope as the current was strong. The dolphin feeder called and they came, three of them. Long before the dolphins of Manu became famous, this was a total privilege. Although the water was relatively clear, there is usually low visibility in tannic water. To see them, I had to be within a metre. They were as curious of me as I of them. Their snouts were long, their heads bulbous, their eyes degenerate and their voices unusual. With my head fully underwater, breathing through a snorkel there were no external distractions and I felt very much one on one with an animal as it came close to 'look' at me with its complex sonar.

I had actually trained dolphins in my past, before I set off around the world. My Galapagos girlfriend at the time was Spanish Canadian and we were up in her hometown of Edmonton over a long, very cold, Christmas and New Year period. Edmonton, at the time, had the largest mall in the world, owned by Arabs.

In it was a dolphinarium, a submarine, some tigers and a seal. I got a job working with the dolphins. I was in the pool with them every day and the trick we were teaching them was for me to be pushed around the pool with their snouts pressing on my feet until they would throw me into the air. It was a bittersweet experience. Bitter to have these four animals, each with totally different personalities cooped up in the confines of a dolphin show facility. Sweet because it was very, very special to be able to interact, so personably with dolphins. All I could do was show them kindness and give them lots of hugs in the water which they seemed to enjoy. I also spent a lot of time with a harbour seal. Just me and him, for hours at a time, alone backstage. That was magical for me too. I even taught it to blow a trumpet and to clap.

Normally left alone, boutus are only occasionally hunted for meat. One of the local myths surrounding them in our area is that if a woman unexpectedly becomes pregnant, the deed can often successfully be blamed on the dolphins who are reputed to secretly climb out of the water at night and lie with women.

Down from Sacha Lodge, still on the Napo River, lies the community of Sani Isla. It is a Quichua community among which we have many friends having worked with them for years in tourism. Tom and Mariela were highly instrumental in securing funds for the community and helping them build and manage their own high-end rainforest lodge. It has been very successful and is in a beautiful setting. The three of us, with a Huaorani Indian, Otobo, were going in for a visit, along with a VIP group who wanted to meet the Quichua, among other tribes. The main VIP was from an extremely wealthy North American family who shall definitely remain nameless, as you just know he has expensive lawyers on speed dial. Then there were two of his friends and a woman, a wealthy socialite, who had done significant work with another group of rainforest Indians in Ecuador. Their party had a guide brought in from Quito, some military survival guide and their fixer, Lazlo, a Lithuanian living in Quito. We knew Lazlo, hence the invite, although I was never able to bring myself to totally trust him. We all paddled in, following a stunning blackwater creek off the main river, until *Challuacocha* lagoon opened up in front of us and we saw the lodge perched on the edge. Seth, a large Canadian, was there to meet us as the naturalist guide. Everything was off to a good start, conversation was healthy, Otobo was his usual entertaining self and we covered jungle topics and the meaning of life. Seth regaled us with stories of wildlife encounters and the amazing number of birds in the area. He was a keen birder; you could tell immediately by the expensive set of binoculars he used. The following day, Seth was asking around if anybody had seen them. No, we had not. An hour later, he was back. Still we had not seen them; he was lost without his optics. The last time he had seen his binoculars, he told Tom, Mariela and I, was when the Quito guide had been using them. Seth was by now very suspicious and getting mad. We all knew it was not the Quichua, we trusted them implicitly but a jungle guide without his bins cannot work. I happened to be sharing a room with the Quito guide and said that I would reluctantly look through his things. Once everyone was in the social area and the Quito guide, as was typical, was resting in a hammock I decided to check. The worst thing that could damage a reputation for a lodge was reports of stealing, we all knew it and the obvious culprits for the missing binoculars might well have been the locals. We knew differently. I rummaged through his backpack. Neatly wrapped in a used T-shirt, I found Seth's binoculars. I detonated and came out of the room to meet the astonished VIPs, Lazlo, the socialite and the Quito guide head on. I was livid and screaming blue murder. Seth got fired up too. I said the guide should be tied up and we would take him to the police in Quito. We were taking him. "Hold on," said the VIP group, "he's *our* guide."

"Not anymore," I said, "he's a thief and we are taking him." Not even Tom or Mariela could calm me down. I was armed to the hilt with passion and loyalty towards my naïve native friends.

One of the lesser VIPs came out with, "How do we know that YOU didn't steal them?"

"Don't go there. Don't go there. Don't even go there," was all I could say.

I was in full rage and I knew I had lost it when Otobo, a member of perhaps the most homicidal tribe on the planet told me, "Pete, *calmate, calmate.*" (calm down, calm down). The trip broke down, we were uninvited, Lazlo was pissed off. Their helicopter was faster than our canoe and so by the time we arrived back in Quito, Lazlo was already well refreshed. We got off the plane, after our long canoe ride and marched straight to his office. It was a tall building, he owned it, lived in the penthouse and had the next floor down as his office. Tom, Mariela and I stormed in, still in our jungle garb. The air was as thick as dough and as black as night. There was no love lost and tensions were boiling. Lazlo had defended the guide when he should not have. We had our words with Lazlo and left. The elevator opened 12 floors below and we walked abreast to the large main entrance like three gunslingers from the OK Corral. Not a word was spoken between us. It was raining a deluge outside. We instinctively paused, when,

SHAZAM! a lightning bolt struck the building and a large chunk of concrete fell off the structure and crashed at our feet. Saved by a millisecond of pausing for the rain. The energy was so intense it was palpable – electric.

Working on one of my latest books saw me south of the Napo River in perhaps the most special area in the entire Ecuadorian Amazon, the Tiputini River. There is a scientific station that operates on the river and Reneé and I were lucky enough to base ourselves there.

Finally, after three weeks of frequent, heavy rain, the forest was dank with moisture. The sun came out and the river level was dropping, sandbanks were becoming exposed. The perfect scenario for a soggy jaguar to dry out on the sand. It was wishful thinking but I decided to go anyway with my native guide, José, upriver in the canoe to look for Amazon River turtles basking on the newly exposed logs. I wanted the shot with *Phoebis* butterflies drinking salt from the terrapin's tear ducts. The skies were slightly overcast and there were no harsh shadows – it looked great. Naturally, we also scanned any bare area on the hope of catching unawares a basking caiman, anaconda, capybara or even that hoped for jaguar.

For more than 20 years, I have been visiting and closely associated with the Amazon yet, within the confines of the *Ecuadorian* Amazon, I had never previously seen a tapir, white-lipped peccaries, giant armadillo or a cat. Either my luck had not been with me or they were all so very rare that they were nearly impossible to see. Having come this time to work in the Tiputini region, bordering the Yasuni National Park, already my luck had changed. After only three weeks, I had under my photographic belt the first three species in the list and had also added two other Ecuadorian firsts the equatorial saki monkey and the grey brocket deer. Working in one of the world's most challenging photographic environments, I was desperate to photograph as many truly wild mammals as possible for the book, instead of resorting to captive animal images, as I and so many other rainforest photographers have had to resort to previously. At the risk of sacrificing captive clarity, I wanted to show wildness – a rarer entity today than some of the animals photographed.

In the early days when I was photographing incessantly in the Amazon, I was always missing jaguar. When in Manaus on a visit, I learned of a military zoo where jaguars were captive. They had a fenced off area of the rainforest where they would allow the jaguars to enter making it a good photographic opportunity in a natural setting. Reneé and I decided to have a look. At the time, until the

Pantanal became known for jaguars, nearly all published jaguar images had been shot at the Belize zoo. We introduced ourselves to the soldiers and paid our photographic fee. The adult jaguars were let out of their cages. Fortunately, for the cats, they had not had their fangs or claws removed which is often the case when people try to keep large felines captive. The cats cowered at the sight of the soldiers. We guessed they had been mistreated. Things were not working out well photographically and I asked to go inside the enclosure, with the cats directly. It was not usually allowed but they agreed. An armed soldier came in with us. Reneé and I crouched as far away as we could from the soldier. We continually spoke to the cats in low mellow tones. They both came to us and, using us as a shield from the guard crouched next to us within a metre. Heartbreaking yet rewarding that they sought comfort in us. I asked the guard to leave. We were now alone inside the cage with the jaguars and they finally got up, moved around a little and relaxed. Yes, I took some images, but it became less important to us while we were with them. We were overcome by a feeling of sorrow and helplessness about their stress and not being able to do anything about it. The soldiers enjoyed the domination we wanted nothing more than to impart empathy.

The big cats are always going to be very difficult subjects in the Ecuadorian jungle, especially as I prefer to not use camera traps, but rather have an actual interface with the subject. For me, it is as much about being with the animal, whatever it may be, as getting the shot. Cats have been much reduced in areas where Huaorani or Quichua Indians roam the forest to hunt. The Quichua, especially, have killed a lot of jaguars using hunting dogs. They simply shoot the cat out of the tree in which the dogs have baled it. Revered yet reviled. Jaguars are strongly represented in Indian folklore. Certain shamans are even believed to be able to metamorphose into black panthers while under the influence of hallucinogenic, naturally occurring drugs, I remember my time spent with the Huaorani where Kempere, a powerful shaman, was well known by the community to be able to undergo such powerful and dramatic transitions.

As we slowly rounded a bend in the dark, sinusoidal river a movement caught my eye on the right. A tail flick. A sleek, long black animal lay on a tiny sand bank – a tayra I thought. Tayras are large mustelids in the martin family capable of running through the canopy to prey on monkeys. I raised the camera as we approached and began shooting test shots. At 40m distance, the 'tayra' stood up, it had been half concealed – it was a black panther! I was ready, and by luck with the perfect camera combination, I excitedly shot away. As we slowed the engine, vibration increased and I was overcome with a fear that my handholding would result in non-sharp images. I bumped up the ISO to increase shutter speed. The animal was everything it was supposed to be, magnificent, evocative, sleek and majestic. Its stare burned through yellow eyes, as it watched us and began walking slowly away. In less than 30 seconds, it was gone. José and I had not said a word but I motioned to him to take the canoe under an overhanging tree at the river's edge to where the panther (a melanistic jaguar) had disappeared. We scanned forward as we bushwhacked, squeezing the canoe under the dense foliage I glanced back to José pleading with my eyes for him to have seen where it had gone. As I did so incredibly, I saw the cat, sitting Sphinx-like, on the edge of the bank no more than seven metres from our canoe watching us. It was curious! My shutter went crazy as we stared into each other's eyes. The canoe was rocking as José tried to bring the stern through the last tangles – the panther was unconcerned and simply followed our efforts with its gaze. Beaching the bow in the soft mud the canoe locked solid and I secured the camera onto my tripod. A minute later, the male panther nonchalantly wandered off to 15 metres distant and lay down to sleep. For a full half hour, we watched nothing more than the occasional ear twitch or talk flick and finally once again, it raised its head to look at us. *This time, he's going to dissolve back into the forest,* I thought but, instead it miraculously stood up and walked straight towards us where it sat down, eight metres away, behind some vegetation and began grooming! It was equivalent to winning the jackpot of wildlife photography, at the very least the Holy Grail of Amazon photography. Still José and I had not said a word to each other as we sat dumbstruck. José is a native of the forest and this was his first ever jaguar sighting! I had been luckier and for me it was number 19 but never had I expected to see, let alone photograph a black panther. None of my professional photographer colleagues, jungle guides or jungle native friends had ever seen one, indeed it was an iconic moment – a once in many people's lifetime's experience. After one hour and 20 minutes in each other's presence, the panther stretched, yawned one final time and melted, in a few steps, into the darkness of the understory as it silently walked away.

My terrapin shot would have to wait and we returned, elated, to the research station for lunch to recount our story to an incredulous audience of hardcore rainforest researchers. They were reckoned to be the first, direct (non-camera trap) professional images of a wild black panther. There was internet in the station and I immediately emailed some low-res images to my agent Larry Minden in the States, reckoned to be the top wildlife agency in the world, Larry is a good friend and knows his business. "Larry," I said, "stop the presses, Scoop! Phone the bank, I've shot the Holy Grail…etc."

"Well done, Pete, you must have really enjoyed that sighting. I don't think I can sell them though."

"Ha, ha," I retorted, but he was right. All the magazines had already, over the years, featured black jaguars, on the cover, inside spreads, you name it. Every image a captive animal but nicely lit and in good condition. My images would not sell because the animal did not look so gorgeous, the background wasn't a smooth, silky green, basically because the public is jaded and there is no value in wildness. It is truly a sad state of affairs. After achieving the impossible, I plummeted to an emotional low point in my career wondering if it was all worth it. The only story left for me to tell was why an image of a *wild* black jaguar would not sell.

# Sharks and Dragons
# Indonesia

My first time in Indonesia was in the early 1990s. I spent the full visa allowance of two months exploring a small part of the archipelago. With approximately 17,000 islands, it is a country that begs repeated visits. I was backpacking and on a very low budget. I began my visit south of Ujung Pandang, as it was known then (now Makassar) on the southwest of the western leg of the oddly shaped Sulawesi Island. I made my way south from there, little by little, changing public transport frequently. The countryside became very quickly more and more rural the further I travelled. My goal was to stay with some old shrimp buddies from Ecuador at the shrimp farm they had set up. It was a perfect base. I made friends with their housemaid, Pur, who, with the help of my phrase book patiently allowed me to quickly become conversational in *Bahasa Indonesia*, the local language. It is actually a very easy language with no tenses or plurals. Tense is implied contextually and for a plural, just repeat the noun. On my first long walk through a nearby village all females literally ran from me screaming *orang bule* (white man or albino) as they fled. It was not offensive but they were so unaccustomed to seeing westerners that they were nervous in the extreme. The men would invite me into their huts for tea. We would sit cross-legged and eventually all the slits in the bamboo walls would be blocked by eyeballs peering into the room as the village kids clambered on to the hut from the outside to stare in at the spectacle. One day I caught a monitor lizard and it regurgitated ten baby mice. I felt really bad for it having lost a meal and moved them to a place that it might find them again after I released it. I loved my stay in Sulawesi and quickly settled into the lifestyle, finding it very calming. It was always the opposite sensation while on a ferry between the islands. I spent long hours on these boats, sleeping on deck where the floor was usually so crowded that if you dared to go to the horrendous bathroom your space had been commandeered when you returned.

On Flores Island, I hiked Mt Kelimutu. The top is a flooded volcanic crater which is divided in half by a thin, rocky septum leaving two brightly coloured lakes sitting next to each other. One lake was a bright turquoise, the other a milky emerald green. I unrolled my fist-sized hammock, found somewhere eventually to string it up and spent a lonely night at the top. I must have come close to hypothermia, as I was as cold as I have ever been and could hardly find the will to do anything about it. From the western end of Flores, I paid a fisherman to take me across the strait to Komodo Island. Loving all things reptilian, I had so desperately wanted to go to Komodo from as early as I could remember. He dropped me off, it was a one-way ticket and I went up to talk to the park guard. Before I even got as far as the hut, I noticed a huge Komodo dragon in slumber, nonchalantly spread-eagle in the shade of the guard's house. A huge bucket list tick. He beckoned to me to come and I walked around the unconcerned monster and climbed the steps. There were no tourists and I asked if they could allow me to stay for a few days. No problem was the answer, for a nominal fee. They set me up with a place to sleep and gave me strict instructions of how to behave around a dragon. I was not to wander off without a park guard under any circumstances. People have been killed and eaten by dragons in the past. These are the largest lizards in the world, excluding crocodiles, growing to about nine foot long and well over two hundred pounds in weight. They lumber sinusoidally over the ground but can put on an impressive sprint over short distances when necessary. On my second morning, it was feeding time. I walked with two wardens and a goat. The wardens carried a long-forked stick each with which to fend off any untoward advances from the dragons and they gave me the free end of the rope tying the goat, which pranced merrily alongside us. We arrived at a clearing dominated by a large tree near a circular fence of wooden posts about two feet tall. The fence was for us and we stepped inside. One of the wardens took the goat, slit its throat and then cut off a leg. The other took the leg, jumped the fence and climbed the tree in a well-practiced manoeuvre. He dangled the leg just out of reach of a slither of dragons that fast approached from all directions. He taunted them with the severed leg from above while the other warden slipped, unnoticed down into the dry riverbed and staked out the three-legged goat. The dragons soon got wind of the ploy and raced down, thunderously, to the meat. The man with the goat leg rejoined us and tossed the limb to the writhing mass of powerful reptiles now in complete feeding frenzy. They were such a different animal from the well-fed dozing lounge-lizard down by the hut. This was a brawl of hissing, tail-whipping, clawing and biting dinosaurian competitiveness. I saw one Komodo slide his mouth over the goat's hind foot, all the way up to the hip and bite the whole leg clean off. It was over in a minute; everything was gone, rope and all. *This* was my bucket list tick. The dragons are no longer fed nowadays.

Continuing on to Bali, it was a different place to what it has become. Obud was not crowded and village women were still often seen topless. Denpasar and Kuta were still bustling, even then, but more as an Australian holiday resort than the real Bali. I headed north and spent New Year with a family in a small fishing village, invited to share in their roast suckling pig, *babi guling*. One of the most treasured mementos from my round the world travels came from Bali. It is a *Kris*, a wavy-bladed dagger. I had the blade made by a local blacksmith, I watched him make it. It is bevelled as well as wavy and is exquisite. Then he directed me to a master craftsman, a wood carver. He built a stunningly beautiful hardwood sheath and for the hilt, from the same wood, he conjured the head of a *garuda*, a mythical bird. It was built specifically for me and has been charged with magical powers. The blacksmith told me that my *kris* will always be my defender and also has the power, should I direct it, to search out my enemy in the night and kill him.

I waited a long time before I saw myself again in Indonesia. In the past several years, I have been many times back to the archipelago. It is a fascinating country, extremely diverse both biologically and culturally. As a diver and underwater photographer, Raja Ampat (The Four Kings) is a magnet. It is an area within the Coral Triangle towards the north of the island group considered as the most biodiverse marine system on the planet. It reminds me of the Amazon rainforest where niches are so narrow and where, if you look hard enough, there is always something very cool to find. Just like the forest, what you do find is often totally bizarre and unbelievable. The most significant ecosystem in Raja Ampat is coral reef where there is a definite trend towards camouflage. It is 'be seen and be eaten'. Coral reefs are well known for supporting myriad brightly coloured fish species and especially in the shallower areas of just a few metres, their colours are truly dazzling as they sway in the swell. Seeking safety at the approach of danger, they move as one in a choreographed dive back between the coral branches for protection. How can you not marvel at the fantastic nature of an ornate ghost pipefish that mingles, head down, with fronds of gorgonians making it almost impossible to find. Its miniscule tubular mouth snapping at any tiny crustacean that it spies. I'm embarrassed to think about how many hours I have spent in the company of clown fish, always 'just one more shot'. Who could not be amazed at the beautiful angelfish, the tangs, butterfly fish, or, one of my favourites, the clown triggerfish? I have led many live aboard snorkel-based trips to the area and it is really fun to do a little diving at night in a few metres of water. It is a different world, gurnard, reptilian snake eels, crocodile flatheads and goatfish can easily be seen. Parrotfish can be often be found wedged into a crevice for the night to sleep, sometimes within a mucous cocoon that they have secreted around themselves for added protection. Even if there were no fish, the area would still be amazing. The corals themselves are beautiful, sometimes covering large areas in a single-species stand. There are an infinite number of invertebrates, from highly ornate crabs to bizarre shrimp, sea fans and crinoids waving in the swells, many species often living their whole lives in association with another unrelated single species. Nudibranchs are what many underwater enthusiasts come all the way to see. There are hundreds and hundreds of species. They are molluscs with naked gills (hence nudibranch), not more than a few centimetres long they are like psychedelic slugs with colours and patterns that simply boggle the mind. Talking of molluscs how about giant clams. They can weigh in at 200 kilograms, be more than a metre long and live to a hundred years. The fleshy mantle that protrudes from the crenelated edge is another example of out-of-this-world colours and patterns. Unsurprisingly, they are the largest bivalve in the world. If we stay on subject, then we come to the best mollusc group of all – the cephalopods (which translates as 'head foot', as the 'limbs' come directly out of the head) they are of course the octopus, cuttlefish and squid. Once again, in Raja Ampat, there are a plethora of species within any individual group. When I used to live in Menai Bridge in Wales, I kept several octopus. They are definitely smart animals and very hard to imagine that they belong to the same group of animals as common or garden slugs and snails. They got to know me as an individual and one would even bang a rock against the glass when it was hungry and wanted a crab. In Indonesia, it is the mimic octopus that is the most sought after. It is able to change its form in an uncanny variety of ways to make themselves appear as something they are not. Squid can often be found on night dives and it is wonderful to watch their mantles flashing a 'language' of colours. For me, not much can match having an interaction with a broadclub cuttlefish. They grow up to 50 centimetres in length and are pretty impressive animals. Like all cephalopods, they are totally aware of your presence, in an almost human-like way. If you behave in a rational way towards them, they accept your good intentions and allow you very close. They may even swim towards you to satisfy their own curiosity, sometimes with two arms raised in front of them as they edge forward cautiously, all the while changing the texture and colour of their skin. Marvellous 'aliens' from the underwater world.

There do not seem to be as many pelagic sharks as one might expect in Indonesia in general largely due, I expect, to huge pressure from finning. Another potentially dangerous denizen of these waters however is the sea snake which, being a reptile, I am fascinated by. Although highly venomous, they are not really very dangerous as they are generally very docile in character. There are several species but the silver and black banded or yellow-lipped sea krait is the most commonly seen. Sometimes I have let them run from one hand to the next in the water to feel their texture; they are very soft. There was one island that I had heard about called Gili Manuk. Apparently, the sea snake capital of the world. I persuaded the clients that it would be worth taking a look and we set sail. It is conical in shape and totally isolated, which is unusual in an archipelago of thousands of islands. I was impressed by the large colony of Christmas Island frigatebirds which I felt must have been out of their normal range. Underwater, not everyone was as elated as I was. Being a snake there is a certain amount of elemental fear that the animal can incite in many folks. To potentially meet one, that is highly venomous to boot, in a three-dimensional environment, in an element that you are less comfortable in than on land, required drawing on reserves of courage before many would join me in the water. We were not disappointed and the snakes were very abundant, mostly however they were the Chinese sea snake, more brownish in colour, longer, more cylindrical and not as soft. Sometimes there were two or three together, sometimes both species. They often swam into my mask as I followed them to the surface to breathe. I had not realised until I spent a lot of time watching them closely how 'snake-like' they still were. They behaved just like a terrestrial snake exploring crevices for food and still with their tongue flicking exploratively in and out, which is what surprised me most.

If we see local fishermen, I will sometimes stop the boat and we'll go and take a look to see what they are up to. They usually enjoy the novelty of strange visitors and like to show off their water skills wearing nothing more than a pair of shorts and some homemade wooden googles. Unlike us who have an abundance of respect for the fragility of a coral reef the locals walk all over it, breaking corals and stand on the coral bombies to rest. It's hard to blame them as it is their back yard. I have watched them beating a vine with a rock in the bottom of one of their dugout canoes. Then they set a net, in a circle, around a patch of reef the size of a tennis court. The crushed vine is taken under water and waved in front of and inside any coral holes. It leeches a powerful toxin; the fish are stunned and float to the surface. If one is trapped, the coral is simply broken to catch it. Others flee but hit the net in their escape bid and are hauled on to the boat. I once watched a fisher catch a hawksbill turtle. Against the rules, I bought it from him, paying a good price and took our boat to release it far away. It all sounds bad what I am describing and so it is but not as bad perhaps as the way we procure our own seafood.

A look at local fish markets often gives a good idea of the health of the nearby reefs. Mostly, I see that the more highly prized pelagic species such as the tunas are few and far between and there seems to be an abundance of less desirable parrotfish for sale. It is an indication of overfishing. Probably commercial fishers have depleted stocks of the pelagics forcing the locals to fish closer inshore on the reef. Once parrotfish start to appear in the catch it means the reef is on a downward spiral. They keep the reef clean; they are the caretakers. Over-exploitation is rampant. A market in Jakarta, that I usually visit, is a wild bird and animal market. It is humungous and houses tens of thousands of mostly wild-caught birds for sale in cramped and grossly overcrowded cages. Owls are common, being caught for pets, made all the more popular since Harry Potter. Wild animals too abound, civets, fruit bats, tokay geckoes and terrapins to name but a few. It is seriously depressing and my blood boils with rage as I walk around feigning the chipper, upbeat, curious tourist with his camera. I continuously fail to understand how we as a species can see no wrong in raping the natural world. Something has to give. Plastic is another major problem globally and I wager that there is no 'better' example of the problem than in Indonesia. All plastic, ever produced in the world since its production 100 years ago is still here. Much of it now reduced in size to micro plastics. The Indonesian culture is a throw away culture where wrappings and plates were once banana leaves that biodegraded. Now, with plastic there is no 'away'. It is not an excuse though, adults after all can easily learn new ideas. As much as the inadequate garbage consciousness in the community I blame the big producers, Coca Cola for example, for irresponsibly continuing to produce plastic without an adequate waste disposal regimen as is legally in place for treatment of other hazardous materials. Production and adequate, ecologically sound, disposal techniques should go hand-in-hand. On one trip to the archipelago, we specialised at looking at marine plastic pollution. It was ghastly and the closer you got to the holiday beaches the more prevalent it became. On Bali, we visited a huge landfill area of mostly plastic refuse. It was totally toxic. I was surprised to see cows grazing on the landfill but shocked to learn that the cow's owners pay for the grazing rights to the land fill boss! What is wrong with us?

I have been up to West Papua, previously known as Irian Jaya, quite a few times now for various reasons. One time had nothing to do with the ocean. A single client and I decided that we wanted to go and see the Dani people of the Baliem Valley. West Papua is the western half of the Island of Papua on which Papua New Guinea makes up the east. It is Indonesia, but only politically. The people rightly consider themselves Papuans. Through political trickery, they were incorporated into Indonesia to access oil and minerals. Much blood has been spilt, in what has been termed cultural genocide, in the ongoing conflict for independence. The Dani are an interesting race characterised by the men sporting large pig's teeth through their noses and a long, upright penis gourd covering their phallus. The women are semi naked, wear a woven string skirt that always looks like it is on the point of slipping down and as part of their apparel, a large string bag which hangs from their forehead down their back. They looked fearsome but were actually very welcoming. They smoke heavily despite the low thatch on the huts trapping dense smoke from the cooking fires which they also inhale. I could hardly breathe inside. I took what I could in the way of photographs and once again had the uneasy feeling of me documenting yet more cultural extinction. One thing I shall never forget is the practice of grieving that the women undergo. If a loved one dies, the woman cuts off the top half of a finger. I was told that she first smashes it with a rock to pulverise it and then slices it off. It is a symbol of the pain of losing a spouse or relative. I photographed one woman who had done this five times.

Another memorable time in West Papua Reneé and I were heading to Cenderawasih Bay on the Bird's Head Peninsula. We were to begin the trip from Biak Island and decided to go several days early. It was disappointing as there was little to see. I met a professional bird tour guide revisiting after many years hiatus. He lamented the massive decline in numbers of birds, as well as their habitat loss since his last visit. We travelled the island; people were friendly and we visited many fishing villages as we usually do. We saw live turtles waiting for slaughter and kids with their goggles spearing little barber fish in the shallow reef, descaling them then threading them on to a line for dinner later on. I saw sago palm, the local starch, packaged neatly into large bundles for transport. I saw lots of parrotfish in the market and clown fish in plastic bags ready for the aquarium trade. It was the big Independence Day celebration while we were there which was very festive and all the locals were caught up in the event. I probably counted almost a dozen birds of paradise made into headdresses. Hence, the tour guide's lament.

Our trip began as we boarded a traditionally built *phinisi* sailboat, an icon of Indonesia. Fitted as a tourist live aboard it was full of character and very appropriate to the area. Our objective was to find whale sharks. As a marine biologist by training, with a long affinity for sharks, I had seen whale sharks before, I'd even helped tag them with satellite tags in Galapagos, but *never* did I expect to interact with so many, for so long, as I did now.

From Biak Island, we set sail south into the deep recess of Cenderawasih Bay, a long-isolated ancient sea complete with its own endemic wonders. We dove along the way, in gin clear, tropical waters of 30°C – bliss. Highlights were frequent. In general, Papua is not a particularly safe place to travel. The crew of our vessel however knew where we could dive safely and where encounters with the natives of the region would be welcomed. The dive sites were varied, some dominated by a riot of brilliantly coloured soft corals, others by large stands of cabbage corals but each with extreme levels of biodiversity. The claim-to-fame of the Coral Triangle, an area of ocean that encompasses parts of Indonesia, the Philippines, Papua New Guinea, The Solomon Islands, Malaysia and Timor L'este, is that it is home to a staggering 500 coral and 1000 fish species. Although huge international efforts are in place to conserve the area, pressures are high. As mentioned, overfishing, the use of gill nets and fish poison, coral destruction by dynamite fishing and trampling along with a host of other problems is seeing a reduction of biomass on the reefs. Indonesia is also one of the world's largest shark-finning nations yet; it was encouraging, back in 2002 when the Indonesian government declared a large area of western Cenderawasih Bay a marine reserve. Bordered by lush tropical rainforest, draped on mist-topped limestone cliffs, the surrounding forest is also home to tree climbing kangaroos, cassowaries, cuscus and egg-laying mammals. It was further encouraging, once we reached our destination, to witness the respect that the local fishermen hold for the whale sharks that we had travelled so far to see, believing that the whale sharks are harbingers of good luck.

Camping out on large, anchored, floating fishing platforms, known as *bagans*, the fishermen use a series of generator-powered lights to attract small baitfish, *ikan puri*, and squid to the large nets suspended below the *bagan* at night. Once or twice a night, these nets are manually hauled in the hope of a bountiful catch. Whale sharks sense the capture and are attracted to the platforms to reap some of the spillage as reward. The fishermen have also traditionally thrown the sharks tidbits in payment of their 'service' of being lucky and everyone is happy. This practice has recently evolved into something of an, as yet, very low-key tourist industry (we didn't see another such vessel the entire trip). We approached the *bagans*, in the evening of arrival to the area, asking who had seen any whale sharks that day. For those fishermen, we offered them payment to 'keep' the fish close by offering rewards during the night. There would be a bigger payment if they were still there for us to get in the water with them the next day. The fishers are paid enough to see the relationship as worthwhile (as well as the local chief and head policeman), visitors have an incredible experience and, best of all, the whale sharks are not hunted for their fins. A win-win all around.

So, what's it like swimming with the world's largest fish? Whereas in most other whale shark destinations, the animals are continuously on the move and the human experience is often one of watching it gracefully glide past, here, in Kwatisore Bay (a smaller bay within Cenderawasih Bay), these gigantic animals actually interact with divers and snorkelers. Once in the water the visitor simply 'hangs out' close to the *bagan* and the whale sharks come. While on scuba, different individuals would stay with me, even as I drifted in the slight current, away from the *bagan* and swim repeated circles around me with an apparent sense of curiosity, either for me or, perhaps more likely, my bubbles. I could spend a full tank of air alone with a whale shark as if it was only the two of us left on the planet – magical! Closer to the *bagan* one could choose what sort of interaction to have. In my case, with a wide-angle lens on my camera, I put myself as close as possible to the gentle stream of water, full of fishy bits, being pumped into the ocean by the men above me. I became part of the furniture and it was not unusual for one, two or three whale sharks to 'stand' vertically in the water with huge mouths wide open under the stream of water jostling for position next to me. Sometimes another, unseen, individual would 'sneak up' from behind and gently, ever so gently, nudge me out of the way to get in on the action. They were conscious of exactly where I was and the space I filled in their world and were so utterly respectful of me and so gentle that I was amazed. When in open water with them, if you held position, they would meander by, often less than a metre below me, and, even though the head had cruised by long before, the last flick of the tail as they passed would contort unnaturally, if necessary, to avoid contact.

Nearly all the individuals we encountered were subadult males. Some were tagged (many by Brent Stewart who was with us on the trip) in an ongoing scientific study to learn more about these charismatic beasts. Incredibly, very little is known at all about the world's largest fish. 'Our' individuals could not count as a population (as they were all males). It was more of a gathering really. But where do they come from? Where do they go? Where do baby whale sharks grow up? How long do they live? Where are the females? A study by the Charles Darwin Research Station and the Galapagos National Park suggests that the northern isles of the Galapagos archipelago might be an important breeding ground for the species. There, for example, it is nearly all, gigantic, adult females, up to 12 metres and 20 tons, that one sees while diving. It remains an incredible truth that while whale sharks are being slaughtered for their fins in certain areas (they command some of the highest prices in Asian fish markets), we know almost nothing about their ecology and hence how, or where best, to protect them.

In Cenderawasih Bay, it seems that whale sharks are doing OK – at least they are revered. The locals even love to jump into the water with them, just to watch them go by. The sharks have great potential to provide an all-important economy to the Papuan fishing communities whilst providing some jaw-dropping experiences for adventurous eco-tourists. It is a heart-warming story of how controlled eco-tourism can bring benefits to on-the-ground stakeholders as well as to the wildlife directly.

My last few hours, after several days with the sharks, before we returned north, were the best. One large male came into the feeding fray from behind me and this time, instead of a gentle nudge, lifted me high and dry for a second out of the water by scooping me up and perched on his nose! I was gracefully lowered back to the water, made eye contact, gave an apology and edged away only to find a new, sub-adult male had arrived. The youngster was enveloped in a confetti-like bouquet of startlingly yellow golden trevallies, small golden fish that were swarming around the shark with some 'piloting' the animal a few inches in front of the mouth. It was truly exquisite and the whole experience shot to my top-ten best-ever wildlife encounters. Yes, they are fish, but I love fish! Yet, in the case of the Cenderawasih whale sharks and for the second time for a 'mere' fish, I also gave them 'honorary mammal' status.

# Afterword
# South Africa

I am in Covid-19 lockdown as I write this, wondering how travel will look in the coming years. I recall the infinite number of hugs I have had around the world, from old men in ponchos to toothless women selling vegetables, our physical contact, from completely different worlds, bridged by nothing more than a smile. Perhaps that will all change as we embrace social distancing. The world, in my view, was certainly out of kilter with pressures too great on Nature to be sustainable. What is sustainability apart from a euphemism? What does 'sustainable development' mean? Develop half, leave half? Do it again, develop half of what was left, leave half? Perhaps the reset that is needed will tame the rampant onslaught of globalisation, perhaps we will become more compassionate towards wildlife, perhaps we will begin to grow a little of our own food and eat what is in season locally, perhaps the amazing indigenous cultures we have seen will retire back into their traditional ways. If not, then I am thankful that I have no children to inherit the collective destruction that we will leave them. My choice is made; I will do what I can to leave the world better than I found it. You, of course have a choice too. I always promote the idea of getting involved in conservation locally. In my case, having lived in Ecuador for 34 years, local to me was the Ecuadorian Amazon rainforest and the Galapagos Islands. It all may sound glamorous but really it is not, it was just an extension of my back yard, both places I lived in for about three years each. I have published eight books between the two areas, each one with conservation messaging. That's what I do, I'm a photographer and it is one of the most effective ways to deliver my skill set to the public. Of course not everybody is a photographer (although there are infinitely more today than when I started and everyone has a smart phone). You could write. If there are any issues that bother you, wetlands being drained for agriculture, roadside verges mowed too often by the council such that wildflowers never get a chance to blossom or seed, school kids made to wear rubber gloves before they get their hands 'dirty' in a school pond-dipping outing, neighbours poisoning wildlife or governments allowing import and consumption of threatened species, all it takes is a pen to do something about it. OK, maybe a computer and an email account, but you understand my point. You could write to your local politician to encourage the municipality to move away from sterile, pesticide sodden, lawns in public areas. Write to the local newspaper. There are so many issues, yet so many voices. I feel very strongly that I have a voice and I will crusade for what I believe is right, the deeper you get involved in an issue you will find others there with you and strength will be gained from kindred spirits. There have also been many times when I have volunteered, working with rescued manatees in Belize, photographing snakes for the Quito vivarium, photographing new frog species on an expedition with researchers, things I believe in. Anybody can be useful to conservation. If you are a carpenter, you can build wooden sign boards in nature reserves for natural history information. If you are an accountant, you can offer some time to an NGO to help with their bookkeeping. Conservation organisations always need IT help. If you have no recognised skill set, you can sign up for local beach clean ups. Every little helps and each new pair of hands is a new recruit in the army.

Having moved now to the Western Cape in South Africa, Reneé and I volunteer a huge amount of our time (especially her) trying to mitigate the negative human-induced/baboon interactions in our community. Basically, the baboons were being severely harassed and we decided to stick up for them as nobody else was doing so. Little by little, we are changing mindsets.

After all of the sermon above, (I really don't mean to preach it is simply that conservation can be accomplished in so many ways) one of the best examples I can think of where an 'ordinary' individual is making a difference comes from my sister Cath. I had come back from a live aboard trip to Indonesia where a group of scientists, artists, Oceanic Society staff, philanthropists, local NGO staff, a cameraman and myself were specifically looking at marine plastic pollution. It was atrocious. I told my sister. Then, a week later, she went to the local premiere of the film 'A Plastic Ocean'. The uncomfortable diatribe was enough to change her outlook completely, she no longer wanted to be a part of the problem and she set up, from her spare bedroom in a semidetached house in Bristol, an online business 'The Plastic Free Shop: Plastic free choices for everyday living'. It has become a huge success and given an outlet for others to express their choice when buying a product. It is making a difference.

I believe we only get one life and I have lived mine hard in an attempt to see and experience as much as possible. I have no regrets and would repeat it all again if there were not so many other things still out there that continue to drive me. There is a lot that I haven't even brought up in this book which I am privileged to have experienced. For example, I helped capture many black as well as white rhinos, I was a member of a capture team to relocate a whole herd of elephants, I have caught, tagged and swam with many sharks around the world, I spent two years habituating leopards (non-baiting) all stories perhaps for another book. My work in conservation photography has earned me a certain level of respect which I value enormously. My biggest ever accolade though came to me unexpectedly. I was in Switzerland, giving the Ecuadorian Ministry of Tourism's keynote address at an international travel conference. An Ecuadorian student, there to help with logistics, came to me and shyly introduced herself, claiming it was an honour to meet me. I returned the compliment and we went back and forth until she said, "No, really, it is an honour to meet you. In my university, they taught us how Pete Oxford has changed the way Ecuadorians view their own country."

*Reneé swimming with a whale shark in West Papua, Indonesia*

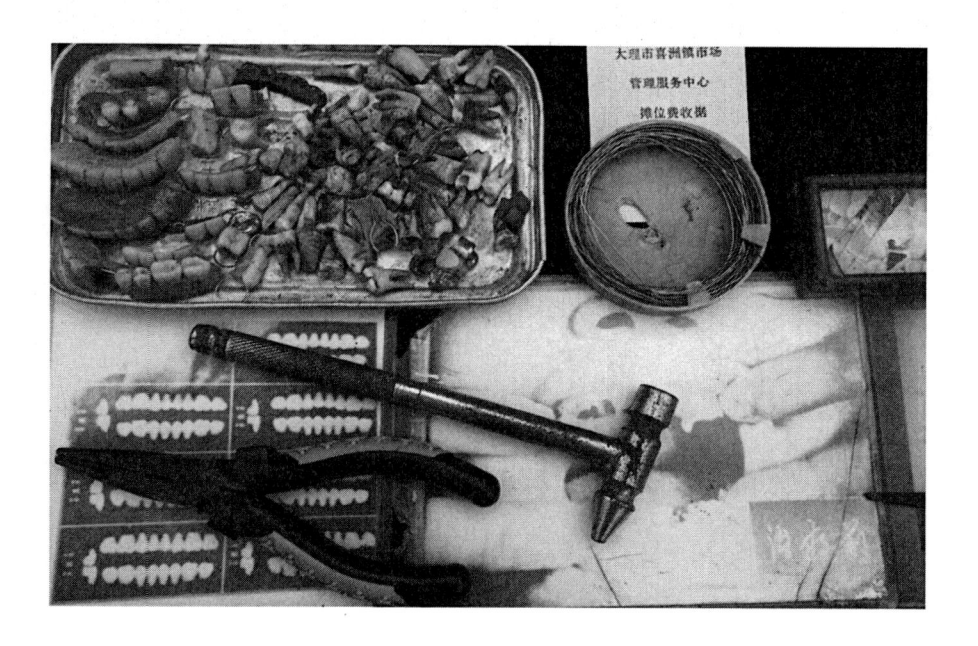

*Local dentist stall Xizhou market, Yunnan Province, China*

*Pete with sloth clinging to paddle for release in Ecuadorian Amazon*

*Pete with Kazakh and golden eagle used for hunting, Mongolia*

*Reneé working on her laptop in the Ecuadorian Amazon with a naked Huaorani*

*Pete and Reneé's wedding in the Amazon, Ecuador*

*Pete with giant tortoise on Wolf Volcano, Galapagos, Ecuador*

*Pete and Reneé travelling by ox cart to photograph sifakas in Madagascar*

*Hunted walrus, Chukotka Peninsula, Siberia, Russia*